W9-BFK-881

PROFILES IN
COURAGE FOR
OUR TIME

PROFILES IN

COURAGE FOR

OUR TIME

INTRODUCED AND EDITED BY

CAROLINE KENNEDY

HYPERION

NEW YORK

Copyright © 2002 The John F. Kennedy Library Foundation

THE COLLECTED WORKS OF W.B. YEATS, VOLUME 1: THE POEMS, REVISED, edited by Richard J. Finneran. Copyright © 1940 by Georgie Yeats; copyright renewed © 1968 by Bertha Georgie Yeats, Michael Butler Yeats, and Anne Yeats. Used with the permission of Scribner, a Division of Simon & Schuster, Inc. A. P. Watt, Ltd. on behalf of Michael B. Yeats.

All rights reserved. No part of this book may be used or reproduced in any manner whatsoever without the written permission of the Publisher. Printed in the United States of America. For information address: Hyperion, 77 W. 66th Street, New York, New York 10023-6298.

LIBRARY OF CONGRESS CATALOGING-IN-PUBLICATION DATA

Profiles in courage for our time / edited and introduced by
Caroline Kennedy.—1st ed.
    p. cm.
   ISBN 0-7868-6793-0
    1. United   States—Biography. 2. Legislators—United   States—Biography. 3. Courage—United States. 4. United States—Politics and government. 5. Northern Ireland—Politics and government.

CT220 .P76 2002
973'.09'9—dc21
[B]

                                       2001051894

Book design by Richard Oriolo

Hyperion books are available for special promotions and premiums. For details contact Hyperion Special Markets, 77 West 66th Street, 11th floor, New York, New York, 10023, or call 212-456-0100.

FIRST EDITION

10   9   8   7   6   5   4   3   2   1

ACKNOWLEDGMENTS

T HERE ARE MANY people who have made this book possible—first and foremost, the winners of the Profile in Courage Award, and the distinguished writers who have illuminated their deeds.

I am so grateful to the members of the selection committee, who have given their wisdom, judgment, and time to make this Award worthy of its name: Senators Thad Cochran and Olympia Snowe, Dave Burke, Marian Wright Edelman, Antonia Hernandez, Elaine Jones, Paul Kirk, and David McCullough; and their predecessors, Senators John Culver and Alan Simpson, Theodore C. Sorensen, Jill Ker Conway, and Charles U. Daly. I would especially like to thank our chairmen, John Siegenthaler and his predecessor, Richard K. Donahue, for their leadership. As always, to my uncle, Senator Edward M. Kennedy, for keeping this so close to his heart.

The staff at the John F. Kennedy Foundation has worked

hard over the last twelve years to support the Committee's work and help us to select the most courageous and deserving public servants. Shelley Sommer, Michele Kane Forster, Karyn Wilson, and Tom McNaught have led that effort. They are now joined by John Shattuck and Deborah Leff, whose vision will lead the Library in the years to come.

The Library is indebted to Bob Miller and Gretchen Young at Hyperion, who made a commitment to this project more than a few years ago, and have believed in it ever since.

My contribution to this book could not have been made without the help of the wonderful Joanna Shea and Claudia Slavin.

Finally, I would like to thank Janet Elder, for her inspired guidance and encouragement, and Esther Newberg, whose tireless efforts brought us all together.

Most of all, and always, I am grateful to my husband, Ed, who has done so much for the Library, and whose love and support make everything possible.

CONTENTS

PROFILES IN
COURAGE FOR
OUR TIME

INTRODUCTION

It was the dream itself enchanted me:
Character isolated by a deed
To engross the present and dominate memory.
—W. B. YEATS

L AST SUMMER DURING the debate on the Patients'
Bill of Rights, I took my daughter, Rose, to see her Great-
Uncle Teddy at work in the United States Senate. When we
arrived, he was speaking on the floor, so we waited in the
colorful hallway outside the Senate Chamber. We spotted a
few senators talking quietly with their staff members. Around
a corner, throngs of visitors shuffled past as pages and interns
ran for the elevators, and lobbyists waited by the marble
busts—a typical morning in the Capitol.

Thrilled to see us when he emerged from the chamber,
Teddy led us up stairs, around corners, into side chambers in
search of his colleagues and friends. We seemed to be at the
end of our tour when he grabbed Rose's arm and said, "You
haven't seen the Senate Reception Room." Off we
went again, loping to keep up, until we turned a corner and
stopped. I looked up at the ceiling and saw portraits of leg-

endary nineteenth-century senators, Daniel Webster, Henry Clay, John C. Calhoun—men who had followed their conscience in pursuit of the national interest—as I listened to Teddy tell the story of how my father had gotten the idea for his Pulitzer prize–winning book, *Profiles in Courage*. My father's own political career, that of his brother Bobby, and now for so many years the work Teddy has done, inspired a generation of Americans to believe in the power of government and to share the conviction that politics can truly be a noble profession. As I stood in that room, I felt a continuity of spirit reaching across time and into the future as I looked at Teddy and Rose.

This book is part of that continuum. I am grateful that so many writers of distinction brought their insights and wisdom to illuminate the acts of courage chronicled here. My father believed in the power of words to lead, to inspire, and to bring about change in the world. My mother took great pride in the fact that the Kennedy Library is the home of the papers of Ernest Hemingway, whose definition of courage as "grace under pressure" was my father's favorite. This book is a celebration of my parents' love of literature, as well as their commitment to public service. I hope that the stories here will inspire another generation to believe in the power of words, the importance of public service, and the necessity of political courage. For it is in words that deeds live on.

In *Profiles in Courage*, my father told the stories of eight senators who acted on principle and in the national interest, even though it put their own political careers at risk. One was Daniel Webster of Massachusetts, the greatest orator of his time, who voted for the Compromise of 1850, which prevented the South from seceding and preserved the Union for an additional, and critical, ten years. His vote placed him at odds with his constituents and his party, and it cost him a chance to be president. Another was Thomas Hart Benton, the fiery Missouri senator who fought to keep slavery from expanding West despite representing a slaveholding constituency that ultimately dismissed him from office after thirty years of statesmanship. Perhaps the most dramatic story is that of Edmund G. Ross, newly elected from Kansas, who followed his conscience, rather than the wishes of his party, and cast the deciding vote against the impeachment of President Andrew Johnson, knowing it would cost him his career. "I . . . looked down into my open grave," Ross later wrote of the moments before he cast his vote. Neither Ross nor the seven other Republican senators who voted with him were ever returned to the Senate.

Each of these men displayed a rare form of courage, sacrificing their own future, and that of their families, to do what they believed was right for our country. Their example comes down to us across the years, their stories are part of our history, and their spirit lives on. The John F. Kennedy Profile in Courage Award is presented annually to an elected official who carries on this tradition. When we created the award in 1990, some doubted we would be able to find politicians worthy of the honor. They were wrong. This book tells the stories of men and women at all levels of government, in all parts of our country, across the political spectrum, who have all stood fast for the ideals of America.

The courage celebrated here comes in many forms. It is the courage to compromise, as well as the courage to stand alone, the courage to cross party lines and build consensus, as well as the courage to stay the course. Sometimes one single selfless act sums up a career. At other times, a politician must follow the law, or his conscience, over a course of time, hoping that ultimately his courage will be recognized when passions have cooled.

At first, and then again last year, we sought to honor politicians like those in the original book, whose singular acts of courage in protecting the national interest put their own career at risk. When President Gerald R. Ford pardoned former President Richard Nixon, barely one month after taking office at the height of the Watergate scandal, he was almost universally condemned. Yet that act of conscience in the national interest, though it may have cost Ford the presidency, has stood the test of time.

Many of the stories in my father's book revolved around the crisis of slavery that tore our country apart in the nineteenth century. The modern struggle for civil rights has produced counterparts of equal bravery. There are men like Congressman Carl Elliott from Alabama and Congressman Charles Weltner of Georgia. Elliott fought for equal opportunity in education and was redistricted out of his congressional seat in retaliation for his principled stand. Weltner took an oath to support his party ticket until segregationist Lester Maddox became the candidate for governor, whereupon Weltner followed his conscience and resigned his seat, rather than violate his oath or his belief that segregation was wrong.

The Committee revisited the civil rights movement in 2001 on the fortieth anniversary of the Freedom Rides, when we presented Congressman John Lewis with a Lifetime Achievement Profile in Courage Award. In spite of brutal beatings and more than forty arrests, Lewis has never wavered in his commitment to civil rights, human rights, nonviolence, and securing for all Americans perhaps the most fundamental right in a democracy: the right to vote.

Local battles are often among the most intense political fights, for public servants are placed in conflict with friends, neighbors, and colleagues with whom they share a lifetime of experience. Often too, their family's security is at risk. Rage, anger, and hostility can be directed not only at public officials, but also at those they love. Inspiring courage was demonstrated by Judge Charles Price when he ruled against another judge's defiantly unconstitutional courtroom display of the Ten Commandments. The Award was given to County Attorney Nickolas Murnion, who stood alone for the rule of law against the irrational and heavily armed Freemen, and to School Superintendent Corkin Cherubini, who took on an entrenched system of race-based tracking in the schools of Calhoun County, Georgia.

Other awards recognize that new forms of courage are required to meet the challenges of our changing political landscape. In modern times, regional interests often become subsumed by special interests. Some of today's most difficult conflicts revolve around those who would bend the system to serve their own ends. The politicians who take them on do so at grave risk. These battles may require the courage to battle party leadership rather than local constituents, yet the fight is just as fierce and the stakes are just as high. Congressmen Mike Synar and Henry B. Gonzalez, Governor Jim Florio, and Senators John McCain and Russell Feingold were willing to risk their careers to preserve the integrity of our system.

New groups of Americans—women, African Americans, Latinos—have entered the political system, embracing a different kind of courage: the courage to compromise. Those entering the political system from historically disenfranchised groups are often taking a great risk simply by running for office. Once elected, they frequently are pitted against established and powerful interests. At times, they risk not only their political advancement but their physical safety, even though they remain popular with their constituents. Former California State Senator, now U.S. Representative Hilda Solis, who brought the issue of environmental justice to the forefront on behalf of the people of her ravaged district, exemplifies this kind of courage.

The courage to compromise was honored in a different way when we presented a silver lantern to the Irish Peacemakers in a special ceremony in 1998. As political leaders who signed the Good Friday agreement described the fear they overcame in reaching out to their historic enemies in the spirit of peace, we were all reminded that the need for leadership is constant and continuing. These men and women from across the political spectrum gave life to the principle that each citizen has a responsibility to contribute by answering the call of his own conscience. As we work to spread democracy around the world, we must also recognize and reward international acts of political courage that may exist within systems different from our own.

Political courage is celebrated in this book, but there are other forms of courage that share its spirit. In the aftermath of the terrorist attacks on the World Trade Center, the extraordinary bravery of our public servants—police officers, firefighters, search and rescue teams, and elected public officials— reminded all Americans how much we depend on courageous leadership in times of crisis and how grateful we are to those who live their lives with honor.

My father ended his book with the following words that bear repeating now: "In whatever arena of life one may meet the challenge of courage, whatever may be the sacrifices he faces if he follows his conscience—the loss of his friends, his fortune, his contentment, even the esteem of his fellow men— each man must decide for himself the course he will follow. The stories of past courage can define that ingredient—they can teach, they can offer hope, they can provide inspiration. But they cannot supply courage itself. For this, each man must look into his own soul."

CAROLINE KENNEDY
October 1, 2001

I dedicated my public life to insuring that the sons and daughters of the working men and women of this nation would have the opportunity to achieve the highest level of education commensurate with their ability, unfettered by economic, racial or other artificial barriers . . .

There were those who said that I was ahead of my time, but they were wrong. I believe that I was always behind the times that ought to be.

—CARL ELLIOTT, SR., 1990

CARL ELLIOTT, SR.

by Michael Beschloss

CARL ELLIOTT WAS born poor in 1913 in Jasper, Alabama, not far from Birmingham. The oldest of nine children, he was the descendant of farmers and Confederates, none of whom had ever finished high school. His grandmother filled his ears about rebel glories. "Until I was six or seven years old," he wrote in his memoir *The Cost of Courage* (Doubleday, 1992), "I thought the South had won the Civil War."

In the northern Alabama hills, Elliott grew up loving books, working in his father's fields, earning money for his family by trapping muskrat, possum and raccoon and going to watch politicians: "The speaking might start at ten o'clock and last until noon—any speaker worth his salt was good for at least two hours. . . . The women in the community would kill a goat or cook a pig, and everybody would eat until they were full. By then most of the afternoon was gone."

From an early age Elliott hoped to run for the U.S. Congress. As he watched the pols who came through Jasper and nearby towns, he tried to learn the tricks of their trade. At thirteen, he was awestruck at how Senator "Cotton" Tom Heflin could mesmerize a crowd by gasconading about the Wall Street "thieves" who had stolen the cotton farmers' money. After warming up, Heflin "went after the blacks . . . then the Jews, then the Catholics, playing them all like the keys on an organ, raising that big fist of his to the heavens and shaking his long gray hair."

Elliott wished he could one day speak as powerfully as Heflin: "But . . . I could not hate like he could. Hate is a powerful force, and a man who knows how to tap it, well, he can go a long way with it. . . . That was something else I saw in the faces of the crowd that day—the frenzy of hate—and that shook me."

At seventeen, with his best friend at his side and a check for twenty-five dollars in his pocket, Elliott put everything he owned in a cardboard box and walked to the University of Alabama at Tuscaloosa, where the two spent their first night in the rain, sleeping under a truck. Some classmates derided Elliott as a "hillbilly" and moved away when he sat near them in class.

The aspiring politician knew that Senators Lister Hill and John Sparkman and other Alabama greats had assumed their first leadership role by serving as student body president at Tuscaloosa. As a law school student, Elliott campaigned as the tribune of those shunned by the university's fraternities and sororities. To boost his candidacy, he threw a dance for non-sorority girls: "Almost eight hundred and fifty showed up, most of them girls that had never been invited to a dance in their lives. And those old gals had the biggest time I'd ever seen, just cutting up and dancing those old country dances. Yes, sir, it was a real night for the have-nots."

The candidate of the have-nots won his first election by a vote of two to one. A gaggle of Elliott's supporters hauled two barrels of whiskey onto the back of a pickup truck in front of the student union building and raised glasses in triumph. The old-guard university president, Dr. George Denny, looked on in disgust: "The modern student has grown to be nothing but a pig."

Since arriving in Tuscaloosa, Elliott had been startled to find students who lacked access to fraternity or sorority "courting rooms" instead lying on blankets on a hillside, "doing things I'd never seen before. Not that my mission was to pull them off those blankets, but I thought those students should have as proper a place to court as their wealthier classmates." Elliott used student funds to buy fifty "courting benches." He said years later, "They got heavy use, and I think some of them are still there."

Elliott also thought that students should own the high-priced college bookstore. Dr. Denny fought him tooth and nail. Elliott discovered that Denny had a quiet financial interest in the supply company that owned and operated the store. "The college ended up hanging onto its ownership, but we got them to slice the markup on the books they were selling to students."

In 1936, during his final semester, Elliott went to Washington to testify before Congress on behalf of federal scholarships for college students. Thanks to a scrawled note from his senator, Hugo Black, whom he had met as a boy, he was granted an audience with President Franklin Roosevelt in the Oval Office: "He asked me a little about my background and

I told him. We talked some about the bill, about how we both felt it was a tragic waste to see young people with ability and potential miss the chance for an education simply because they had no money." FDR later sent him an autographed portrait, inscribed, "To a New Voice in Education."

The earnest, smooth-faced young man returned to Jasper, ambitious to practice law and run for Congress. Most of his clients were struggling coal miners and farmers, causing one friend to call him "Old Coal and Potatoes." He recalled, "I knew just why Franklin Roosevelt was such a popular man. He was aware of these people and he felt for them, and they knew it. I was a New Deal man long before there was a New Deal, and I was definitely one thereafter."

In 1940, thinking himself not quite ready to run for Congress, Elliott instead ran for county judge but lost to the incumbent by three hundred votes. The next day, he said, "I went back to my law office, licked my wounds a little bit, then got to work to start paying back my debts from that campaign." Then he married Jane Hamilton, a federal clerk in Jasper. For their first date, Elliott had taken her to a wrestling match.

With a namesake son at home, after Pearl Harbor Elliott entered the U.S. infantry. But while training in Tennessee, he suffered a climbing accident and was honorably discharged. By 1948, he had been appointed a Jasper city judge and had three children. It was then he decided to make his move.

At the age of thirty-four, Elliott declared for Congress against a fifth-term Democrat named Carter Manasco. Under the banner "From Farm Boy to Congress," he made eighty-five speeches in three months: "I focused real hard on education, telling those miners and farmers that there was no reason on earth their children shouldn't have schooling of the same quality as that of children who live in large cities." He won, spending twelve hundred dollars in the process: "After six years of dreaming, I was finally on my way to Washington, D.C."

The Eighty-first Congress, convened in 1949, was swept into office along with Harry Truman in his surprise presidential victory that year. Elliott's new House colleagues included future Presidents John Kennedy, Richard Nixon and Gerald Ford.

Elliott was determined not to go native. Since he was a boy, what he had cared about was "seeing that folks got what they deserved, good or bad; seeing that the less fortunate weren't denied at least the same opportunity to get an education, earn a decent income, have a home and raise a family as people who happened to be in better circumstances." He was determined never to be "mesmerized" by power or prestige.

He later wrote, "A Congressman holds a seductive position in a very seductive city, and it's easy to see how some men lose sight of why they're here or of what their priorities are. I never hit a golf ball in my life. I went to as few parties as possible, although those still kept me busy enough to wear out two tuxedos during the time I was in Washington."

Elliott managed to obtain only his third-choice committee assignment—Veterans' Affairs, under the chairmanship of the notorious Mississippi racist John Rankin: "I had no taste for Rankin's virulent racism, but . . . I'd learned early on in life that you can only afford to get offended about so many things, so you've got to pick and choose the spots to spend your steam on. Hopefully those spots are on something you can change.

God knows there was no changing John Rankin." He quickly concluded that there was "one secret to John Rankin's success—he was simply one of the best parliamentarians on the floor of the House. . . . He could play those thousands of legislative strings like a harp."

Elliott aspired to be not just a congressman from Jasper but "a national Congressman—an *American* Congressman. . . . The way I saw it, somebody's got to mind the store, and if Congress doesn't do it, if every man's just looking out for himself and his friends, nobody's tending the store. I wanted to hear what *America's* problems were."

Elliott soon discovered that a congressman of loose ethics could make a lot of money from lobbyists and special interests: "Lord knows I could have reached out and grabbed some for myself back then. If I'd taken all that was offered me, both legitimately and otherwise, during my years in Congress, I'd be a rich man today."

One constituent offered Elliott a bribe to get him a post office job in Winston County. He asked Elliott what the price would be. "There ain't no price *to* it, you sorry son of a bitch, and I'll throw you out this goddamn window unless you leave my office immediately," came the reply. "It's three floors down to that sidewalk down there, and that's where your ass will be if you don't leave my sight right now."

The idealistic freshman congressman told President Harry Truman at the White House that he wanted to work for federal aid to education. By Elliott's account, Truman told him, "Aw, Carl, you don't want to fool with that. There's no politics in education, no future. You've got to be practical about these things. There's probably never going to *be* any federal aid to education . . . in your lifetime." Both Truman and Elliott knew that conservatives saw federal aid to schools as a dangerous means of allowing Big Brother to control citizens' lives.

Truman advised the young congressman, "Get you a dam built down there somewhere. Now *that's* something I can help you with. . . . That'll help you get reelected. . . . And you'll have none of the problems that come with this education business."

Elliott took Truman's advice. He concentrated on roads, dams, housing, rural electrification and veterans. Still he kept his eye on education. In 1951, he won appointment to the House Committee on Education and Labor. In every congressional session during his first decade in office, he proposed some form of aid to students. "I knew this would take time, and I was right. But hell, it took me twenty-seven years to get to Congress. I could handle another ten to get this done."

Elliott considered education "like a religion to me. I believed totally in its ability to empower every man to explore the limits of his potential." In 1958, he and his Alabama colleague Senator Lister Hill were key champions of the $900 million National Defense Education Act, also known as the Hill-Elliott Act. Passed after the national scare over the launching of the Soviet satellite *Sputnik* and American lassitude, the bill was the first serious federal effort to aid education.

"We were hanging our hat on the need for scientists in particular," he said. "But our aim was much broader than that. The forty thousand grant-in-aid college scholarships we proposed were aimed at the immediate goal of producing scientists, engineers, mathematicians and linguists. But the program we hoped to put in place was going to last much longer than any particular crisis." Senator Barry Goldwater was warning that the bill would allow the federal camel to get its nose into local tents. As Elliott recalled, "I couldn't admit it at the time, but I prayed Goldwater was right."

One of Elliott's early peers on Education and Labor was the thirty-four-year-old John Kennedy of Massachusetts. He admired JFK's grace in dealing with his painful back injuries: "Maybe it's the fact that I was raised by a man with a crippled leg, but I've always felt an affinity for people with any sort of physical disability, especially when I see them working through and with it the way my father had."

When Elliott came to Congress, the issue of race was becoming the focal point of American politics. As he later recalled, before the mid–twentieth century, it was "still relatively easy" for a Southern liberal to "skirt the issue of race." But the national Democratic party was beginning to fracture over segregation and voting rights.

At the Democratic convention of 1948, white Southerners had walked over the Harry Truman civil rights plank, crying, "We bid you goodbye!" Fifty-two Southern Democratic congressmen bolted the Truman ticket for the Dixiecrats led by Strom Thurmond of South Carolina. Elliott recalled how Sam Rayburn of Texas had said, "Those Dixiecrats are as welcome around here as a bastard at a family reunion." But Thurmond carried Alabama that year. "It was frighteningly clear to me that the fight down here had only begun," said Elliott. "But I hoped it would burn itself out."

In the 1950s, the Supreme Court ruled in *Brown v. Board of Education* that "separate but equal" schools had no place in American society. In Montgomery, Rosa Parks refused to go to the back of the bus. Little Rock Central High School was integrated by troops sent by a reluctant President Eisenhower. The fires of rebellion were being stoked in every American city.

White Southerners in Congress were under ferocious pressure to take their stand with the segregationists of Dixie. Elliott said, "By then the biggest challenge facing a liberal in the South was figuring out some way to make the voters at home look away from or see beyond the issue of race alone, so he could find his way back to Washington and do some work that really meant something . . . for blacks and whites alike. If you took a firm stand at home on race—the *wrong* stand— you could be assured you would not be making a stand anywhere else on anything. You'd be out of office."

Long afterward, Elliott told a reporter, "Anybody who had a grain of sense knew that the blacks had to be given their rights. The question was, how were we going to do it. Then the question locally was, what can we do and still live with our own particular situation?"

By the 1950s, he observed, "There was no room left in the middle. . . . A course of reasoned moderation had become a tightrope almost impossible to walk. . . . I saw . . . a South that seemed to be slowly losing its senses." Elliott felt that he had to find some way to "appease" the reactionaries "without sacrificing your own principles. Not only did you face that challenge with your constituents at home, but you faced it as well with your colleagues in Congress . . . from the South."

In March 1956, Southerners in Congress issued the notorious "Southern Manifesto," declaring that after *Brown v. Board of Education*, "meddlers" and "outside agitators" had acted against the Constitution to upset the "Southern way of life." The petition was signed by 101 Southerners. Lyndon Johnson,

Sam Rayburn, Albert Gore and Estes Kefauver of Tennessee refused to sign. Carl Elliott did not.

"Yes, I signed it," he said in 1992. "I can say now it was an evil thing, but I could not say it then. And I honestly did not feel it then as strongly as I do now." At the time, Elliott had "reservations" about the Supreme Court's demand that school desegregation be ended "with all deliberate speed." He recalled, "I knew things had to change. . . . But I was afraid things were happening too quickly, too fast, with too much force."

Elliott consoled himself by telling himself that "the aid-to-education bill I was working on was something that could heal and strengthen us all, black and white, as we let go of the past. . . . But I also knew time was slipping away. . . . don't want to sound like I'm making any excuses. Given that time, that place and those circumstances—with none of the knowledge that comes after forty years of hindsight—I'd probably make the same decision again."

In 1960, racist Alabamans were denouncing the education act Elliott had worked so hard for as a "nigger-loving" bill. That year, Elliott endorsed his old friend John Kennedy for the Democratic nomination for president. "In the same way that young liberal Democrats in my day had worshipped Franklin Roosevelt, I saw this new generation completely smitten by JFK."

After Kennedy's election, Speaker Sam Rayburn enlisted Elliott to help enlarge and modernize the critical House Rules Committee, chaired by the reactionary Virginian "Judge" Howard Smith, which for so long had been a graveyard for progressive bills, especially those to advance civil rights. Rayburn had chosen Elliott precisely to blunt the race issue: "It was understood that while I would vote for just about every liberal reform Kennedy had in mind, when it came to specific civil rights legislation, I would side with Smith and his crowd."

But not all Alabamans were mollified. The *Alabama Journal* said in the spring of 1961 that "Alabama has special reason to resent this blow against the South, this liberalism run wild and turned loose to foist all sorts of alien schemes upon the nation. It is a pro-Negro plan . . . to carry out some of the wild schemes put into the Democratic national platform." The paper said that, as a member of the new Rules Committee, more even than other Alabamans who had endorsed the reform, Elliott would have to "face" the people and explain why he had "deserted" them "in an hour of crisis."

As Elliott recalled, "It was pretty clear the other shoe was about to fall. When it did, it would be worn by a fellow I hadn't paid much attention to till then—a man named George Wallace."

Elliott had first met the pugnacious little man from the wire-grass lands of southwest Alabama in the early 1940s. Wallace was an undergraduate at Tuscaloosa. As Elliott recalled, "He was a very intense young fellow, clearly on the make . . . He told me he knew all about me, told me how much he thought of me . . . He talked about all the books he'd read on politics, and all the plans he had for himself. . . . Finally Jane pulled me into the car, and this boy was still talking as we pulled away, telling me I was the greatest man that's ever been and maybe we'd cross paths again."

Elliott had watched Wallace "punch his way through state politics in the 1950s, making a name for himself by staging showdowns designed to build his reputation. . . . I knew he didn't stand for anything that was constant. . . . As the saying goes in these parts, he'd become anybody's dog that would hunt with him. Votes were just about all George Wallace cared about, and when he latched onto the racist whirlwind of the late fifties, well, he had himself just about all the votes he could imagine." In 1958, bested for governor by the race-baiting John Patterson, Wallace had famously said, "Boys, I'm not going to be out-niggered again."

When Freedom Riders and other civil rights workers were attacked in Birmingham and Montgomery, Elliott felt "repelled by the violence" but he also "resented these 'activists' coming into Alabama from other places, fanning the flames that were already frighteningly high."

Even three decades later, Elliott angrily remembered how James Farmer of the Congress of Racial Equality had said he was counting on the "bigots" in the South to do his work for him: "Well, I resented that approach. . . . Maybe things never would have changed if they hadn't been shoved along. But at the time, I felt that a lot of these protesters . . . were opportunists eager to provoke and bring out the worst side of the white South."

Elliott knew there was trouble ahead for him. The 1960 census had forced Alabama to lose one of its nine congressional districts. The state legislature decreed that all Alabama voters would decide which of the nine Democratic nominees chosen by each district would survive. Elliott recalled that "in an election where people are looking for one name *not* to vote for, the publicity I'd gotten put me in a bad position." Elliott made it through, winning seventh place, "which was not too comforting."

He was more nervous about the state's new governor, George Wallace, who had campaigned by saying, "Niggers hate whites and whites hate niggers. Everybody knows that deep down." He foresaw that Wallace would try to consolidate his control of the state by purging elected officials of potential adversaries. In September 1962, after winning the Democratic nomination, which was tantamount to election, Wallace had appeared on Elliott's doorstep in Jasper. He bloviated about his plans for Alabama and gave the congressman a cheerful ultimatum—he had better join him.

As Elliott later recalled, "I'd spent my career in Congress building a record I could be proud of . . . and I was not about to let that record be sullied by shifting toward the likes of Wallace." He considered Wallace a surly "upstart." He said, "George, you don't need me, because I don't agree with your stand on almost everything you've talked about." Wallace retorted that he did want him.

Elliott brought him up short, saying, "You and I are on completely different sides." Wallace tried to resume the conversation, but Elliott stopped him. He warned, "George, don't piss on my leg."

At his inaugural in January 1963, Wallace fired a famous shot across the bow of Alabama moderates like Elliott: "In the name of the greatest people that have ever trod this earth, I draw the line in the dust and toss the gauntlet before the feet of tyranny, and I say, 'Segregation now! Segregation tomorrow! Segregation forever!' "

Elliott was appalled by what he had heard. In March, he told young Democrats at a Jefferson-Jackson Day dinner in his district that extremists like the John Birch Society were "a motley crew of malcontents and troublemakers who deserve the scorn and contempt, if not the pity of every responsible American." The *Montgomery Advertiser* replied that it could not understand what had "impelled" Elliott to "alienate so many voters needlessly."

That winter and spring, Kennedy was pondering whether to send to Congress the most sweeping civil rights bill in American history, which would open public accommodations to every American. He called Elliott to the Oval Office and asked whether he had "overlooked any chance of accommodations with the leaders of the South."

Elliott said that there wasn't: "I'm sorry to say I've recently finished a campaign in Alabama and there is absolutely no spirit of accommodation there on civil rights at all." With a melancholy face, Kennedy replied, "I just wish I was smart enough to do this thing without the country becoming disrupted over it. But there is no choice. It's either respond to the desire and insistence of these people to have their rights or have the country face revolution."

That June, Wallace stood in the door of the University of Alabama in his theatrical, vain effort to forestall the Kennedy administration's plan to enforce the law ensuring integration. The governor's staff had asked Elliott and other moderates whether they would join him in the defiant gesture. Elliott replied that he had refused to stand symbolically with Wallace the previous fall and had no notion of changing his mind now.

Still Elliott was not eager to commit political suicide. He continued to vote the Southern way on civil rights. He killed a bill to establish a federal department of urban affairs that, so Kennedy had promised, was to be headed by Robert Weaver, a black man. While pledging to support Kennedy's reelection, he publicly declared that JFK was "dead wrong" to assume that civil rights laws would calm racial turbulence in the South.

In the summer of 1963, despite Kennedy's intense unpopularity in Alabama over civil rights, Elliott flew in with him on a trip from Washington to a new Tennessee Valley Authority building at Muscle Shoals. From Air Force One, he pointed down at his old hometown of Vina and told the president, "There's hardly anybody living here. Maybe three hundred people. And there's nobody living here that has ever had a bath in water drawn from a central water system."

"Now Carl, this trip hurts you politically," said Kennedy. "I know it does. I'd like to find a way to show my appreciation." Elliott asked for new water systems for Vina and a neighboring town. The president got it done. That November, he was murdered.

By 1964, it was President Lyndon Johnson who was pushing the civil rights bill through the House and Senate. As Elliott recalled, "I stood against civil rights, believing it was too much too soon, hoping this Wallace madness would pass away, having faith that some less confrontational steps toward integration could then be taken, and knowing I wanted to be around when they were." Still he believed that the law was the law and must be obeyed.

Elliott was running for reelection. Wallace was testing his standing with Northern and border-state segregationists in presidential primaries in Wisconsin, Indiana and Maryland. Before appearing at the University of Maryland, he asked the entire Alabama congressional delegation to join him on the platform. With Wallace wildly popular at home, Elliott felt that refusal would mean political death.

"That was one of the lowest points of my life," he recalled. "Simply sitting on that stage, lending any kind of validity at all to George Wallace, made me realize how desperate I had become. It physically hurt. When I got back to Alabama the next day, I went right home to Jasper. That was the only day during that race—in fact, it was the only day during any race in my life—that I did no campaigning at all. I just couldn't."

Despite Elliott's cave-in in Maryland, a hard-right group known to be allied to the Wallace machine sent out a million sample ballots, delivered by state troopers, listing each of the nine names in the at-large congressional election, except Elliott's. Wallace denied to Elliott that he was behind the assault, but the damage was done. As the ninth man in an eight-man race, Elliott was defeated. Lingering campaign debts ran twenty thousand dollars.

Elliott could not overcome his feeling of injustice: "It was hard . . . to swallow the idea that I was a loser. I could work to pay off that debt, but the taste of defeat was not so easily erased, especially a defeat like that one. If I'd been whipped fair and square, that would have been one thing . . . But there was so much that was just plain wrong about what happened. . . . I had to do something, but I wasn't sure just what it would be."

In 1965, after "Bloody Sunday" in Selma, where civil rights demonstrators were attacked by state troopers and a civilian posse led by Sheriff Jim Clark, Lyndon Johnson sent a bill to Congress to ensure that black Americans could vote. With the bill's passage in August, Elliott imagined that thousands of new black voters might make it possible to end the Wallace era in Alabama.

When the Alabama Senate refused to rescind a one-term limit on the governorship, Wallace decided to run his wife, Lurleen, for the job in 1966, with himself as her "number-one assistant." The governor knew, but his wife did not, that she was suffering from terminal cancer.

Elliott announced his candidacy for governor. He was eager to show that there was a place in Alabama for white moderates. Over his shoulder he looked nervously at another candidate, Attorney General Richmond Flowers, a liberal who would challenge him for the loyalties of moderates and blacks. At the start, he told voters in Birmingham, "We must have racial peace. We must seize the leadership from the self-serving extremists on both sides who use the race issue as a whipsaw for . . . personal gain."

Elliott found that "the campaign turned pretty ugly pretty fast." His enemies, including the Ku Klux Klan, scrawled "NEVER! NEVER! NEVER!" across billboards emblazoned with his name. Shots were fired at some of his campaign workers. In Bessemer, Alabama, local toughs shoved him off the stage as he was threatened with arrest for public speaking without a license.

Then, despite Elliott's hopes for an endorsement and support from the Johnson White House, Martin Luther King came out for Flowers, followed by most of the Alabama black establishment. As Elliott recalled, "I didn't stand a ghost of a chance after that day." He kept fighting, but his crowds grew smaller and fundraising flagged. In the final week of the campaign, he called House Speaker John McCormack in Washington and told him that he wanted to cash in his congressional pension in order to pay thirty-eight thousand dollars for television advertisements.

"That's crazy," McCormack said presciently. "The time will come when you'll need this money to live on."

Elliott spent the money. But on election night, Mrs. Wallace avoided a runoff, drawing more votes than Flowers, Elliott or the eight other candidates combined. Elliott found himself a half million dollars in debt. His political career was over, and in Wallace's Alabama, he was now an official outcast in a state where the political moderate had abruptly grown extinct.

Elliott set up a law-lobbying firm in Washington. The firm benefited from his closeness to the Johnson White House but failed when Richard Nixon became president in 1969. He swallowed his pride, returned home and asked a dozen Alabama colleges and universities, including his alma mater, to let him teach English, history or political science. Dependent on Wallace for funding, they turned their backs.

"I had pretty much become a political . . . untouchable," he recalled, "and I know that had to be hard for my children to see, no matter how much they believed in me and the things I stood for."

With his son Carl and two friends he formed a law partnership in Jasper that specialized in winning damages for coal miners who had black lung disease. He also represented the Creek Indian nation against the federal government. Within ten years, he managed to cut his campaign debt in half, but his life continued to spiral downward. An investment in his brother's chicken farm collapsed. In 1974, the century's worst tornado tore apart his house, which was uninsured because Elliott lacked the money. He suffered a heart attack. His son Carl died. So did his wife.

"My circle of friends had grown so much smaller over the years . . . My career and business had shrunk to almost nothing. . . . I still had the burden of debt pressing hard on my shoulders—and on my soul," Elliott recalled. "It was torture to know I owed any man something I was unable to pay."

By 1988, he was confined to a wheelchair with diabetic neuropathy. "For more than twenty years, my world had been shrinking pretty steadily, my life closing in to a tighter and tighter circle," he wrote in 1992. "Now it had finally pulled pretty much inside the walls of my home, which is where I have stayed almost entirely since then."

In the ramshackle house, going blind, he strained to read poetry and history by the light of a naked bulb. A visitor observed that "the sorghum voice remains rich, but time has withered the body. His skin is gray as putty."

"His life became an absolute economic nightmare," recalled his lawyer and friend Julian Butler, who fended off creditors. "We would string it out in court. Sometimes we had a friendly judge who would not set cases." In 1989, Wil Haygood, a black reporter from the *Boston Globe* descended from Alabamans, interviewed him and wrote a sympathetic story called, "Twilight of a Southern Liberal—Carl Elliott: Flat Broke and Nearly Forgotten."

When the John F. Kennedy Library announced establishment of the Profile in Courage Award, Butler and Mary Allen Jolley, an old congressional aide, assembled material on Elliott and sent it to Boston. After five thousand nominations, Elliott was told that he would be the first recipient. More than thirty relatives and friends flew up to Boston for the ceremony on May 29, 1990, which would have been John Kennedy's seventy-third birthday.

Senator Edward Kennedy declared, "He persevered despite the fact that his stands were anathemas to the conservative climate of Alabama at the time. Ultimately they cost him his career . . . We hope the Profile in Courage Award will bring him at least some small measure of the recognition and respect he deserves."

Elliott replied, "There were those who said that I was ahead of my time, but they were wrong. I believe that I was always behind the times that ought to be."

He told a reporter, "I'm happy to have the award because it'll help me pay some debts before I leave this world. It'll also help me eat. . . . I regret that I'm in debt, but I can't regret the cause."

Elliott indeed passed along his twenty-five-thousand-dollar award to some of his creditors. He donated his Tiffany-made silver and glass lantern to the Carl Elliott Regional Library in Jasper. An old political enemy sent him an apology and a hundred-dollar check.

"I never swapped an old friend for a new one," Elliott said, "and I guess in the beginning people saw that as a mark of courage."

He also heard from George Wallace, by now in a wheelchair himself, after being shot during the Maryland presidential primary campaign of 1972. As Elliott remembered, the letter "began with congratulations for the award, but he quickly turned it around to himself, talking about the subject of civil rights and the good work he'd done for that cause" when the black vote surged in Alabama in the 1970s and 1980s.

At the bottom of the letter Wallace had scribbled the percentages of blacks who had voted for him in his last gubernatorial election. "That's just like him," observed Elliott, "always positioning himself, always adjusting and arranging the facts to suit his situation, always gauging the wind and trying to get himself out in front of it."

Jacqueline Kennedy Onassis, by then an editor at Doubleday, urged Elliott to write a memoir and found him a collaborator, Michael D'Orso, a staff writer for the Norfolk *Virginian-Pilot*. D'Orso recalled, "What I saw was a man with great pride and great strength who basically had nothing left."

In 1992, Elliott published his memoir under the title *The Cost of Courage: The Journey of an American Congressman*. After it was published, Wayne Flynt, a history professor at Auburn University, said, "History is vindicating Carl Elliott now. But history doesn't pay your bills." When motion picture companies asked about making the book into a film, Elliott said he was willing if they would pay off a few of his bills.

In January 1999, four months after the death of his nemesis George Wallace, Elliott died at the age of eighty-five. He was always proudest of his role in passing the National Defense Education Act, which helped more than fifteen million Americans to go to college.

Principal sources: Profile in Courage Award Files, JFK Library, Boston; Carl Elliott, Sr., and Michael D'Orso, *The Cost of Courage* (Doubleday, 1992); Wil Haygood in *The Boston Globe*, 2/28/89, 5/30/90; Jim Yardley in *The Atlanta Journal-Constitution*, 5/17/92.

President Kennedy knew, with Plutarch, that human beings are moved, not so much by abstraction and theory, as by the acts and lives of other human beings. He believed that public officers are trustees and servants of the people. He believed that public life must be lived for the public good.

The nation needs to promote and support the high calling of public service; and young people need to know that. Let public officers know that the people expect from them nothing less than the best they have to give; and let the people demand just that.

—CHARLES LONGSTREET WELTNER, 1991

CHARLES LONGSTREET WELTNER

by Bill Kovach

THERE HAD NEVER been a time when Charles Weltner was unaware of who he was and, more important, where he came from. He was reminded of it every time he heard his name: Charles Longstreet Weltner. A big name for a little boy. But it ran deeper than his identity because he was the namesake of one Confederate general and the great-grandson of another general. Most of us are familiar with his namesake, Lieutenant General James Longstreet. But Weltner's blood ancestor, Brigadier General T. R. R. Cobb, was Georgia's icon of the Confederacy. He not only wrote the definitive legal treatise defending slavery but was the principal author of the Confederate Constitution. He died at the head of his unit, Cobb's Legion, defending Stonewall Jackson's position at Fredericksburg. And from family portraits, it appears that Charles Weltner inherited the general's dimples in his upper lip and in his chin as well as an instinct for legal reasoning.

As a child his friends would tease him when they stretched his name to sing-song lengths—Chaaa-rulsLooongstreeet-Weelltner—but he was confident of their envy of his special place in Southern history. In reflective moments as an adult, he would recall the feeling for the Confederacy that this accident of birth engendered. It contained, he once wrote, "all the elements of gallantry, chivalry, courage, and Greek tragedy that have fascinated modern man for centuries . . . The courage of Southern men and women, in the face of impossible odds, cast about the whole era a glow that even the underlying shame of slavery cannot dim."

But that personal history became problematic as he came of age in the 1950s. By then, the romantic glow was fading for those living in an urbanizing South that was finally breaking free of the Confederate legacy that had long held the majority of citizens in rural political servitude.

In 1954, four years out of Columbia Law School, Weltner felt the first pangs of change when the U.S. Supreme Court issued its historic opinion in *Brown* v. *Board of Education*, declaring the separation of races in the schools unconstitutional.

Like most white Southerners of his time, Weltner was unprepared for this rejection of a central tenet of his society. Like others who were part of a privileged class, the social, racial and political tensions that had been building to a boil since the end of World War II had largely escaped his notice. The decision hit like a scalding bath and political leaders reacted with threats to end public education rather than mingle races in the classroom. Resolutions, memorials and manifestos of repudiation clattered down like hailstones on the region. No single responsible political voice in Georgia was raised in support of the *Brown* decision. No officeholder missed a chance to enumerate its evils.

Weltner allowed himself to fall back on his newfound legal craft for argument asking, "Where is the legal appeal?" to avoid confronting the moral question of legally imposed inequality that the decision raised in front of the conscience of every white Southerner. Instead, he busied himself in the cause of the social and economic leadership of Atlanta. The aim was to overthrow the county unit system that perpetuated rural control of state politics. Herman Talmadge, who was governor then, said the county unit system (which counted votes in such a way that a single rural county's vote would count as much as 100 votes cast in Atlanta) would "stop the nigger bloc at the county line."

While the number of Atlanta blacks was growing, their history of allegiance to the party of Lincoln and voting solidly with the Republicans meant they were as yet not part of this struggle. But inexorably, the campaign against the county unit system began to draw the new young black leadership of Atlanta's civil rights movement—people like Vernon Jordan, Andrew Young and Julian Bond—into the politics of the Democratic Party.

By 1960 Weltner had helped form something called the New Forum to provide support for the campaign of John F. Kennedy, a campaign the state party leaders were ignoring. Kennedy didn't carry the black vote in Atlanta, but he made a big dent in it and gave added impetus to the legal battle that eventually overturned the county unit rule. The gathering momentum of these movements and the new urban organization created an entirely new context for the 1962 elections. As a key part of the strategy to defeat rural control of state politics in Georgia an attorney named Morris Abrams convinced Weltner to run for Congress and use the issue to continue to build on the urban Atlanta vote inspired by Kennedy's presidential campaign. "I believe that I am," Weltner later wrote, "the only person who ever became a candidate for public office without the urging of thousands of his friends."

But history was on his side. Shortly after he began his campaign the U.S. Supreme Court ruled in a Tennessee lawsuit, *Baker* v. *Carr*, that unequal treatment of rural and urban voters was unconstitutional. Within months, a federal court in Georgia ruled that the County Unit Rule was also unconstitutional. The newly empowered Atlanta voters helped Weltner defeat James C. Davis, the eight-term segregationist representative from Stone Mountain, the birthplace of the modern Ku Klux Klan.

The Charles Weltner who went to Washington as a member of the Eighty-eighth Congress was not so much a representative of the New South emerging to confront festering issues of race. He was more a representative of a renewal of the old New South of commercial and economic development preached by Henry Grady in the nineteenth century.

With Betty Jean, his wife of twelve years, and their three children, Weltner settled in Bethesda, Maryland; his ambition was to build a career as a progressive representative inspired by his association with the youthful vision of the Kennedy campaign. At the top of his agenda was Atlanta's desire to gain more federal dollars for transportation, housing development, urban renewal and even international trade. Issues of race were secondary.

But the rising tide of change that was challenging his personal history and that of his region were not to be easily held at bay. In April, there began the nonviolent campaign for equal rights led by a young black minister from his own hometown by the name of Martin Luther King, Jr. Soon it would consume the American political system in an often bloody struggle for fundamental change.

Within weeks President Kennedy sent federal troops into Alabama to restore order, rearranging his own political agenda to introduce major legislation on civil rights that would eliminate discrimination in restaurants, hotels and other places of public accommodation.

Like an evil reincarnation, the Old South rose again in resistance. Southern opposition to the bill in Congress was virtually unanimous. The Georgia congressional delegation closed ranks in opposition—including Charles Weltner. But there were hints in his first important speech on the bill that he was struggling to accommodate change.

In a characteristically brief speech on the legislation, he began to define himself as something more than a traditional Southern rejectionist.

Slightly built, five feet ten inches tall, wearing a dark blue suit, white shirt and red tie, his long, slender fingers fluttering the two pages on which his speech was written, Weltner spoke his words deliberately and precisely.

"[W]e must recognize that all governmental, or publicly supported or controlled facilities must be made available to all citizens," he said. "The Fourteenth and Fifteenth Amendments, forged in the bloodshed of a century ago, are [also] the law of the land. Their guarantees must extend to every citizen.

Nor can there be any justification for withholding or denying any of the rights there secured on grounds of race or color. Particularly, the right to vote must be extended to all persons, without regard to color, who can qualify under fairly administered standards. Those who seek, by harassment, subterfuge, or intimidation, to deny the ballot to others do nothing but invite Federally supervised voting procedures. Unless justice is done at the courthouse, it will be done at the Capitol. . . ."

Those who knew the region from which Weltner came recognized the speech as a signal that Atlanta was no longer ruled by the sentiments of Stone Mountain. Instead of the harsh, defiant voice of George Wallace echoing the Rebel Yell that inspired often murderous violence in the South, his soft, cultured tones of reason gently filled the House chamber. Yet, as if mindful of the weakening political limb on which he walked, the hesitancy that restrained him when he first confronted the school desegregation decision asserted itself. He retreated into legalisms about the constitutionality of President Kennedy's proposals.

"Is it fair that some Americans are admitted, and others turned away?" he continued. "Is it fair that some Americans are welcomed on one side of a store, and rejected on the other? If we seek fair play, then we must acknowledge that it is lacking here. [But] is the remedy found in a public accommodations law of nationwide application? . . . I think not. I do not think that prudence dictates such a mandatory rule as the national public accommodations proposal, and I cannot support it. . . .

"Our nation can overcome its problems—but we must solve them, not ignore them. Long-term solutions are still to be found, not in hastily passed statutes, but in a full and fair opportunity for every American to attend a good school, to earn a good income and to achieve full development of his own talents and abilities. . . ."

Sara Craig, Weltner's administrative assistant, remembers this as a time when her normally sure-footed and assertive boss was at a loss to reconcile the personal and political forces tugging at his attitudes, beliefs and history.

"You could literally see him struggling to find his way through his own conflicted feelings and a divided constituency—and then he had his own agenda that was more in step with the urban agenda of the country than the rural agenda of Georgia," she recalls.

His personal conflict was sharpened when President Kennedy convinced a strong supporter and advisor of Weltner's, Atlanta Mayor Ivan Allen, Jr., to speak out for the legislation at a Senate committee hearing. Unlike Weltner whose constituency included two rural counties outside of Atlanta, Mayor Allen owed his position to the Atlanta power structure, which was anxious to change the city's Old South image. Even so, Weltner recognized it was a risk no other Southern official of his stature was willing to take.

Georgia's senators, Richard Russell and Herman Talmadge, scorned tradition when they refused to introduce the mayor or even attend the committee meeting. So it fell to the most junior member of the delegation to extend that courtesy and to accompany Mayor Allen into Room 318 of the Senate Office Building where the hearing was held.

One moment in the tense hearing particularly struck Weltner as he sat at the mayor's side. It was when Democratic

Senator John Pastore, in an effort to rescue the mayor from a sarcastic assault by Senator Strom Thurmond, announced himself "humbled" by the mayor's appearance.

"I think," Senator Pastore told the mayor, "that President Kennedy, when he wrote *Profiles in Courage*, must have been thinking of men such as you."

After attending church on Sunday, September 15, Weltner took his three children, ages ten, eight and three, to see the battlefield at Fredericksburg where their great-great-grandfather died. They returned home to hear a radio report that a dynamite blast had killed four young black girls attending Sunday School in Birmingham, Alabama. Once again Weltner was the lone voice from the deep South that felt compelled to examine publicly the sharpening pangs of his conscience on the issue of race:

"Mr. Speaker, there was a time when a Southerner was 'moderate' for what he did not say. There was a time when silence amid the denunciations of others was a positive virtue. But, in the face of the events of Sunday, who can remain silent? Those responsible for the deed in Birmingham chose a Sabbath morning as the time, a House of God as the place, and the worshipers within as the victims. I do not know what twisted and tortured minds fashioned this deed. But I know why it happened. It happened because those chosen to lead have failed to lead. Those whose task it is to speak have stood mute. And in so doing, we have permitted the voice of the South to preach defiance and disorder. We have stood by, leaving the field to reckless and violent men.

"For all our handwringing and headshaking, we will never put down violence until we can raise a higher standard.

Though honest men may differ as to means, can we not affirm as a great goal of this Republic the concept—equality of opportunity?"

Weltner spoke more boldly than any other congressman from the Deep South to condemn his regional colleagues. But he was still unable to take the next step to announce himself in favor of the civil rights legislation. This time even his legal instincts failed to help him bridge the gap between the moral standard he pronounced and the practical step he would propose. The arc of his rhetoric dropped sharply as he fell back on exhortation:

"Mr. Speaker, we need not so much new paragraphs on books of the law, as new precepts in the hearts of men. We need to raise, and to follow, this standard—as old as Christianity and as simple as truth—'Let right be done.'"

This speech catapulted him to the attention of the country as a rare responsible voice of a new generation of Southerners. Although he pulled up short on the legislative question, the depth of his repudiation of the rhetoric of George Wallace and Orville Faubus was singular.

A FRESH VOICE FROM THE SOUTH, headlines announced, WELTNER DECRIES MOB ACTION.

But as it turned out, the impact of these changes proved fleeting as events seized the reins of the political process.

The drive for equal rights legislation was stalled. The massive quarter-million-person March on Washington in August and Dr. Martin Luther King's "I have a dream . . ." speech couldn't bring the Kennedy bill to a vote. Three months later the president was assassinated.

Civil rights legislation may have stalled, but it was far from dead. Weltner returned to the Eighty-ninth Congress to find that Lyndon Johnson had placed Kennedy's Civil Rights Act at the top of the agenda. By January 31 the bill was before the House and after a week of debate, the bells rang to summon members to a final vote. As Weltner recalls in his autobiography the roll call had reached the Ws as he entered the House Chamber,

"Watts. 'No.' "

"Weaver. 'Aye.' "

"Weltner. 'No.' . . ."

"I should have been glad it was over. The days and nights had been long, the debate wearing, and the issue itself was stale from overdiscussion and overemotion. I should have felt a sense of relief that the House might now turn its attention to other fields . . .

"The question had come and the vote was cast. Yet I sensed no finality about the matter. Instead, there was a vague lack somewhere, as though something were left undone that needed doing."

Without Weltner's support the House passed and sent the bill to the Senate where a filibuster led by Georgia's senior senator, Richard Russell, one of the most powerful members of Congress, awaited. But Lyndon Johnson knew the Senate even better than Richard Russell, and he was not going to be denied on this bill.

President Johnson broke the filibuster and on July 2, 1964, Charles Weltner was asked, yet again, to declare where he stood on equal rights.

Those who knew him best remember the church as a signif-

icant force in the evolution of his thinking during the five
months the civil rights bill was being considered.

"We were churchgoing folks," Betty Jean, his wife at the
time, said. "The church nearest us was a northern Presbyterian
Church . . . A very liberal church. The minister there was Dr.
Carl Pritchard and he just firmly believed segregation was
wrong and every Sunday he talked about the civil rights issue.
It wasn't pounding-the-pulpit preaching. It was carefully
thought out, intellectual. Why it was wrong. Basically, it was
unchristian."

Wyche Fowler, who would later become U.S. senator from
Georgia and ambassador to Saudi Arabia, and described as
Weltner's closest friend, agreed and added, "He got his sense
of right and wrong from his mother's side. She was a very strict
Calvinist—in church everytime the door opened, twice on
Sunday and once in the middle of the week. And she raised
him that way."

Reporters in the press gallery above the Speaker's rostrum
were watching Charles Weltner as the members filed into their
seats. They had watched this member of a Deep South delegation struggle with issues of race and equal rights for a year and a
half now. The fact that he had asked for an opportunity to explain his vote before the roll call suggested news was about to
be made. But they could read nothing in his appearance, he
wore the usual dark suit, white shirt, hair cut as it was in his military days. Nor could it be detected in his demeanor. His
hooded eyes, as usual, gave nothing away. The way he shifted
in his seat and fiddled with papers on his desk was no indication because everyone knew Weltner could never stay still.

The press gallery couldn't hear eighty-one-year-old Carl Vinson, the dean of the Georgia House delegation, as he leaned down to ask Weltner if it were true that he planned to vote "yes" on the bill. Unheard also was Weltner's response that he was and the old veteran, shaking his head slowly and referring back to the day Mayor Allen testified for the bill, whispered, "Profiles in courage and all that, I'd hate to see you cut short a promising career." Vinson returned to his seat as Weltner walked slowly to the well of the House:

"Mr. Speaker, over four months ago, the civil rights bill came to the floor. The stated purpose, equality of opportunity for all Americans, is a proper goal. But I questioned its means, and voted against passage. Now, after the most thorough and sifting examination in legislative history, this measure returns for final consideration. It returns with the overwhelming approval of both Houses of Congress.

"Manifestly, the issue is already decided, and approval is assured. By the time my name is called, votes sufficient for passage will have been recorded.

"What, then, is the proper course? Is it to vote 'no,' with tradition, safety—and futility?

"I believe a greater cause can be served. Change, swift and certain, is upon us, and we in the South face some difficult decisions.

"We can offer resistance and defiance, with their harvest of strife and tumult. We can suffer continued demonstrations, with their wake of violence and disorder.

"Or, we can acknowledge this measure as the law of the land. We can accept the verdict of the Nation . . .

"Mr. Speaker . . . I will add my voice to those who seek reasoned and conciliatory adjustment to a new reality.

"And finally, I would urge that we at home now move on to the unfinished task of building a new South. We must not remain forever bound to another lost cause."

Before he finished his brief speech, the Clerk of the House had flipped to the end of his roll call sheet and drew a red check mark through Weltner, C. L. to signify the only "yes" vote that would be recorded by a congressman from the Deep South.

His fellow Southerners sat stunned by the speech. His Georgia peers who, to a man, voted no, were shaking their heads, convinced young Charles Longstreet Weltner had signed his political death warrant.

And maybe he had. William Faulkner once wrote of the South, "The past is not dead. It is not even past." But with that vote the scion of the man who had offered moral and legal justification for slavery and willingly died defending it had finally shed that burden of his past.

As he told his constituents in Hapeville, Georgia, a few months later:

"How well I knew what would happen if I dared vote for the Civil Rights Bill. This district, after reapportionment, is three to one white in voter registration. Only one out of four of my constituents is Negro. How well did I realize that whatever career might be ahead for me would fall into grave jeopardy. But my career was not the issue; my future was not the question; my safety was not the cause. There was a greater issue, a larger question, a higher cause. Indeed, at stake was the highest cause in the affairs of men—the cause of simple justice for every American.

"And so, on that afternoon in July, when the bells rang in the House Chamber—on that day when they called my name, I voted 'aye.' "

The day after that vote three black students trying to integrate the Pickrick restaurant near the heart of Atlanta were met by the owner, Lester Maddox, who was armed with a pistol and waving a pickax handle.

"Get out of here and never come back," he shouted as he drove them away.

His pickax handles—Pickrick Toothpicks he called them—became a symbol of segregationist defiance.

Overnight Georgia became the showcase of the region's deadly struggle to break the hold of the past when Charles Weltner, the rising star of a new kind of Southern politician, qualified to run for reelection to a third term in Congress, and the newly notorious Lester Maddox, accompanied by a gang of his ax-handle-wielding followers, qualified to run for governor. Among the dozen or so papers candidates signed that year was a new one-page mimeographed oath pledging to support all the nominees of the party in the November general election.

Overcoming fears that his votes for civil rights legislation would end his career, Weltner won the Democratic nomination to his third term in Congress. Already at thirty-eight one of the most promising of a new generation of political leaders, the talk among his supporters that night was of his potential someday for the number two spot on the national ticket.

His assistant, Sara Craig, remembers that all the others in

the headquarters in downtown Atlanta were reveling in the sense that with this election a new South had finally begun the process of relieving itself of the burden of history.

Charles Weltner wasn't part of the celebration. He seemed more burdened than ever.

"We were so busy celebrating our victory," she now remembers. "We had the nomination won and that meant the election was as good as over and we paid no attention to the fact that Lester Maddox had won the Democratic Party's nomination for governor. We didn't, but Charles had."

Always a restless man, on this particular night Weltner seemed unable to find a comfortable spot as he moved from place to place exchanging one cigarette for another, sitting for a moment, flipping his brown loafers on and off his feet.

Wyche Fowler, his youngest staff assistant, was the first to understand why. He recalled the night this way: "We were celebrating his third term, but Charles seemed distracted. The last thing he said to me that night was to call a press conference for eleven o'clock in the morning. I said, 'What for?'

"And he said, 'I'm resigning.'

"I said, 'What? Why?'

"He said, 'Because I've made this commitment to support all nominees of the party and I can't do that for Maddox. I've fought him all my life.'

"I said, 'You can't resign. You can't just *resign*. I mean, you're resigning from the race?'

"He said, 'No, I'm resigning from Congress.'

"You know I'm only twenty-six and I'm talking to him like I'm his elder but I'm sure I wasn't very forceful."

The press conference was called for eleven o'clock the next

morning, but Fowler and Sara Craig and other members of the staff met with Weltner at ten to try to talk him out of his decision.

"He sat there cool as a cucumber and said, 'I have no alternative. I won't violate my oath.' His sense of righteousness—his critics called it self-righteousness—was what he thought was his commitment to himself."

So, on October 3, 1966, Charles Longstreet Weltner sat before the television cameras in Atlanta to announce his decision. His face, made even more rounded and boyish than usual by its puffiness for lack of sleep, was not raised to look into the cameras. Instead he methodically read through his prepared statement, which recalled the new loyalty oath that he and all other Democratic Party candidates had routinely signed, and he concluded: "Today the one man in our state who exists as the very symbol of violence and oppression is the Democratic nominee for the highest office in Georgia. His entire public career is decidedly contrary to my deepest convictions and beliefs. And while I cannot violate my oath, neither can I violate my principles. I cannot compromise with hate. I cannot vote for Lester Maddox. Therefore I am withdrawing as the Democratic nominee for the House of Representatives.

"I love the Congress but I will give up my office before I give up my principles. I cannot compromise with hate."

The next morning's *New York Times* declared Weltner "A Candidate of Conscience." The *Washington Post*, in an article by Richard L. Lyons, noted that "political skeptics, not used to such a display of conscience, began speculation that Weltner might be drafted as a write-in candidate for governor. Weltner said he would have no part of it, 'I'm out of politics this November,' he said."

Weltner's congressional office was inundated with expressions of support. In the first week there were 38,000 letters, mostly of support.

One, which seemed to sum up the national reaction to the rare resignation from public office on a matter of principle, said simply:

"Last week I'd never heard of you. Now I'll never forget you."

But, back in Atlanta, there was among many a sense of abandonment, a reaction that Weltner would only become aware of when he tried to reclaim his seat in 1968. It was a reaction summed up by Vernon Jordan many years later as he tried to express the way he felt that July morning.

"I walked down the street from my office on Forsyth Street to his office and when I first went in I was convinced that he had performed a great act of conscience," he said. "But the more I thought about it when we talked, my reaction was that the black people in Atlanta had been screwed."

The state Democratic Party felt the same way, according to Fowler.

"They just thought he was crazy. They didn't have time to get anybody to stand in, so the Republicans won the seat. Only Charles would have considered that a binding oath. It was a mimeographed form. You had to sign about a dozen of these things. They didn't even, most of them, know what they were signing.

"When you're confronted with a moral force," he concluded sadly, "rational people don't know how to deal with it. He was invoking a higher standard in politics."

And so, like a soaring hawk that had lost the thermal, Weltner's career and his personal life spiraled downward.

"He didn't, as we would say, settle down to a very satisfactory life of the mind for at least ten years after that," Fowler said. "He was thirty-eight and he'd been on the cover of *Time* magazine, voices of the New South."

His wife, Betty Jean, remembers it as a disorienting and painful time.

"We moved into a run-down neighborhood in Atlanta, just on the cusp, and our daughter, Betsey, said, 'How can Daddy do this to us? We're living in a slum.' "

The effort to recover his seat in '68, when he discovered the degree to which the black community and the Democratic Party resented the political cost to them of his act of conscience, she remembers was "like a death."

"I don't think we felt we could lose. He had done this right thing and people would appreciate that. And it was awful that they didn't. You feel like you were so let down. It was like a death, at least it was for us. Such a rejection."

Then in 1971 his marriage disintegrated and Charles and Betty Jean were divorced. Charles entered what his friends called his "hippy" period. He returned to his practice of law but he replaced his dark, conservative suits with loud sport coats, if he did wear a coat and tie, and his favored means of transportation became a Yamaha 200 motorcycle. Color: Purple.

Seedy bars along Ponce de Leon Avenue in Atlanta became

his nightly haunts. "Ray-Lees White Dot Lounge" was a favorite spot, and as one friend said, "He'd fall in love with the waitresses down there when he got drunk and they'd call me to come get him. We all thought he was going to kill himself driving drunk on that motorcycle."

He even married one of the women he met at one or the other of the bars. It lasted five months.

But then his dissolute spree ended as quickly as it began. As his friend said: "He sort of, one day, like he always did, said: 'I'm not going to drink anymore.' And that was it. Never drank another drop in his life."

Weltner's career in public life was resurrected in 1976 when Governor George D. Busbee appointed him judge of the Superior Court in Atlanta. He was elevated to the Georgia Supreme Court in 1981. On his desk Weltner kept a quote from Czech President Vaclav Havel that read: "I simply take the side of truth against any lie, of sense against nonsense, justice against injustice."

Chief Justice Harold G. Clarke described Weltner's presence on the court. He was, Clarke wrote, "known for his quick mind and his keen interest in a myriad of subjects. He valued clear and concise language, precise writing, and internal logical consistency. He labored over the opinions that he authored, some of which went through as many as forty drafts. He was conscious that printed words mattered, that they endured."

But, Charles's restless mind and body never changed. Even on the bench in the somber, dignified atmosphere of the courtroom Weltner couldn't stand to sit still. For him that was torture.

He began working on a doctoral dissertation in Biblical

studies from Trinity College. In pursuit of his studies, he taught himself to read the ancient languages of Greek, Hebrew, Latin, Aramaic, Ethiopic, Ugaritic, Akkadian, Syriac and Egyptian Hieroglyphics.

During the interminable oral arguments in the court, he filled the pages of an ever present student notebook with row after row of symbols from one of the many languages he knew.

In July 1990 Weltner learned that he had esophageal cancer which would prove to be terminal, but not before the importance of his life was recognized.

As David Nyhan wrote in the *Boston Globe* in May 1991: "Anytime you pick up the phone on a quiet Sunday night at home, and a strange voice starts talking about something that happened to you 25 years ago, your heart skips a beat. In the case of Charles Longstreet Weltner, the voice he heard a week ago Sunday was . . . explaining how an act of political courage in 1966 has been found worthy of the 1991 John F. Kennedy Profile in Courage Award."

As Weltner's daughter, Susan Weltner Yow, recalled the event, "Dad said it was like someone had been reaching into the dustbin of history and—blowing on his fingers like blowing off dust—just picked me out."

His friend, Chief Justice Clarke, received approval of a plan to temporarily step down and allow the dying Weltner to assume the position as Chief Justice of the Georgia Supreme Court. It was a post held by another of Weltner's nineteenth-century ancestors, Chief Justice Joseph Henry Lumpkin.

Weltner then set about what his children (who now include two girls by a third marriage) describe as "the act of dying with dignity."

"We were all surrounding his bed and he said at one point, 'Hey, I'm trying to die here,' " his eldest son, Philip, recalled. "He wanted to get it over with and get onto the next thing. I told him, 'Everything we do we do for you, Dad.' He smiled."

His second son, Charles, remembers him playing the concertina.

"He played the concertina the night before he died," he said. "He played 'Waltzing Matilda.' We were all gathered around and he played 'Waltzing Matilda' and then he said, 'Oh, go on home. I won't die tonight. I'll die tomorrow.' And he did."

In his memorial tribute to Weltner, Judge Clarke wrote:

"On the first day of arguments after Chief Justice Weltner's death, I opened the drawer in front of my seat on the Supreme Court bench expecting to find a pencil and notepad. Instead, a page from a small yellow pad stared back from the bottom of my drawer. The page bore Charles Weltner's handwriting, and in a way typical of him, contained words written in Arabic and in English.

" 'ALAM BEK A'N'

"Farewell, World!"

I'm proud to be a politician in a free society. It is the accolade of one's neighbors not the dictate of a system or a man. The courage attributed to me is the reflection of those I serve. For all the licks anyone takes by choosing, there is the elation of having achieved for good purpose what none thought possible. And such feeling far exceeds whatever the hurt for having tasted the battle.

—LOWELL WEICKER, JR., 1992

LOWELL WEICKER, JR.

by E. J. Dionne

I NEVER QUARREL, SIR," declared Senator Thomas Hart Benton, one of the heroes of *Profiles in Courage.* "But sometimes I fight, sir; and whenever I fight, sir, a funeral follows, sir." Henry Clay said Benton had the "hide of a hippopotamus," and Benton once insisted: "I despise the bubble popularity that is won without merit, and lost without crime."[1]

Days after Governor Lowell Weicker, Jr., pushed through an income tax in Connecticut that was despised by voters who had never before had to pay one, the very unpopular governor described the choice he faced in risking political conflagration.

"Did you want war or an endless series of firefights?" he asked. "I chose the former."[2]

[1] John F. Kennedy, *Profiles in Courage* Memorial Edition (New York: Harper and Row, 1964), pp. 72, 84, 88.
[2] Judith Gaines, "Weicker Survives Odyssey," *Boston Globe,* Aug. 25, 1991, p. 41.

Weicker spent an entire political career waging and risking war. If he was described as "muscle bound by morality" or as believing, as a Connecticut Democratic state chairman once put it, "that the Lord speaks directly to Lowell Weicker, and only Lowell Weicker," he seemed not to mind.[3]

"I used to call him in every now and then," said Howard Baker, the Republican Senate leader who had served with Weicker on the Watergate committee, "and said, 'Now, Lowell, you can only be a moral giant once this week.' " Baker once described Weicker this way: "That's the only man I ever met who would strike a match to look into a gas tank."[4]

Weicker's tax war made him so unpopular that he received a call one day from his neighboring governor, Mario Cuomo. "I understand your pain," Cuomo said. "So I have decided to offer you political asylum in the state of New York."[5]

Like Benton, Lowell Weicker was a party maverick who took risks for principle and was prepared to leave his party— and many in his party were glad to see him go. Few feuds were more amusing than the one between Weicker and conservative columnist William F. Buckley, Jr. In 1988, when the Republican Weicker lost his Senate seat to Democrat Joe Lieberman, Buckley created his own political action committee, Buckpac, to raise money in support of the *Democrat*—or, more precisely, to beat Weicker. The feud even made it to William Safire's language column. Safire could not resist citing Buckley's rococo attack on Weicker: "His pomposity and tergiversations on

[3]Michael Specter, "In This Corner," *New York Times Magazine*, Dec. 15, 1991, p. 144.
[4]Specter, pp. 145, 142.
[5]Michael Specter, "Weicker Trying to Corner $1 Billion in New Taxes," *Washington Post*, July 14, 1991, p. A8.

every issue make his running as a Republican an anomaly we ought to correct."[6]

It was a puzzling contest during which reporters wondered in print whether Weicker and Lieberman were each in the wrong party. Weicker attacked Buckley's "ultra-conservatism" and his "ilk" in the Republican Party. Lieberman carefully welcomed Buckley's support and occasionally sided with Ronald Reagan on issues where Weicker had not. Yet Lieberman insisted that Buckley's views were not his own. "I don't believe Bill Buckley is supporting me because he agrees with me on a lot of issues," Lieberman insisted. "He's supporting me because he's fed up with the Weicker record as a lot of Republicans in the state are."

In a clever formulation designed to appeal to all parties, Lieberman—who eventually won by some 5,000 votes out of 1.3 million cast—would declare: "Lowell Weicker is not a real Republican. He's not a real Democrat. He does what he wants to do when he wants to do it."[7] *Good + bad?*

In almost any context other than that of a harshly negative campaign, Lieberman's assault might be seen as a high political compliment. There's a name for a politician who does what he wants to do when he wants to do it: independent.

In that, too, he was like Benton, who also ended his political career as a man without a party. And like Benton, Weicker has never been an easy man. He has never been one to play down his own gifts or his own courage. Commenting on an address he had just given, Weicker said exactly what he

[6]William Safire, "On Language," *New York Times Magazine*, Sept. 25, 1988, p. 20.
[7]Gwen Ifill, "Sen. Weicker Scrambles to Keep Seat," *Washington Post*, Oct. 29, 1988, p. A12.

thought. "That was a good speech," he declared. "That was one hell of a good speech."[8]

But there was courage, and a thundering outrage that millions of Americans discovered when the Watergate hearings were televised in 1973. Weicker's Republican affiliation did not take him off the case of Richard Nixon, who had helped Weicker in his 1970 Senate race. When Weicker called for the resignation of top Nixon aide Bob Haldeman, Nixon fumed and suggested that Barry Goldwater demand that Weicker disqualify himself from the committee. Nixon insisted that Weicker was "like a judge who has a prejudice in advance."[9] Behind closed doors, according to the White House tapes, Nixon told his aides that he wanted them to get the goods on Weicker. "I think we've got to play a tough damn hard game on him," Nixon said.[10] The game turned the other way.

In the Senate, Steve Roberts wrote in the *New York Times*, Weicker was "a prowling, growling gusher of Paris-born, Yale educated indignation." He "delights in kicking over traces and pricking balloons, and his energetic eccentricities have led to a rapid turnover of his staff." It didn't bother him that his colleagues might use words such as "headline hunter" and "dilettante" to describe him. As Roberts put it, "He is not interested in compromise or consensus, and there is only one way he can win: by making his colleagues so frustrated they will give up the fight."[11]

[8]Specter, "In This Corner," pp. 145, 142.
[9]Fred Emery, *Watergate* (New York: Times Books, 1994), p. 295.
[10]Stanley I. Kutler, *Abuse of Power: The New Nixon Tapes* (New York: The Free Press, 1997), p. 290.
[11]Steven V. Roberts, "Gadfly Says What Others Will Not," *New York Times*, Nov. 20, 1981, p. B8.

Perhaps that is just the way of a certain breed of New England politician. Weicker, a wealthy patrician, began in politics as the first selectman—in smaller New England towns that's the mayor—in the affluent community of Greenwich. He was elected to the Senate in 1970 the same way he won the governorship twenty years later: in a three-way contest with a minority of the vote. The flames of Vietnam, which indirectly consumed Richard Nixon, produced a searing split in the state's Democratic Party. The veteran incumbent Democrat, Thomas Dodd, had been a loyal supporter of the Vietnam War. But insurgency was the order of the day in the Democratic Party. Dodd lost his party's nomination to Joe Duffey, a Protestant minister who built a powerful grassroots organization that included in its ranks a young law student named Bill Clinton. Dodd ran as an independent, and Weicker edged past his divided foes. Just three years into his term, Weicker found himself at the center of the Watergate storm and quickly became a national figure. He was reelected in 1976.

In fact, it's possible to argue that Lowell Weicker presided over the last stages of the tax revolt, and it's a fitting role for someone who found himself in opposition to the predominant trends in his party. By the 1980s, the revolt against taxes was what the Republican Party was all about.

The beginning of the national rebellion against taxes can be dated with some precision: it started in 1978 when California voters, outraged over property taxes driven ever higher by inflation, passed the tax-cutting Proposition 13. For the next twenty years, it was nearly impossible for a political candidate to run for office without insisting that tax increases would never, ever be on the horizon. Better still, as

Ronald Reagan showed in 1980, for a politician to promise deep tax cuts.

Reagan turned tax cutting into the ideology of the 1980s. Reducing taxes was not simply popular, in Reagan's hands it became a moral crusade. Cutting taxes, he said, would restore growth to a stagnant economy. And tax cutting would also restore the virtues of work, savings and investment. All voters who had never much liked paying taxes in the first place could now understand their desire for lower rates as sound economics rooted in sound values.

All this made no sense to Lowell Weicker, and the 1980s were for him a time of deep discontent. A man whose heroes had been Republican liberals such as Jacob Javits, Clifford Case, Edward Brooke and Charles "Mac" Mathias, Weicker was to find himself in permanent opposition to his own party and his own president.

In an interview in December 1980, even before Reagan had taken the oath of office, Weicker was already casting himself as a "counterbalance" to other Republicans. Anticipating by two decades Vermont Senator Jim Jeffords's rationale for leaving the Republican Party, Weicker expressed open uneasiness about the Republican takeover of the Senate and the White House in that year's elections. "I have mixed emotions," he said, "because many of my own principles, I think, will fare a lot worse under a Republican setup."[12]

He was right. In March 1982, he told an Associated Press reporter: "This has been the toughest and loneliest period in

[12]Diane Henry, "Weicker 'Purring' for Now," *New York Times, Connecticut Weekly,* Dec. 21, 1980, p. 1.

my political life. We're being tested by the right, and by the Democratic Party." Political conservatives, Weicker said, want to run it all. "And they are."[13] Courting all the opposition he could get, Weicker declared himself "unwilling to accept a Republican Party in the mould of Reagan."[14]

And opposition he got. He was challenged in 1982 not only by a strong Democratic candidate, Congressman Toby Moffett, but also by Prescott Bush, Jr., brother of then Vice President George Bush. Weicker survived, taking his party's nomination and narrowly beating Moffett in what was a very Democratic year. Six years later, Connecticut Democrats, always outraged that they had lost to Weicker in the first place, defeated him with Lieberman—with all that help from conservatives like Buckley, who had never liked Weicker, either.

But just two years after his Senate defeat, Weicker was back, seeking vindication and action. In 1990, he sought Connecticut's governorship as an independent—or, more precisely, as the candidate of "A Connecticut Party" as he called his insurgent movement. Weicker was Ross Perot two years early and, like Perot, his hope was to ride into office on popular disgust with the two major parties and politics in general.

He ran strong until he confronted the tax issue. Connecticut voters knew their state faced grave budget problems and feared that politicians might finally impose an income tax on them. Connecticut had rebelled against an income tax once

[13]Ann Blackman, "Moderate Republicans Getting Frustrated," Associated Press, March 8, 1982, PM Cycle.
[14]"Connecticut: Bird in the Hand," *The Economist, American Survey*, Jan. 30, 1982, p. 30.

before. So fierce was the popular reaction to the state's first income tax, passed in 1971, that it was repealed before it ever took effect.

Weicker spent most of the 1990 campaign dodging the issue. He refused to rule an income tax in or out. But his Republican opponent John Rowland—he was eventually elected governor in 1994—used Weicker's imprecision as the surest evidence that Weicker intended to do precisely what the voters didn't want.

Ultimately, Weicker was forced to make one of those campaign promises (or sort-of promises) that live for years. In a television advertisement directly attacking Rowland, Weicker told the state's voters: "Long before your negative ads, I was opposed to an income tax. The people of Connecticut and I know it would be like pouring gasoline on the fires of recession. And nobody's for that."[15]

He narrowly won—and almost immediately decided that his state's wretched finances could be cured only by an income tax. On February 13, 1991, he proposed a 6 percent flat income tax. He also proposed cutting the state's 8 percent sales tax almost in half, reducing corporate taxes, and abolishing taxes on capital gains and dividends by making them part of a taxpayer's gross income.

His rhetoric reached high. "Few in a generation have the chance to make history," he declared. "Everyone within and without this chamber starts at that threshold this evening."

"Neither you nor I signed on to muck around in the mis-

[15]Specter, "In This Corner," p. 145.

takes of the past," he told the state legislature. "We're in the future business."[16]

And almost as soon as he was finished, the future looked difficult, indeed. Structurally, Weicker's budget was hard to resist. With the state facing a $2.4 billion budget gap in a $7.4 billion budget, dramatic action was hard to escape. The proposed tax cuts appealed to business and, in principle, to lower-income families who would pay lower sales taxes and be exempted from income taxes on the first $25,000 of their income.

But it became apparent quickly that for most voters—and thus for most politicians—all the rest of Weicker's budget was detail. The one issue that mattered was the income tax, and the opposition was fierce and immediate. Richard Foley, Jr., a state representative and the state Republican chairman, immediately pronounced Weicker's proposal "a declaration of war on the middle class."[17] And over the coming months, much of the middle class in the state seemed to agree.

The battle was fought out over six months. Weicker vetoed not one, not two, but three budgets passed by the legislature that were financed by increases in the sales tax rather than an income tax. He called them "art forms" based on "gimmickry."[18]

Weicker began with the problem that he was an independent governor with no natural partisan support in the legis-

[16]Kirk Johnson, "Weicker Proposes an Income Tax in Fiscal Overhaul for Connecticut," *New York Times*, Feb. 14, 1991, p. 1.
[17]Ibid.
[18]Judith Gaines, "Weicker Survives Odyssey," *Boston Globe*, Aug. 25, 1991, p. 41.

lature. But he also confronted two parties with their own problems. As Judith Gaines wrote in *The Boston Globe*:

> It was a classic stand-off. Republicans insisted that the state's fiscal problems were the result of overspending, not tax policy. Democrats, who were generally more sympathetic to Weicker, worried that the tax would be too onerous in the current recession and complained that it did not represent genuine tax reform—just another tax. And so the impasse continued.[19]

Making the problem even more difficult was a split among Democrats between moderates who feared the political impact of supporting Weicker's plan, and liberals who shared Weicker's desire for tax reform and saw an income tax as inevitable. But even the liberals worried about the impact of the tax on middle-income taxpayers.

The climax came in late August during a seventeen-hour debate in the General Assembly. Even to the end, the fate of Weicker's plan—now substantially revised in the search for votes—was problematic.

The Senate acted first in a session "punctuated by long pauses for closed-door meetings."[20] At 3 A.M., the roll was called. Eighteen Senators voted for the tax bill and eighteen voted against. That put the deciding vote in the hands of

[19]Ibid.
[20]Michelle Jacklin, "After Battle Royal, An Income Tax," *Hartford Courant*, Aug. 23, 1991, p. 1. This account draws heavily on Jacklin's excellent reporting, and also on a fine background feature by Mark Pazniokas and Bill Keveney, "Final Hours: A Seller's Market in a Minefield," *Hartford Courant*, Aug. 23, 1991, p. 1.

Weicker's lieutenant governor, Eunice Groark. She voted yes, and the bill was passed. For the next twelve hours, Weicker gleefully referred to the bill as the "Groark income tax."[21]

The bill went to the House, which had approved the income tax earlier. The House Speaker, Richard J. Balducci, was working closely with Weicker, twisting arms as necessary. But as the *Hartford Courant* reported, "It became clear that income tax supporters had badly underestimated the difficulty of passing an income tax a second time in the House. That miscalculation almost doomed the entire budget proposal."[22]

At 8:27 A.M., the House began voting. Reporters heard gasps in the chamber as the lights went up on the tally board. The budget failed, 81–69. Balducci's eyes brimmed with tears.

And then he and Weicker went to work again, concentrating on three Republicans and three Democrats who could be persuaded to switch. At 1:15 P.M., the bill was brought back for debate, and at 3:15, the vote was tallied: the income tax, now down to 4.5 percent, had passed, 75–73.

Weicker was ecstatic. And signed the bill immediately. "God bless the legislature of Connecticut," he said. "God bless our state of Connecticut."

But even God Himself could not guarantee popular support for an income tax, and the next months were miserable for Weicker and all who had voted with him. Weicker was trailed by demonstrators bearing "Impeach Weicker" signs, and other, less polite messages. One legislator who supported

[21]Pazniokas and Keveney.
[22]Jacklin.

the tax had a bullet fired through her window. Some 40,000 citizens gathered for an angry rally to stir support for income tax repeal.

But the tax was not repealed, and by August of 1994, the state was running a surplus of $169 million. Weicker's popularity never recovered and he did not seek a second term. His successor was the very John Rowland whose campaign had pushed Weicker into making the anti-income tax statements that voters held against him. But when Rowland took office, he cut the income tax. He did not repeal it. Economic good times combined with a sound tax structure to create fiscal happiness for the state. And Rowland was easily reelected in 1998.

To say that Lowell Weicker ended the tax revolt would be an exaggeration. Tax cutting remains popular enough that President Bush got a very large reduction through Congress in 2001. Governors and mayors all over the nation still fear that when they raise taxes—let alone impose new ones—political punishment is sure to follow.

Still, it's worth noting that two years after Weicker's income tax odyssey, President Bill Clinton imposed an income tax increase for top earners—and, after the Democratic disaster in the 1994 election, won reelection handily. In 2000, Bush's tax cut was never at the top of the electorate's priorities. Voters still don't much like taxes, but their reactions, as Weicker assumed, are more pragmatic than dogmatic. To use a favorite Weicker word, voters respond to "facts."

Many conservatives still resist seeing Weicker as any sort of hero, partly because of his personality, but mostly because they can't abide seeing any politician who raised taxes transformed into a profile in courage for doing so. Weicker's old nemesis, William F. Buckley, Jr., put the conservative case plainly in 1992. "Governor Weicker time and again vetoed efforts by the legislature to diminish or to remove his new tax," Buckley wrote. "Question: Why is that a sign of courage? By conventional standards, to be courageous is to do that which is correct, against the demagogic tide."[23]

Not surprisingly, Weicker sees the demagogic tide flowing the other way. Asked after he announced his retirement if he had been surprised at the passionate opposition he encountered, he replied calmly, "I expected it." And he blamed the reaction (also not surprisingly) on the anti-tax sentiment let loose in the Reagan-Bush years.[24]

If you ask Lowell Weicker what he regards as his most important achievements, neither Watergate nor his struggle to get an income tax passed top his list. In an interview in November 2001, Weicker said he's most proud of the work he did on legislation for the disabled, the handicapped, the mentally ill and the mentally retarded. Treating the handicapped as first-class citizens, he said, "was the next great civil rights victory."

His second proudest achievement—this won't surprise his pro-Reagan foe Bill Buckley—was in resisting cutbacks proposed during the Reagan years in health programs, particularly in the National Institutes of Health. This is one area, at least, where a Weicker so out of tune with his former party got to see it switch to his side: Republicans, including former House Speaker Newt Gingrich, eventually pushed for *expanded* funding for the NIH.

[23]William F. Buckley, Jr., "The High Cost of Courage," *National Review*, July 6, 1992, p. 62.
[24]Elizabeth Ross, "Weicker on Taxes, Politics and His Legacy," *The Christian Science Monitor*, Oct. 18, 1993, p. 8.

Watergate ranks only third on Weicker's list, and his income tax victory comes after that.

Weicker remains frustrated that he never had a chance to govern once the revenues from his income tax began pouring in. He rates as his biggest disappointment "the fact that I couldn't go ahead and implement priorities for Connecticut." One of those, he says, would have been dealing with "racial isolation" in the public school system and the unfairness of public school funding. "I never brought that one home," he says.

But he says he's not disappointed that few voters ever came up to him to say: Thanks for the income tax. "They didn't then and they don't now," he told CNN's Jeff Greenfield in June of 2000. His satisfaction comes from the fact that even ardent foes of his tax have never found a way to do without it. "The answer lies in the fact that when somebody comes up to me moaning about the income tax, I [say] well, go and repeal it," he told Greenfield. "We can't, because quite frankly, the state needs the revenues." And still does.

Weicker remains what he's always been: a Mugwump who doesn't feel any particular fondness for either political party. (He endorsed Democrat Bill Bradley for president in 2000.) And he worries that in state politics, at least, the two parties collaborate too much and challenge each other too little. "If you have no competition in economics, you get high prices and bad products," he says. "If you have no competition in politics, you get bad ideas and bad candidates." But he readily concedes that his dream of a strong, moderate third party that could challenge the other two is a long way from achievement.

And he remains troubled that his former political home is now so inhospitable to people of his perspective. Asked why he didn't leave the Republican Party earlier, Weicker flatly rejects the question. "The real question," he says, "is what happened to the Republican Party itself." When he started in politics, "the moderates and liberals were legion." Like so many who abandoned their earlier allegiances, Weicker insists—Benton again comes to mind—that his party did all the changing, not him.

If you ask Weicker what advice he'd give a young man or woman about to enter politics, his response is characteristic: "Do the same thing I did."

His point is that a career in politics, now disdained, is honorable, and that starting at the bottom (and not expecting to start at the top) is as wise in politics as it is in other endeavors. "My whole life was politics," he says. Elective office, he adds, "should not be used as a way to cap your career." Far better, he says, "to learn the ropes from the ground up."

In this sense, Weicker breaks ranks with much of the anti-politics protest movement that saw "career politicians" as always being the enemy and outsiders—a billionaire like Perot, a pro wrestler and Weicker fan like Jesse Ventura—as always providing the answers. Here, after all, is a proud career politician who likes government and bemoans the fact that "the main business of politics now is not government, it's getting elected."

But you can't do anything if you don't win elections, right? True, but Weicker insists on the paradox that you can't do anything if winning is the *only* thing that matters. Where politics is concerned, Vince Lombardi may thus have it wrong.

"For God's sake," Weicker thunders, "don't be afraid to lose. If you're not afraid to lose, you'll make your mark in politics."

We need to restore the essential balance between rights and responsibilities, between entitlement and duty, that has always been the creed of our political faith.

I don't believe in carrying those who can walk; neither do I believe in refusing a hand to those who stumble.

I believe instead that all of us must accept responsibility—for ourselves, our families, and our communities. And if we are fortunate enough to be chosen for public office, we must accept the responsibility of making difficult decisions.

We don't get to choose the times in which we live, but we do get the chance to determine how we respond to those times.

—JAMES FLORIO, 1993

JAMES FLORIO

by Anna Quindlen

T HERE WAS A time, during the early 1990s, when it was
virtually impossible to drive through the state without seeing them. On the Turnpike, the Parkway, the back lanes of
hilly Warren County or the flat strips of macadam that ran like
black ribbons of tedium through the southern Pine Barrens,
on the rutted roads around the projects in Camden and Newark, on the backs of Lincoln Continentals and old Volkswagen
vans and pickup trucks and Jeeps, there were the ubiquitous
bumper stickers. Impeach Florio. Florio Free in '93. Dump Florio. Dump Florio. Dump Florio. They were like roadside mark-
ers: you have now entered New Jersey.

"There was a time there when sometimes I thought my
first name was actually Dump," says former Governor James
Florio, sitting behind the desk in his law office in Newark.

This is a story of guns and money, political passion and
political pressure, people who believe in being left alone and

people who believe in government intervention for the greater good. It is a story of ideologies rocketing headlong toward one another down an alley of legislation, and the resulting crash and predictable pileup. It is the story of American politics at the end of the twentieth century, of pressure groups and polls and political contributions and the covert manipulations of elected officials and the electorate itself.

It is the story of how Jim Florio won the John F. Kennedy Profile in Courage Award and lost the governor's race.

And in some sense it is the story of the kind of accidental big issue that changes the lives and careers of some political figures forever. When Florio was elected governor of New Jersey in 1989, his legislative profile was that of a garden-variety liberal with a penchant for environmental issues, a former member of Congress who had made the Superfund legislation that cleaned up the worst toxic dumps his crusade. During the gubernatorial race much of the rhetoric focused on car insurance rates and clean water, not guns, although Florio had made it clear in interviews and at public forums that he felt more restrictive measures were needed to keep certain weapons out of the hands of criminals. "I met him about six months before he was elected," recalled Rev. Jack Johnson, then the chair of New Jersey Citizens to Stop Gun Violence, a coalition of gun control groups. "I talked to him a little bit about it at a breakfast, and at that time it didn't seem to be of significant interest to him as part of his agenda."

But during a campaign stop in North Camden, Florio recalled, a county prosecutor told him that he didn't feel comfortable sending investigators, lawyers and other staff members into the neighborhood because he feared for their safety. "The bad guys have more firepower than we do," the prosecutor told the Democratic candidate. It was the sort of grassroots moment of truth that spoke to Florio, who had been in public life for two decades at the time and yet could barely conceal his distaste sometimes for the old-fashioned insider deal making that was the backbone of his business. Florio had made a career out of looking to the opinions of people outside the process for clues to what really mattered, a way of life that had earned him a reputation for being diligent, hardworking, and a little superior. Hearing this lawyer speak of his fear of the streets, the gubernatorial candidate began to think about crafting legislation that would outlaw the assault weapons he believed were the choice of criminals, not hunters or collectors.

Florio knew that gun control was, as he puts it, "the third rail of American politics—touch it and you die." But those who knew him were unsurprised that he was willing not only to touch it, but to embrace it. Profile writers made much of the fact that he had dropped out of high school to join the U.S. Navy, was a product of the rough-and-tumble streets of Italian immigrant New York, hid a tattoo of the American flag on his arm beneath the dress shirt and the suit jacket. But his demeanor as an elected official belied that biography, was more topcoat than T-shirt. From his early years in the State Assembly, he had been better known as a politician with a marked touch of the pedagogical, a bit of a policy wonk who seemed most comfortable behind the podium. A stiff, often unyielding man with the uneven features and flattop hair of the second-banana leading man in a '30s movie, he was also often described in terms of the boxing career that had marked his face, and his temperament. He'd learned to box in the

Flatbush section of Brooklyn and had a creditable career as a middleweight in the service until he took on a fighter who outweighed him by 12 pounds. The wired jaw, the awry features: the legend of a stubborn David who foolishly kept coming at Goliath was born.

On the gun control issue he could be forgiven the perception that he was not utterly outmatched. While the National Rifle Association had long been feared for a political clout out of all proportion to its membership numbers, New Jersey was scarcely a gun stronghold, not Idaho or Montana. The polls showed that as many as eight in ten of the state's citizens supported curbs on the kind of guns available and the ease with which guns could be purchased. And the statistics on gun deaths, particularly in the cities, were rising year after year, the bad guys winning because, as the Camden prosecutor had said, their firepower was superior. As Florio was running for governor the murder of five children in a schoolyard by a crazed gunman in Stockton, California, had set the stage for more curbs on the possession of guns, particularly assault weapons.

So only a few months after his election, Florio waded into what would be the morass of a political lifetime. With the support of a then-Democratic State Senate and Assembly, the governor crafted a bill that would be, at the time, the toughest gun control legislation in the United States. It banned semi-automatic handguns and rifles, those capable of firing more than 15 rounds of ammunition at once, guns that account for only 1 percent of civilian firearms but are used in about 10 percent of those crimes involving guns. And it did it with language that sidestepped the pitfalls of previous bills. Other gun measures had banned certain weapons by make and model; gun companies had merely modified those guns slightly to make them legal despite the prohibition. But the Florio measure not only banned specific firearms, but banned others of the same type or that were "substantially identical," making the usual gun company tinkering useless in meeting the stringent provisions of the New Jersey bill. And while other legislation had grandfathered in formerly legal weapons, the Florio bill provided that anyone who owned a gun on the list had a year to sell it out of state, disable it by removing the firing pin, or hand it over to the police. It was exactly the kind of measure that made the gun lobby crazy, then and now, especially that last part: hand them over.

The fracas that ensued stretched over four years, countless speeches, and numerous demonstrations at the governor's mansion in Princeton at which he was repeatedly likened to Adolf Hitler. The first salvo from lawyers for the NRA and its New Jersey affiliate, the Coalition of New Jersey Sportsmen, was an immediate court challenge to the constitutionality of the section of the bill that required gun owners to give up their weapons without reimbursement for their cost. A year after Florio's bill had passed, an appellate court rejected the gun lobby lawsuits.

But the coalition had better luck with the legislative branch than it had with the judicial or the executive. In the midterm elections of November 1991, the Republican Party, which has historically been more friendly toward the interests of the NRA, took back both the Senate and the Assembly in New Jersey. There was little mystery to the reason for that result; the NRA and the coalition contributed more than $250,000 to the campaigns of those candidates they knew were hostile to gun control, including a $25,000 donation to the Assembly Republican majority. In short order a new law was passed eviscerating the initial ban and removing the "substantially identical" provision. The *New York Times* editorialized, "The repeal embarrasses the legislature and insults the public."

Florio was expected to veto the altered bill, but decided that instead of simply doing so from the state capitol in Trenton he would travel the state drumming up public opinion and convincing voters of the wisdom of the original ban. It was a page taken from his past life as a member of the House of Representatives. He had been a member of the congressional class of 1974, a polyglot group of mostly liberal Democrats elected at a time when the Watergate scandal and resignation of President Nixon had sent American confidence in the integrity and openness of politicians plummeting. Many of those elected were young populists who eschewed party bosses and organizations and preferred to hold town meetings and open forums to try to take their ideas directly to the voters. "Sometimes it's just a waste of time to try to persuade the insiders," Florio says. "The insiders respond more expeditiously to outside pressure."

So he made dozens of appearances from one end of the state to another, picking up creatively culled opponents to the repeal: not just those who belonged to gun control organizations, but teachers who taught in schools in which students had been wounded, doctors and nurses who had treated gunshot victims in emergency rooms, ministers and priests who had presided at funerals. He spoke at the spot where a 15-year-old girl was killed with a semiautomatic, holding up a gun like the one used in the fatal attack as friends and family members sobbed at the sight.

While many legislators in Trenton vowed to override the governor's veto of the weaker bill, almost immediately there were signs of softening support for that position. A month after Florio's veto was announced, a five-term Republican assemblyman who had voted to repeal the assault weapons ban said he had done so largely because of NRA pressure and threats that he would be unseated in the next election, adding, "I was wrong." James S. Brady, the press secretary to Ronald Reagan who was seriously injured in the assassination attempt on the former president, came to the governor's office in his wheelchair to show his support just days before the State Senate was to vote on override legislation. Former Governor Tom Kean, a moderate Republican whom Florio had defeated in 1989—and who had defeated Florio in Florio's first try for statewide office in 1981—came out in support of the tougher gun control bill, throwing down the gauntlet to more conservative members of his party.

By the time the State Senate acted in March 1993 the pendulum had swung convincingly Florio's way, and the members voted unanimously not to override the governor's veto. The unanimity was not all that it seemed; 26 senators abstained on the issue, clearly paralyzed by competing pressure groups and ideologies. But the moment was seen as a considerable victory for gun control groups and for the governor. Only minutes after the vote, the Attorney General of the United States, Janet Reno, called to congratulate Florio. The governor reported that she had said she hoped the outcome in New Jersey boded well for the Brady Bill, the federal legislation to require waiting periods for handguns named after Jim Brady. It was, the newspapers reported, a "dramatic conclusion" to years of discord, struggle and political back-and-forth.

But it was too soon to consider the matter concluded. That has been the history of the gun control and gun ownership issue in this country, an ebb and flow as unpredictable as school shootings or high-profile murders. It is difficult to remember, given its current slash-and-burn virulence, that it is a relatively new controversy, largely a creature of the late twentieth century. The first really significant piece of gun control legislation passed in 1911 in New York, a statute called the Sullivan Law requiring a permit from the police for possession of a handgun. And although gun regulation issues became a rallying point for some women's groups in the years immediately after suffrage, it wasn't until more than 50 years after Sullivan that a major piece of federal legislation was enacted, the Gun Control Act of 1968 proposed by Lyndon B. Johnson. The history of that bill would hint at battles to come; it took more than five years of debate and disagreements to produce laws substantially diluted by compromise and NRA lobbying, yet it was considered one of the most inflammatory and controversial bills of the 1960s. And when it was enacted into law, the issue of gun control vanished from the national radar screen for years.

Assassination attempts have often driven the issue: the Johnson measure was a reaction to the murder of John F. Kennedy by Lee Harvey Oswald, who was armed with a gun he had ordered from an ad in the official NRA magazine. (Ironically, President Kennedy accepted a life membership in the NRA during his time in the White House, although Shelton

Stern of the Kennedy Library once noted, "Membership in the NRA in 1962 does not mean what it does today.") The killings of Robert F. Kennedy and Martin Luther King, Jr., both shooting deaths, briefly revived interest in gun control statutes, but with the national focus on the Vietnam War, the years between 1968 and 1980 were fallow periods for the issue. But the availability of firearms burst into national prominence again after John Hinckley shot at Ronald Reagan in 1981 and James Brady's wife, Sarah, became a nationally known advocate for gun control. Still, the most significant piece of gun legislation passed in the 1980s was a revision of the 1968 act that substantially weakened it. The NRA had learned to use both its substantial campaign war chests and its single-issue voters to persuade elected officials that gun control was a losing issue.

The success of the gun lobby highlighted once again the considerable disconnect between the sentiments of the people and the influence of interest groups that had inspired Florio and the House members who entered Congress with him to turn to politics. For while the country's strongest gun control measure was being dismantled, opinion polls showed over and over again that the vast majority of American voters favored such controls. And during the years that Florio was fighting the New Jersey gun control fight, public opinion on the issue was hardened by a flood of violence, both local and national. Children accidentally killed playmates with guns found in unlocked cases and closets. Teenagers committed suicide with parents' guns. Men gunned down their coworkers in offices and hallways.

The gun lobbyists in New Jersey complained bitterly that an accident of timing had sideswiped them: in the months after legislators had replaced Florio's tough bill with an eviscerated version, the killing of four federal officers in Waco and the bombing of the World Trade Center had once again ratcheted up public distaste for easy access to weapons. The assistant Democratic minority leader referred directly to that climate during the Senate vote to override Florio's veto of the weaker bill, saying, "only three kinds of people need assault weapons: cop killers, drug dealers and terrorists." One of the NRA lobbyists, Rodger Iverson, shouted from the gallery, "and freedom fighters," and stormed from the chambers.

Florio could also take comfort in a peculiar political synergy that had grown up around the issue. While once police and sheriff's officers aligned themselves squarely with the NRA on the question of government curbs and regulations on guns, that alignment had shifted in the years before Florio was elected governor. A public relations battle had erupted around the question of "cop killer bullets," a particular kind of Teflon-coated ammunition originally designed to penetrate cars. Television reports revealed that the bullets could penetrate body armor and bulletproof vests as well, and Mario Biaggi, a former New York City police officer who had become a member of Congress, sponsored a bill that would control the use of the ammunition. When the NRA strongly opposed the legislation the alliance between law enforcement and gun advocates was shattered. "There was a break in the traditional monolithic groupings where the issue was concerned," Florio recalls. When the governor announced his veto of the weakened gun bill, he was surrounded by a phalanx of police officers, a vivid indication that the old alliances were gone.

It was a daunting combination for those who felt fiercely enough about holding on to their guns to style themselves as freedom fighters. The man in the street did not support them; neither did the police. Even some of their own members were doubtful about the need to protect weapons like the Ruger Mini-14, which became the focus of NRA efforts in New Jersey even though the high-powered semiautomatic had been used in two highly publicized shootings during the 1980s. One shooting instructor in southern New Jersey, an NRA member for 20 years, was quoted in *Time* magazine on the Florio gun measures as saying, "I see no reason that hunters need semi-automatics."

Appealing to the public's sentiments about the Second Amendment was a losing prospect for the NRA by the time Florio triumphed in the State Senate. And the ability to influence legislators with campaign contributions had been significantly affected by public opinion on guns: some politicians felt the money simply wasn't worth it if 80 percent of their constituents felt they were supporting a losing, even reprehensible cause. The New Jersey debacle was a turning point for gun lobbyists; at the time most reporters styled it a defeat. But instead it would come to mark a change of tactics, and the new tactics the gun lobby would choose to defeat those who supported gun control would find their perfect object in the personality and the policies of Jim Florio.

In some ways, given the opinion polls, gun control was the least of Florio's worries. When he took office in 1990, he was faced with two enormous fiscal crises. He contended that the Republican administration that preceded him had concealed huge budget deficits and that maintaining state services and programs would require an immediate infusion of new revenues. And he became the heir to a lawsuit about school funding that had been bouncing around Trenton for years. The New Jersey Supreme Court settled it soon after Florio was elected in a sweeping decision; the justices ruled that the gap in property values had grown so great between poor areas and wealthy ones that the state was obliged to step in and address the subsequent disparity in spending per pupil, and to find a way to make spending in its 30 poorest school districts comparable to that in its 54 wealthiest areas.

Florio had campaigned on a promise not to raise taxes, but the two crises combined to lead him to almost immediately push through the legislature nearly $3 billion in new taxes, and to overhaul school funding in the state. Two weeks after the court ruling, the legislature passed Florio's Quality Education Act, which went beyond the demands of the court ruling to increase funding to more than 300 rural and urban school districts and to cut back state aid to more than 200 of the richer districts. The state sales tax was raised from from 6 to 7 percent, and staffing in government offices was cut back. The wave of public antipathy that followed was almost palpable. Within six months of his election the governor had become a state bogeyman, and one newspaper story after another quoted salesmen, housewives and other ordinary voters using the word "impeachment." Although he also promised to cut the Trenton bureaucracy to offset citizen fury, Florio's approval rating plummeted; by November of 1990, less than a year after he'd been elected governor with a resounding majority, Florio

had a 23 percent approval rating. And when Senator Bill Bradley narrowly averted defeat in a race against neophyte Christine Todd Whitman, the same Democrats who had passed
Florio's tax package began to call him a liability. *USA Today*
described him as the nation's "most vulnerable governor."

His allies evaporated; the old breed of local pols who had
read that he once said some of them should be "on a post
office wall" were happy to cut him loose, especially with constituents whose voices grew shrill when they spoke of him.
The skill at taking his case to the people that was on display
during the battle over guns was little in evidence when the issue
was taxes, and the man who had always been a bit wooden,
sometimes dogmatic, rarely charismatic, badly needed the human touch. At the time Florio himself acknowledged his lack
of public relations savvy; "If I was grading myself," he told a
reporter, "I'd give me good high marks for decisiveness. I'd give
me less than high marks for bringing people along."

And while Florio had been able to style himself the brave
David against the NRA Goliaths in the gun battle, the tax package and the public reaction reversed the roles. Led by a postal
worker named John Budzash, a group with the vaguely poetic
name of Hands Across New Jersey became the epitome of the
little guy fighting big government, holding rallies full of
middle-class residents infuriated by the tax increases and the
redistribution of state monies to poorer school districts. While
a pastoral letter signed by clergy from the New Jersey Council
of Churches called opposition to the tax package "uninformed," even racist in its assumptions that poor districts
would squander increased funding, it was Hands Across New

Jersey that was cast as the voice of the people in the wake of the tax increase. Press coverage of the group was largely credulous; one story likened its gatherings to Woodstock, another to the civil rights movement. But peace and love were not the order of the day at the group's highly publicized events, whose numbers often fell far short of the trumpeted expectations. "I remember a couple of those big tax revolt rallies," recalls Rev. Jack Johnson of the gun control coalition. "I have never seen such hostile crowds. There were lots of state police around, and the governor needed them." At one State House rally, vendors sold color photographs of the governor in full Nazi regalia, echoing the fascist Florio pejoratives often used by the gun groups.

That was not, it developed, accidental. Even in its early days Budzash expressed concern about special interest groups "trying to muscle their way in" to Hands Across New Jersey, and there were several such groups in evidence, including speakers at the 1990 State House rally from the Sportsmen's Coalition. Jon Shure, Florio's press secretary, began to notice a peculiar phenomenon as he traveled the state attending town meetings with his boss. No matter how far afield from their hometowns the meetings were held, people affiliated with the gun groups would attend. But they would ask questions about the salaries of administration members or the plans for a local garbage incinerator. In 1990 a reporter for the *Asbury Park Press* reported that a lobbyist for the NRA, Richard Feldman, had become active in the citizens tax group. The lobbyist insisted he was working on his own time and that he had deep feelings about the tax plan as well as about gun control. "They went undercover on the gun issue," gun control advocate Dorothy

McGann recalled. "It was insidious. They went after him on the tax issue instead."

Although Rev. Johnson says it was apparent to his members "from the get-go," it took some time for the extent of the gun lobby's involvement in Hands Across New Jersey to be revealed to the public. Richard Miller, the chairman of the Coalition of New Jersey Sportsmen, told a *New York Times* reporter in 1992 that members of his organization turned out to increase the crowds at tax revolt rallies. "I spoke at a lot of the Hands rallies," he added. In 1993, Richard Feldman finally came clean with a reporter for the *Gloucester County Times* about the extent of his activities with the group. He admitted that he had written press releases, helped organize protests and made certain that there were vocal Florio opponents at the governor's public events. His was not the only stealth presence. Taking advantage of a loophole in state law, the NRA was able to finance a $100,000 phone bank to get out the anti-Florio vote two days before the gubernatorial election in 1993, and to keep its involvement quiet until after the results were in.

It was the wave of the future for gun lobbyists, a backdoor strategy: find the Achilles heel. Carolyn McCarthy, the member of Congress from Long Island who ran for office after her husband was killed and her son wounded by a gunman on a commuter train, believes that the NRA was responsible for the literature attacking her position on abortion rights during her last campaign, even though the literature wasn't identified as being sponsored by the group. "It was a loser for them to go after me, of all people, on gun control," she said last year. "They had to find someplace else where I was vulnerable."

Sponsors of the anti-Florio phone bank wouldn't say whether they told voters that the NRA was paying for their effort, either. The group's director of state and local legislative affairs crowed at the time, "Since it was so successful, I want to keep it to myself."

Once the gun lobby had attacked its foes head-on, insisting they were protecting a righteous Second Amendment right to bear arms. But the public not only did not care, in most cases they did not agree. Finding the other, more mainstream chinks in a candidate's armor proved more successful. The anger over the tax hikes in New Jersey was real and potent, and Hands Across New Jersey had among its members many, many voters who were truly mobilized by opposition to, even hatred of the governor and his policies. (Although it is worth noting that the group's co-founder, John Budaszh, resigned after he complained that it had become too closely aligned with the Republican Party and had lost sight of its grass roots.)

But it is also true that the movement was in some considerable measure shaped, even financed, by individuals and organizations opposed to gun control who found the back door more conducive to victory than the front. While the voters thought they were witnessing the rise of a citizens movement, what they were also seeing was the outline of a well-financed and well-organized lobbying effort. The NRA, aware of their lack of public support, insisted that it was keeping a low profile during the gubernatorial campaign, but after it was over they ran an ad that boasted, "Jim Florio ran against the NRA and lost." In an article about the issue in the *New Jersey Reporter*, former press secretary Jon Shure concluded, "If the NRA deserves the credit it wants to get for the work it did, then the reality is this: It helped to undermine Jim Florio by playing a role in portraying him as a politician under fire because people believed he made a promise not to raise taxes and broke it, when the group's real complaint was that Jim Florio made a promise to ban assault weapons, and he kept it."

The 1993 gubernatorial election in New Jersey marked a turning point in gun lobby tactics, an end run that proved more successful than a frontal assault. It also put paid to the governor's political career. Although Bill Clinton called Florio the Resurrection Kid as Election Day approached, and although the governor's poll numbers increased week by week during the campaign, he lost to Christine Todd Whitman, who had come so close to defeating Democratic Senator Bill Bradley at the height of anti-Florio fever. Florio himself ran for the Senate in 2000, but lost in a primary to investment banker Jon Corzine. Guns were scarcely an issue; the two men agreed on the need for stricter national gun controls. But money was more important than ever before; Corzine used his considerable personal fortune to mount what was the most expensive Senate race in American history. Florio is more saddened than angered by the overwhelming role of fund-raising in public life today. "The financial imperatives are such that if you're on the point on any issue you're going to make someone unhappy," he says a former aide told him not long ago. "And you can't afford to make anyone unhappy.

"In the eight years since I've been out of office," he added in 2001, as members of Congress debated campaign finance reform, "the influence of money in the process almost makes it a process I wouldn't want to be a part of, and a process in which it would have been impossible for me to prosper."

But he believes he did prosper. He says that when he and his wife walk along the beach at the Jersey shore in summertime, people who can remember when those same beaches were closed because of medical waste and who know how hard Florio worked to clean them up come up and shake his hand and thank him. He believes the long-range benefits of spending more on schools in impoverished districts is beginning to pay off in some of the state's cities, and that the tax increase was still the only way to put New Jersey on a sound financial footing.

And he thinks he won on guns, or, more accurately, that the people who elected him did. Each week seems to bring another sad confirmation of that fact: the school shootings, the gang murders. In the wake of the shooting spree by two students at Columbine High School in Colorado there was another wave, of interest and of rhetoric, about the need for better gun laws. "I never had any doubt that it was the right thing to do," Florio says. "What strikes me is the timidity of leaders who are unwilling to take on the issues because they're not willing to undertake the public education required. I knew that when people understood, they would support this, and they did."

Despite her claim that she would roll back the ban on assault weapons, his successor, Governor Whitman, never did. There was little legislative pressure for her to do so. "Even Republicans in New Jersey are no longer out there catering to the NRA," Florio says. Occasionally, on the back of an old Toyota or a dusty van, he will see one of the surviving emblems of the storm that swirled around him, a tattered "Dump

Florio" bumper sticker. He shrugs, and refers back to the remarks he gave in 1993 when he was awarded the Profile in Courage Award. "The first thing I learned as governor is that you can't please everybody," he said that day. "The second thing I learned is, some days, you can't please anybody."

My mother advised me to stay out of politics: "You'll make the Americanos angry," she said. But she also told me, "First, respect yourself." Always, I remembered the words of Santa Teresa, so beloved by my mother, "fear not." And it was this kind of teaching that led me into public life and . . . enabled me to see that no one, least of all myself, should or even could be silent in the face of injustice.

Once I got into politics, I learned this very early: people will respond to you if they can believe what you say. People will trust you if you keep your word. People will respect you if you respect yourself. If you lay out the problem accurately and if you propose a reasonable solution, people will give you a chance, notwithstanding your heritage or race.

—HENRY B. GONZALEZ, 1994

HENRY B. GONZALEZ

by Pete Hamill

I N H I S L A S T years in the public eye, a tough old man named Henry B. Gonzalez brought immense happiness to many Americans who had never met him. Engulfed in solitude on the floor of the House of Representatives, Gonzalez talked to all of them, and with his blunt words, his ideas, and his combative stance he cheered people who lived far from his own part of the country, the region along the Texas border with Mexico. To be sure, his language, often as subtle as an ax, frequently roused loathing among a much smaller group: the powers that be. But their condemnation was proof to Henry B. Gonzalez that he was on the correct path, as a Congressman and as a citizen.

For in his final years, as he had done from the beginning of his career, Gonzalez was speaking for all those people who lived on the wrong side of American towns, from San Antonio to New York. He spoke for those who lived in the worst housing and worked at the worst jobs and dreamed the grandest dreams for their children. And his essential philosophy was as old as the American nation: to afflict the comfortable and comfort the afflicted.

His face in those last years was leathery and baroque, full of knobs and whorls, gullies and ravines, a face as scoured by time as certain hills in the American Southwest. His hooded eyes sometimes burned with righteous anger but more often twinkled with amusement. He always planted himself like an old welterweight, shoulders sloping, chin down, prepared to absorb any punch thrown at him, and then come back swinging. You saw him, lonely and majestic, on C-SPAN or in some clip from a congressional hearing and you thought: Some old man. Some American.

In his last decade, the man his admirerers called Henry B. was, for many of us, an astonishment because he so totally resisted the prevailing slickness that was debasing our politics. He had come out of a hard Depression childhood and had survived into the era of sound bites and voice coaches, when grown men from both parties wore makeup in the halls of Congress and waited for polls to decide what they believed. Their rhetoric was usually a stale mayonnaise of euphemism and evasion, punctuated by savage partisan outbursts ordered by their advisers. Most of them toadied to campaign contributors, or to the infantry of their "base," no matter what that constituency might be, and rented themselves to both groups. Henry B. was never for rent. Henry B. toadied to no man on the planet.

It could have been no other way, given the facts of his biography. The Gonzalez story most properly begins in mid-sixteenth-century Mexico, long before there was a New York or a Washington, D.C., or a dream of American democracy. The Gonzalez of that time found his way to what is now the state of Durango (where John Wayne would shoot many Westerns four centuries later) and planted deep roots in that harshly beautiful place. By the nineteenth century, the family was prosperous from mining. In the 1860s, the grandfather of Henry B. Gonzalez took up arms to fight beside Benito Juarez in the war against the French invaders who had imposed an unemployed Austrian archduke named Maximilian as the Mexican emperor. In that war, Juarez, a full-blooded Zapotec Indian from the state of Oaxaca, insisted that the Indian and the Mexican *mestizo* was the equal of any European, and better than many. He was a proud liberal, and a reformer. His moral force was his greatest weapon in the war that established forever the sovereignty of Mexico. The story of that heroic struggle—and the fighting Gonzalez heritage—was absorbed by Henry B. Gonzalez through all the long evenings of his San Antonio childhood.

In a way, the betrayal of the liberalism of Juarez led to the birth of Henry B. Gonzalez in San Antonio. By 1910, a former Juarez general named Porfirio Diaz had become the virtual dictator of Mexico. A mystical intellectual named Francisco Madero crossed the border that year (from San Antonio exile) and began the long agony of the Mexican Revolution. All over Mexico, the poor and the dispossessed rose in rebellion, attacking haciendas, sugar mills, mining companies, and all symbols of state authority. In Durango, Leonides Gonzalez was mayor of the town of Mapimi. The anarchic rage of those called by Mexican novelist Mariano Azuela *los de abajo* (the underdogs) drove remorselessly toward the Mapimi city hall. Leonides packed his bags and his family and left for exile in San Antonio.

Leonides quickly found work as the managing editor of *La Prensa*, the only Spanish-language daily newspaper in San Antonio. He was paid little, and housing was almost impossible to find in a city crowded with other refugees. In one shack, the floors were made of hard-packed dirt and there was no running water. Eventually, as they earned more money, he and his wife (her maiden name was Barbosa) settled on Upson Street in the Prospect Hill section of the city's west side. They were not rich, or even middle class, but in a house with books on the shelves, they were not poor either. At home on May 13, 1916, Henry Barbosa Gonzalez was born.

His childhood was crucial to the career that followed. In his home, there were six children, one aunt, and many visitors. His father, Leonides, as editor of the newspaper, often hosted visiting intellectuals from Mexico and some of the leading Mexican-American citizens of San Antonio. They talked politics, of course, and news of the ongoing Revolution. But there were other subjects for their kitchen table discourses. Years later, Henry B. remembered hearing passionate discussions in Spanish about Kant and Hegel, Descartes and Carlyle, without understanding anything about what was being said. And, of course, there was talk of Benito Juarez. And Pancho Villa. And Emiliano Zapata. To a boy, these images of revolution and resistance were naturally more vivid than the abstractions of philosophy.

At the same time, young Henry B. was coming up against the prevailing American bigotries of the era. He learned the hard way that some Americans thought of him and his father and his family as "greasers," or "messicans." His skin was brown, the color of the earth, and people with pink skins too often treated him as if he were dirt. At his kitchen table, he struggled to understand this stupidity. He was too young to understand that the bigotry had been there for a long time, and was growing worse with the swelling tide of refugees from the violence of the Revolution. The year before Henry B. was born, D. W. Griffith's *The Birth of a Nation* had helped revive the Ku Klux Klan, and a local branch of these fools often rode through the Mexican barrios at midnight, dressed in bedsheets and hoods. Mexicans, after all, were dark-skinned *and* Catholic, representing to the kluxers a double menace to the American way of life. The racist fringe was assisted by the respectable folk at the center. Schools were rigidly segregated. The use of Spanish was punished. Mexican customs were subjected to sneers. And on blazing summer afternoons, Henry B. and his friends were barred from public swimming pools.

At his kitchen table in the house on Upson Street, Henry B. learned from his father and his father's friends the tale that most of the pink people never learned: how in Mexico the great cities of Tenochtitlan and Teotihuacan, Chichen Itza and Monte Alban and a dozen others had been built by the ancestors of the "greasers" of San Antonio, Texas; how the Olmecs and Maya and Aztecs had developed great civilizations, with systems of writing, mathematics and astronomy, with refined art and architecture, while many Europeans were still painting themselves blue in caves. To come from such people was a thing of pride. And those descendants of Mexicans who chose to call themselves "Spanish" instead of Mexican were denying a more glorious truth. Besides, Leonides Gonzalez was a refugee, not an immigrant; when things settled in Mexico, they would all go home again.

Still, the boy was living in the United States, not Mexico, and it was small consolation in the here and now to be told that Texas itself was once part of Mexico, along with all the land west to the California coast, land that had been stolen at gunpoint in the American war against Mexico of 1845–48. History was the past. Young Henry B. was living in San Antonio in the 1920s and thinking about the future. To reach that future, he would have to overcome a number of obstacles in life, but the first, and most important, was fear.

"Fear seemed pervasive, hanging as a heavy fog all around my childhood world," he said at the John F. Kennedy Library in 1994, when accepting the Profile in Courage Award. "The fear of abject poverty, of dread diseases like tuberculosis, and the fear linked to a hostile, alien neighborhood, speaking with a harsh and unfriendly-sounding, incomprehensible language. There was the terror of being dragged to that first day of school—to its forbidding-looking strange adults and unknown classmates. Not knowing English, I was compelled to spend a whole year in 'low first' grade."

Then he discovered in an aunt's missal what he always remembered as a "heavenly message," a kind of epiphany. It was a prayer written by Saint Teresa de Jesus, and the words in Spanish said:

Nada te turbe
Nada te espante

Todo se pasa,
La paciencia todo lo alcanza
Quien a Dios tiene la falta
Solo Dios basta.

"Those words were so powerful," Henry B. said more than seven decades later, "that even to this day I cannot do [them] justice in English."

Still, he gave the translation a try:

Let nothing vex you
Fear not.
All things soon pass,
Patience conquers all.
He who has God with him wants for nothing.
Our Lord God suffices.

"Those words gave me the courage that was essential to self-respect," he said in old age. "From then on, fear did not overwhelm me."

At roughly the same age, as Henry B. moved into "high second" grade, he made another crucial discovery.

"My wonderful inspiring teacher, Miss Mason, made it clear that if we were born in the United States we were Americans. This was astonishing news, because at home we were being brought up as Mexicans who would eventually go back to the homeland . . . That evening at the supper table I announced this startling revelation: I am an American because I was born here. But my 'nana' (an aunt) harumphed: 'Well, if that's so, if a cat is born in an oven does that make him bread?'

And with that, and the instant laughter and jeers of the crowd of cousins who had just come from Mexico, I was laughed out of the room: 'Ha, ha, he wants to make believe he is a gringo.' "

In spite of the derision, Henry B. began to forge an alloy of his Mexican heritage and his American identity, and followed the traditional path out of the ghetto. It was the same path followed by the American children of the Irish and the Jews and the Italians and all the other enriching streams of American immigration: education. From the age of eight, he haunted the public library. In adolescence, he began to look for the writers whose names he had heard at the family table. For a while, he fell under the spell of Thomas Carlyle and his "great man" theory of history. He devoured biographies, as if looking for models. He read poetry and novels.

But in junior high school, Henry B. still had a thick accent and other kids often made fun of him. There were few English-language models in those days in a segregated city: movies were silent, television didn't exist, and radio was in its primitive beginnings. But Henry B. read in a library book about Demosthenes of Athens and how he refined his skill at oratory by hurling words at the sea with his mouth filled with pebbles. Henry B. did the same at home, far from any sea, using Carlyle as his text, "until Papa thought I was nuts and told me to stop." He then switched to Robert Louis Stevenson (a favorite of the Argentine writer Jorge Luis Borges), reading out loud (without pebbles) while a friend corrected his accent. Sometimes, alone in his room, he would speak to himself in the mirror, while his sisters giggled in the hallway. But Henry B.

never got discouraged by scorn or mockery; he was too busy forging the alloy.

Toughened each day by hard times (the Depression had begun the year he was thirteen), hearing Franklin D. Roosevelt's vow that the only thing Americans had to fear was fear itself, Henry B. Gonzales went on to San Antonio College and then to St. Mary's University School of Law, where he would earn a degree. He helped his father set up a translation service (for the father now had decided he would not be returning to the old country) and added French and Portuguese to his own intellectual tools. He boxed in local gymnasiums. He kept reading, absorbing the true riches of the world, and paid special attention to the Constitution of the United States. In the 1930s, he married Bertha Cuellar of Floresville, who became his *companera* in all the battles of his life and the mother of his eight children. Beyond his labors with his father, he took what work he could find, including a $5-a-week job killing insects for the Austin Exterminating Company. There was no shame to being poor, as people were learning all over the United States in those years; the only shame was to surrender. That was never in the nature of Henry B. Gonzalez.

The war came to America on December 7, 1941. Henry B.'s country needed his linguistic skills and so he did not go off to combat; he worked instead as a military censor. Many Mexican-Americans did go to war, and when the survivors came home in 1945, they were no longer prepared to accept the old bigoted traditions. If you had fought at Guadalcanal or Anzio, at Omaha Beach or the Hurtgen Forest, you would not easily allow some fool to sneer at your accent, your family traditions, or the color of your skin. Henry B. felt that surge of emotion as he wandered through his parish. And for someone raised in the activist era of the New Deal, he began to see that the only solution lay with politics.

He seemed to know in his bones what the good ones learn the hard way: all politics is local. His eyes were set at first on the San Antonio City Council. No Mexican-American had ever been elected to this august body. Like states that had fought for the Confederacy, Texas used a system of poll taxes (where a citizen, in effect, had to pay for the right to vote) and literacy requirements to limit voting by Mexican-Americans and African-Americans. In 1950, Gonzalez ran anyway, made it to a runoff, and lost. But his defeat was a kind of victory; around the west side, Gonzalez emerged as someone to be listened to, and his message was clear: we can do this.

In 1953, he ran again and won. The Mexican-Americans of San Antonio were exuberant, and Henry B. took their needs and hopes with him to the City Council. The first order of business were those swimming pools, symbols of a humiliating exclusion. He went straight at the issue, demanding that the city desegregate those pools, along with every other city facility. The San Antonio establishment shuddered. And some of the yahoos came out of the darkness.

"I came home late one night," Henry B. later remembered, "when all of a sudden I heard something rev up and a car spun by in the darkness of the alley. And I heard two shots, and they hit the door of [my] car. I still believe if they wanted to, they could have hit me."

But he had his motto: *fear not*. And Henry B. Gonzalez

refused to be intimidated. With white liberal allies, and the support of the excluded, he won the battle. The pools of San Antonio were desegregated. So were the other vestiges of Jim Crow in public facilities. Three years later, Henry B. was elected to the Texas State Senate in Austin. This was two short years after the United States Supreme Court ruled on *Brown v. Board of Education*, in effect ending segregated school systems all over the United States, but most particularly in the American South. The governor of Texas was a man named Price Daniel, and he chose the side of resistance. Resistance to the Supreme Court. Resistance to fairness and justice. Daniel and his segregationist allies put together a package of bills whose intention was clear: to maintain the racist status quo. Then the freshman state senator from San Antonio rose in lonely grandeur and began to talk. And talk.

"In those days, you had unlimited debate," Henry B. remembered later, "and when you had the floor you could go on until they adjourn or you drop dead."

He had embarked on one of the most glorious filibusters in the state's history. He talked and he talked and he talked. Other men went home to sleep or out to eat. Henry B. talked. He talked for 36 amazing hours, sucking on lemons and raisins to soothe his throat.

"Once I had the floor, I was determined to hold onto it," he said. "They were determined to wait me out." The press converged to witness the spectacle. The old-line pols were embarrassed, or furious, singled out by some as red-necked neanderthals. "Finally about 4:30 in the morning they came over and said, 'Look, if you will let us pass just one, we will withdraw everything else.'" Henry B. agreed.

The bill that did survive was later defeated. Henry B. had won a famous victory.

He didn't stop there. In 1958, he became the first Mexican-American to run for governor, campaigning against the reactionary Price Daniel. He must have known that victory was impossible, but somebody had to do it first in order that another could someday do it better. Texas had to acknowledge that Mexican-Americans were a crucial political component of the state; so must the government in distant Washington. In only two weeks of that quixotic campaign, Henry B. logged 14,000 miles on the family station wagon, going everywhere, talking to all who would listen. He spent a grand total of $1600 on his campaign. That's *sixteen hundred dollars*, probably a day's worth of lunch in today's extravagant campaigns. And with all those limitations, and in spite of death threats and midnight phone calls, he won 18.6 percent of the vote. That is, a share large enough to provide a margin of victory for other candidates. National politicians were now paying close attention to this man from San Antonio, this Henry B. Gonzalez. One of the men paying attention was John F. Kennedy.

They first met in the early 1950s at a housing conference in Washington, D.C. (Gonzalez was deputy director of the San Antonio Housing Authority at the time). This was fitting, since Gonzalez had made public housing essential to his political vision, a clear, practical way for government to serve ordinary people. "He was a mostly unknown Congressman," Gonzalez said of Jack Kennedy. "I saw and identified with something beneath his shyness: a decency, a concern, a strength. . . . He in Washington, and I down in San Antonio, were on a parallel path—each working in our own way, in far distant places, toward the same general goals—though his were better defined than mine, and his vision far greater."

In 1960, Gonzalez became co-chairman of the Viva Kennedy campaigns, designed to bring Latinos into the presidential contest in an unprecedented way. Gonzalez was learning that any decent politician must respect the good sense of most voters. "People will respond to you if they can believe what you say," he said in 1994. "People will trust you if you keep your word. People will respect you if you respect yourself. If you lay out the problem accurately and if you propose a reasonable solution, people will give you a chance, not withstanding your heritage or race. Some would never vote for the Irish Kennedy or the Mexican Gonzalez; and some would only vote for us *because* he was Irish and I am Mexican; but most would decide the issues on the merits, and us on our ability."

In November 1960, Kennedy won Texas by a narrow margin to become the first Catholic ever elected president of the United States and the following year, with the support of Kennedy, Henry B. Gonzalez became the first Mexican-American ever elected to Congress. Each, in his way, was *un abrecaminos*, a person who opens paths for others, and Gonzalez would often joke (in the most serious way) that Mexicans were the Irish of the Southwest.

But even for the happiest warriors, horror can lurk in the shadows; it is no accident that the Irish and the Mexicans have a refined sense of fatalism. On November 22, 1963, Henry B. Gonzalez was two cars behind the limousine that carried President Kennedy past the Texas School Book Depository in Dallas. He was right there when that immense hole was blown

through America. He was in Parkland Hospital to light a cigarette for Jacqueline Kennedy while she sat in her bloodstained
clothes. He signed for the belongings of Governor John Con-
nally, who was wounded that terrible day. He flew back to
Washington with the presidential party on Air Force One.
Along with millions of others, he wept without shame. And
in the weeks that followed, he grieved. Jack Kennedy's photograph stayed on his wall for the rest of his life, as it stayed
on the walls of humble homes in San Antonio, and all along
la frontera, where it shared space with Nuestra Señora de Gua-
dalupe.

But in the wake of the assassination, Henry B. Gonzalez
did not retreat into cynicism or glib despair. If anything, he
fought harder than ever for the principles in which he believed. Years later, in a 1986 interview with the *Austin American-Statesman*, he admitted that he had only one regret about
the years that followed the killing of Jack Kennedy: his reluctant decision to vote for the Gulf of Tonkin resolution in
1964, which licensed President Lyndon B. Johnson to widen
the war in Vietnam. Johnson, a fellow Texan, was famous for
his bullying, arm-twisting tactics in getting what he wanted.
Gonzalez succumbed. He added his "aye" to those of the
full House, which by a 416–0 vote gave Johnson what he
wanted and opened the door to the national calamity that
followed.

"I never had graver doubts," said Gonzalez in 1986, "and
I swore that no matter who it offended, or anything, I would
never vote out of fear again."

He would stay in Congress for decades, famous for his
personal frugality, his small book-lined apartment in Wash-

ington, his off-the-rack clothing (including an electric blue polyester job beloved by his fans). Every weekend, he flew to San Antonio to be with his beloved Bertha and his children. In San Antonio, he had his own cost-free focus groups, made up of barbers, postal workers, gas station attendants, waitresses, and neighbors. No citizen was too ordinary for Henry B.'s attention. His banker and friend, Bill Sinkin, remembered one such moment, in an interview with the *Austin American-Statesman:*

"I was at Henry B.'s house one Christmas Day, along with a few other friends and supporters, when the doorbell rang. Henry opened it, and there was a man standing there. This man took a bus across town, probably spent his last ten cents, to give Henry a Christmas present—a 10-cent Christmas card. Henry invited the man in, sat him down, gave him breakfast and kept everyone waiting for forty-five minutes. Just took him in like he was his biggest contributor. That showed where his priorities were."

But if Gonzalez had a good heart, and a respect for ordinary people, he was not soft. He is still remembered in Texas for several events in which the old Depression-era boxer came roaring to the surface. In 1963, an El Paso Republican named Ed Foreman called Gonzalez and 19 other House members "pinkos." They had committed a terrible act of subversion by voting against funding the House Un-American Activities Committee. The 47-year-old Gonzalez went after Foreman and threw a long right hand at him. Alas, the punch was a little wide and only hit Foreman in the shoulder.

In 1986, when Gonzalez was 70, he was in a San Antonio restaurant when another Republican, dining at a separate table, shouted that Gonzalez was "our Number One leading damned Communist." Henry B. got up. This time the punch landed, his much younger opponent suffered a black eye, and Henry remarked that in fact he had been quite restrained. "If I had acted out of passion," he said, "that fellow would still not be able to eat chalupas."

But his political passion did not diminish as Gonzalez grew older. In 1989, he rose through the seniority system to become chairman of the powerful House Banking, Finance and Urban Affairs Committee. After 27 years on the committee, he then did something revolutionary: he used his new position on behalf of citizens, not bankers. He demanded that the Federal Reserve Board open its proceedings to public scrutiny (eventually they did) and at one point threatened to impeach Chairman Paul Volcker (he didn't). He hammered away at the corrupt core of the savings-and-loans industry, focusing on the role of Charles F. Keating, and the way he had corrupted five members of the U.S. Senate, four of whom were Democrats. Incredible! The man was attacking his own party! Obviously he was a "flake" or "a loose cannon." A large number of Democrats tried to boot him out of the chairmanship; he fought back and won. More than any other congressman, Gonzalez helped clean up the mess of the S&L scandals, forging the bailout of those people who had been hurt by the scandals, and making certain that Keating ended up in jail

Then he moved onto even larger game. He began to uncover the secret details that caused the American taxpayer to expand the war machine of Saddam Hussein. This scandal came to be known as Iraqgate. Gonzalez discovered that more than $3 billion in loans and letters of credit had been issued by the United States to the Iraqi government, supposedly for agricultural projects but in reality to buy weapons or their components. This scheme was driven by George Bush, James Baker, and others, and was operated through the small Atlanta branch of the Banco Nazionale del Lavoro (BNL). Early in the investigation, when Gonzalez was proposing public hearings, then-Attorney General Richard Thornburgh asked him to stop, citing "national security." Gonzalez gave him the brush, dug deeper, and soon discovered the true scenario: those "agricultural" loans were really a cover for Saddam's attempt to build nuclear and chemical weapons.

The logic was bizarre but also familiar. Since Iraq was then at war with Iran, and Iran was an official enemy of the United States, our enemy's enemy was therefore our friend. The "national security" mask had one intention: to keep American citizens from knowing what was being done in their name. Various U.S. agencies urged the Bush White House to end the secret deal with Saddam, since Saddam was an erratic, brutal thug; Bush and Baker ignored the warnings and went ahead with their arming of the Iraqi leader. Gonzalez was publicly dismissed as a head case and denied access to classified documents. He labored on, while Saddam Hussein continued murdering Kurds in his own country, and finally, in August 1990, invaded Kuwait. In January 1991, after a massive buildup, the Americans and their allies launched Operation Desert Storm. The war was over in 100 hours, but 141 Americans were killed in action, many of them with weapons indirectly paid for by American taxpayers. Bush had a brief moment of glory. Gonzalez said publicly that he should be impeached. The tough old man from San Antonio found no support at all among his colleagues for such a drastic move. But when the history of that era is written, Gonzalez will almost surely be noted as one of the sturdiest of all representatives, one who took the Constitution seriously.

In 1994, the Republicans took control of the House and Gonzalez lost his chairmanship. He was reduced to being the senior Democrat on the banking committee. Gonzalez laughed: "I was always in the minority, even when I was in the majority." Some of the younger Democrats now thought he was too old, and in 1996 started a move to replace him. He faced them squarely, as he always had, refused to beg, offered no deals, and made a rousing speech, saying, in part, "I have served with honor and integrity and success. I have never failed myself, and I have never failed you."

He kept his job. But the following year, he was terribly ill, and stayed home for many months. He made a brief return to the House in July 1998, was warmly embraced by friends and foes, and then chose not to run again. His 37 years on Capitol Hill were over. His son Charles won a race to succeed him, and Henry B. Gonzalez returned to San Antonio and his wife, his books, his friends, his children, and grandchildren. He died on November 28, 2000. He was buried out of San Fernando Cathedral, the same church in which he had been baptized 84 years earlier. Tributes flowed in from Democrats and Republicans, from President Bill Clinton to Texas Governor George W. Bush. Ordinary people wept, lit candles, laid flowers in his name, and remembered a thousand small moments in his presence. Many flags flew at half-mast. A mariachi band played a lament in the cathedral as Henry B. Gonzalez was taken to be buried in the American earth. Some old man. Some American.

I believe to be courageous is to be guided by your own internal moral compass. . . .

All across this nation, ordinary men and women are displaying those qualities of leadership . . .

All across this country, you can find examples of such courage. As was said of the Marines at Iwo Jima in 1944: "Uncommon valor was a common virtue.". . .

In my life, I have tried to demonstrate such resolve—to walk in my fellow man's steps before I led—to care for others before myself—to do what is right regardless of the consequences.

—MICHAEL L. SYNAR, 1995

MICHAEL L. SYNAR

by Steven V. Roberts

IT WAS MAY of 1979. Mike Synar was 28, a newly minted representative from Oklahoma facing his first serious vote. The issue was a bill protecting vast areas of Alaskan wilderness from development, and his background clearly told him to oppose the measure. Many of his relatives were ranchers. He had raised beef cattle to pay his college expenses. And he'd grown up resenting federal controls on public lands. More seriously the National Rifle Association, with 35,000 members in his district, was against the bill. And the presidents of five different oil companies, including one based in his home region, had called him personally and urged a no vote.

But as Synar studied the issue, his views began to shift. His office was covered by maps of Alaska, and as his former aide Sandy Harris remembers: "We really went through that issue in detail for months, and Mike became convinced that the oil industry was being irresponsible. They were intent on drilling wherever they wanted. He just thought they were wrong."

Synar knew the cost of his conversion. The oil companies "were livid at his position," says Harris, "and he heard from a number of family members and supporters, telling him that if he did this, it would be the end of his career." The afternoon of the vote, Synar convened a staff meeting and his closest adviser, an old college friend named Bill Bullard, told him flatly that if he voted for the bill, "I can't get you back here. You'll be a one-termer. Literally."

When bells rang through the Capitol complex, signaling the vote, Mike hurried to the House chamber, with Harris jogging to keep up. Both were fighting back tears. "He was quite emotional," she recalls, "it was very much weighing on his mind, what he was about to do. He turned to me and said, 'You know, this could be the end of us.' " Harris asked: "Are you sure you want to do this?" And the young lawmaker answered: "Yes, it's the right thing to do." Minutes later, when the big electronic board above the House floor flashed a green light next to Mike's name, indicating he had voted yes, Harris says, "there must have been a lot of people thinking, Synar has just committed suicide."

They would have been wrong. Synar was very much alive. "After that," says Harris, "he never seemed to be bothered by the political heat he got from back home." Mike agreed. In an interview with Chris Casteel of the *Daily Oklahoman* almost 15 years later, he reflected on his decision: "You want to know how all this started? It started right there, that day. It set the tone and the dimension and the personality of this office."

That tone and personality reflected the complicated man

whose name was on the door: demanding and devoted, hot-tempered and warm-hearted, an obnoxious bully to some and a beloved buddy to others. "Anger and outrage were an important part of Mike's makeup," says David Cohen, an old friend who is co-director of the Advocacy Institute. So were "passion and fearlessness," recalls Fred Wertheimer, another longtime ally in public interest battles. But even his fiercest critics agreed that when you dealt with Mike Synar, he told you the truth. Professor Ron Peters of the University of Oklahoma sums it up best: "It was a matter of personal honor to Mike to be a straight-shooter."

The oil industry was only one of many enemies Synar made during 16 years in Congress. Tobacco companies, gun owners, cattlemen, miners—they all joined the list. He took on any special interest he felt was draining the treasury, degrading the environment or demeaning the individual. "I'm the easiest-going guy in the world," he once said of himself, "but if you cheat, or take advantage of the system, or run over people, I can be one mean SOB."

Synar was often attacked in Oklahoma as a liberal, or even a Communist, but he was never easy to label politically. He proudly opposed wasteful government spending and was inducted into the Taxpayers Hall of Fame as someone who "would always stand up against the pork-barrel projects pushed by special interests or political back-scratching." If one word can describe him it is probably populist—a foe of concentrated power in all its forms. His district included the hometowns of both Will Rogers and Woody Guthrie (as well as Patti Page and Mickey Mantle), and as he told the *Daily Oklahoman* in 1994: "The best way to describe Mike Synar is the way Warren Burger described himself during his confirmation hearings as Chief Justice. When he was asked, are you a liberal or a conservative, Burger answered: 'Neither one. I call them as I see them.' "

Make no mistake, Mike Synar was a professional politician who spent a lot of money on opinion polls and TV commercials and wanted to win very badly. What made him different from most politicians was that he did not let polls dictate his decisions. He followed the lesson of the Alaska lands debate throughout his career and lectured his staff repeatedly that they should brief him on the substance of an issue, not its political impact. As he liked to say: "When we make a decision in the office, we don't take politics into account. I want to make a decision based on the facts first and then, if there's going to be some political flak, to try to deal with that issue separately."

The way he dealt with the flak was to go home and explain himself. A former congressional colleague, Pat Schroeder, said that Mike "saw his role as being an educator," and that's a good description. There are two ways to be a legislator and they are often in tension: to reflect your constituency, or to follow your own judgment. And when Synar disagreed with his voters, which was often, he would return to the district and make his case at town halls and coffee shops and Rotary Club meetings. "He always felt that he could convince the other side of his point of view—always, always," recalls Tom King, Synar's political consultant. "Often he was wrong about that."

As Ronald Reagan came to power America was turning sharply to the right, and no state felt the change more dramatically than Oklahoma. When Synar was first elected, there was only one Republican in the six-member House delegation, but after the 2000 election there was only one Democrat. The governor and both senators were also Republicans. But as the political landscape shifted, Synar did not. If anything he grew crustier and more confrontational. "His ego was huge, and he didn't try to hide it," notes Jim Myers, who covered Synar for the *Tulsa Tribune*. Town hall meetings turned more frequently into shouting matches. Recalls Tom King: "I kept telling Mike you can't vote like you represent Cambridge, Massachusetts, while you're representing Muskogee, Oklahoma, and expect to win. And he'd say, I won't change. I'll vote the way I think I should."

He didn't change, and in the end, he didn't win. After barely surviving a primary challenge in 1992, Synar was ousted in 1994, the year Republicans gained control of the House for the first time in 40 years. "Mike got caught in a tide, the state was just rejecting the Democratic Party," says Mickey Edwards, a former Republican congressman from Oklahoma now teaching at Harvard.

Within months of his defeat, Synar started suffering severe headaches. Aides remember him gulping down pain pills when he received the Profile in Courage Award in May of 1995, a moment, he told friends, that was the proudest in his life. That summer he was diagnosed with brain cancer and he died on January 9, 1996. He was only 45, but his short life left a large and lasting legacy.

The Mike Synar story begins long before that day in 1979 when he voted for the Alaska lands bill, 90 years before, actually, when his great-grandmother left Pennsylvania and joined the land rush into Oklahoma. She was an unlikely pioneer, a Polish woman with two daughters, no husband and little English, but as family legend has it, she strapped on two six-shooters and staked her claim to a 160-acre homestead on the Deep Fork River. Her daughter Adelaide, Mike's grand-mother, married a man named Synar who fathered six sons and then decamped, leaving the family mired in poverty. Adelaide moved the clan to an inhospitable place called Dirty Creek Bottom and raised her sons in a two-room shack—although in Mike's telling the dwelling shrank to one room. "Both of my parents were desperately poor growing up, desperately," he recalled. "My father says they were so poor, the poor people talked about them."

Still, the Synar boys made a name for themselves. Mike used to boast that between 1939 and 1949, Oklahoma State won the national livestock judging championship for 11 straight years, and every team captain during that period was named Synar. All six brothers saw combat in World War II, and Uncle Stanley was an ace pilot, shooting down two Jap-anese zeroes in a five-second span. Mike's dad, Edmond, was a tailgunner on a B-24 in Europe, and he says now, "We were all damn lucky to get back, that's for sure."

Just after Mike was born in 1950, smack in the middle of the postwar baby boom, Ed moved the family to Memphis where he took a job with a large meatpacking company. At his father's urging, the boy joined the 4-H club and at age nine entered his first speech contest. (Mike used to say he was only seven, but Ed assures me you had to be nine to join the club.) For months, father and son practiced the five-minute speech and Ed recalls that young Mike was a perfectionist. If he made even a tiny mistake he'd start over from the beginning. When the contest was held at the Peabody Hotel in Memphis, Mike beat out a three-time winner who was several years older. "I was hooked after that," he remembered and his dad agreed. The elder Synar spent many years coaching 4-H members but never met anybody as competitive as his own son: "Sometimes he was a poor loser because he wanted to win so bad."

A few years later the family moved back to Muskogee, and Ed joined his brother Steve in a ranching and real estate business. As a young teenager, Mike was asked to speak at the dedication of a local post office, and he met the area's long-time representative, Ed Edmondson. From that moment on, says his father, Mike "got the idea that he wanted to be in politics, and he never changed in that regard." Mike had a slightly different version: As a high school sophomore he was only five feet five inches tall, so he had to abandon dreams of athletic glory and "change direction in my goals in life."

When he arrived at the University of Oklahoma in 1968 he already had a statewide reputation as a champion debater. And Muskogee had a reputation as a tough town. "The guys I knew from there at O.U. were all street fighters," recalls Chris Casteel. Mike admits to spending a lot of time "drinking beer with those bums" at his fraternity house, Beta Theta Pi, but he plunged into student politics during a time when the Vietnam War had the campus in an uproar.

The idealism of the early sixties was still tangible, and a friend of Synar's, Mike Kelly, recalled the scene this way for the *Daily Oklahoman*: "I think all of us were compelled to try to do something, to be active, to try to be part of our political and social order. I guess somebody could nostalgically suggest that came from Jack Kennedy's tradition and possibly it did."

Synar had absorbed something else from the Kennedy tradition, a taste for political hardball, and his buddy Bill Bullard describes how Synar ran the student legislature: "We used to call Synar the 'iron duke' because that was the way he ran congress. Basically, it was Synar's way or the highway. Sound familiar?"

After antiwar protesters were gunned down at Kent State in Ohio, the Oklahoma campus boiled over in outrage, and Governor Dewey Bartlett was under growing pressure to call up the National Guard. Mike was chosen to help mediate between the students and the governor, his first taste of big-time politics. "They sent me out," he recalled, "because I was the frat guy with short hair. I became the spokesman for the student body." He made an impression on a student journalist, Keith White, who later covered Mike's political career for the Gannett News Service: "Mike's was always one of those names you wrote down and said, I've got to watch him."

After finishing college in 1972, Synar spent five years in graduate school: a master's from Northwestern, a Rotary fellowship in Scotland, a law degree from Oklahoma. He hated law school and didn't do very well at it. A few years later when he became the lead plaintiff in a Supreme Court case challenging the Gramm-Rudman budget balancing act, he told me with some embarrassment that he'd only gotten a B-minus in Constitutional law.

As Mike was finishing law school in the spring of 1977, the Democratic incumbent in Oklahoma's second congressional district, Ted Risenhoover, was suffering through a damaging spate of news stories about the heart-shaped waterbed he kept in his Washington apartment. Synar always insisted that he tried to get someone else to run against Risenhoover, but it's pretty likely that he was itching to do it himself. When he came home in February of 1978 and announced that he was entering the primary his father bellowed: "You're gonna do what with that goddamn $50,000 education I gave you?"

Mike was always deeply loyal to his dad, and often referred to him as his best friend, but Mike also described his father as a cautious and conservative man who wanted his son to be a tax accountant and a lawyer involved in the family business. When I asked Ed Synar about Mike's candidacy he replied: "Hell, I wasn't surprised, but I didn't think he ought to do it. It would take a lot of money and he didn't have any."

But he did have the Synar name. The six brothers had served as county extension agents and owned businesses in the area. Uncle Stanley had run for Congress in 1946 and Uncle Harry was dean of agriculture at a local junior college, so their nephew had a ready-made political network. But there was a hitch: Stanley had lost partly because he was a Roman Catholic in a heavily Protestant region, and when Mike went to see one local power broker, the man brought up religion. Mike said he had been raised Episcopalian, a compromise between his Catholic father and Methodist mother. As Ed Synar tells the story, the man replied good, that solves the problem, because no one in that part of the state "understood what an Episcopalian was anyway."

Still, by July, Mike's campaign was stalled. "We hadn't moved an inch in the polls," he recalled, "and we were flat broke." One evening a meeting of his closest advisers was just about ready to have him quit the race when his dad took the floor. "This family's name is Synar," he snapped, "and we don't quit." A plan was hatched: Mike would mortgage 20 acres of land he owned and 30 head of Angus beef cattle to finance the rest of the campaign. Three banks turned him down but at the fourth, an officer told him: "You've got it." When Mike allowed as how the man did not know him, the banker replied: "But I know your family, you're good for it." As Mike described the moment: "I remember my hand was shaking when I signed the note for $100,000."

Synar had something else going for him that the incumbent couldn't match—the boundless energy that later became his trademark on Capitol Hill. He told me after the election that he had met 150,000 people personally. "There's not a town in the district I don't know five people in," he boasted. "I go to Pawhuskie and I see the Sears man. I go to Bunch, and I see the school superintendent. Bunch, Oklahoma, population 26. But that's what they want." He was right, that's what they wanted. Mike defeated Risenhoover in the primary and sailed to victory in November.

At the time I was working for the *New York Times* in Washington, and I decided to write a series of stories about one new member and how he was adjusting to congressional life. A friend suggested Mike, saying he was the youngest member of the class. He wasn't, he was the second-youngest, but he still made an ideal subject: smart enough to know what was happening to him, wide-eyed enough to tell me about it.

In my first article, written from Muskogee in December of 1978, I quoted Bill Bullard about his friend's appeal: "I think what Mike represents is a coming out of—or an alternative to—the Nixon syndrome. I think a lot of people see Mike as a bright, shining sort of guy, the sort of Congressman they thought they should have." Bullard was struck by the folks who dropped by the office after the election to wish Mike well. "People keep coming in here and saying to Mike, 'go up there and don't change.' That's why they elected him. What they're afraid of is that he'll become another politician."

Those fears were unfounded. He never did become "another politician." And he was always bothered by a contradiction he kept hearing from his constituents. Those were the days of the growing tax revolt that helped elect Reagan two years later, but just as people were denouncing the evils of big government they were lining up for their own share of the federal pie. From the beginning, Synar demonstrated another trait that always marked his career: a willingness to tell people things they didn't want to hear.

When I interviewed him in January, in his new office on Capitol Hill decorated with Norman Rockwell prints his parents had given him for Christmas, he said sternly: "It might make me unpopular, but we can't deliver the goodies the way congressmen used to."

Two months later, as we traveled together through his district, he returned to the theme. A banker in Vinita had lectured him that "socialistic" congressmen from the Northeast were bankrupting the government, but the area was littered with federally financed projects: a dam in Grove, a sewer system in Big Cabin, a health center in Claremore. He hated hypocrisy, and as he was leaving the Vinita City Hall, Synar draped his arm around the shoulders of Bill Castor, the city attorney, and cracked: "Don't tell me again you want a balanced budget, not if you keep asking me for all these things."

Nothing got Synar angrier than the waste of government money. One pet peeve was the project to develop synthetic fuels, which he derided as "corporate welfare." But it was a favorite of Jim Wright, the representative from Fort Worth and the number two Democrat in the House who later became Speaker. When Synar opposed the synfuels plan, which was eventually abandoned as impractical, he lost an important friend. The same thing happened with the Tennessee Tombigbee waterway, a huge canal backed by important lawmakers from Kentucky and Mississippi. Synar considered it an "idiotic boondoggle" and refused to support it. A delegation from home paid a visit, suggesting that Mike was obligated to back the project in order to curry favor with its powerful sponsors who would then look favorably on money for eastern Oklahoma. He remembers telling his visitors that he felt no such obligation and wouldn't budge.

After his election, Mike made a pilgrimage to the home of Carl Albert, an Oklahoman who had retired as Speaker just two years before. The conversation left a lasting mark, and Synar often quoted the advice he received from Albert that day: "You have to decide whether you're going to be an Oklahoma congressman, or a congressman from Oklahoma." The implication was clear: would you consider just local interests or also national interests? And to Mike the choice was also clear: he would be a congressman from Oklahoma who tried to reflect and represent the world beyond his home region. But he also cherished another bit of advice he got from Albert: "He told me that the worst thing a politician can do is fear his own constituency." In other words, if you disagree with the folks back home, if you vote your conscience, or the national interest, spell out your reasons and trust people to understand, even if they don't change their minds.

An early test of Albert's advice came during Synar's first year, when he voted for legislation implementing the transfer of the Panama Canal back to Panama. A poll showed 90 percent of his district opposed the transfer and he received 750 postcards denouncing the bill. But he still thought the legislation was in the "best interests" of the country and that his voters had been "misinformed" by right-wing propaganda. He tried to explain his stance back home but he made little headway. As the wife of a retired Air Force colonel told me one day in Sallisaw: "I feel he's on pretty shaky ground with the people of Oklahoma."

That was often true, but those same people also respected his forthrightness, and Synar's staff was always struck by the reactions he received from his constituents. "We'd go back home," said Amy Weiss, who ran Mike's last campaign, "and people would say, 'Goddamn Mike, you're totally wrong, but you're standing up for what you believe in and I'll give you my vote.' It was incredible." Political scientist Ron Peters says this helps explain how Synar survived as long as he did. Because voters saw him as candid and principled, "he bought himself some slack," even with his opponents.

There was another secret to Synar's survival: his emphasis on constituent service. Like many new members in that era, he realized that more and more lives were being touched by the federal government. As one congressman put it at the time, "We've become the complaint window in the government department store." And answering those complaints efficiently gave folks a reason to vote for Mike, even when they clashed on the issues.

During his first year in office, Synar stationed 8 of his 14 staff members back in Oklahoma, and 3 of them lived and worked in small towns scattered around his sprawling district. The local coordinator for the Vinita area was a fast-talking blonde named Cindy Chestnut, the wife of Synar's college roommate, who called herself the congressman's "barometer."

Here's what I wrote about her in March of 1979: "Every week she roams through the towns and villages, stopping at cafés and city halls, taking the pulse and tapping the mood. And every week she gets a new flood of complaints—about Social Security, veterans benefits, disability payments." As Chestnut explained: "Money's the name of the game a lot of the time. Federal money reaches all of our lives, one way or another." Like her boss, Chestnut was frustrated with voters who told her to cut the budget, but keep their favorite programs intact. We were chatting over lunch one day at the Pioneer café when a local lawyer heard Cindy's lament and just laughed: "When the congressman's in town, everything's a federal problem."

There are two other keys to understanding Synar, and one was his district, an area that covered the entire northeastern corner of Oklahoma. Yes, it was conservative, but it was also poor, with a history of worker resentment against the mining and oil interests that dominated the economy. In the early part of the twentieth century there was a large Socialist vote in this region and David Cohen of the Advocacy Institute suggests there was a "class-based component" to Mike's appeal that tapped into that left-wing tradition.

Sandy Harris describes the heritage of the district in slightly different terms: "It was a very populist district. They hated everything big—big government, big labor, big oil, big business." In that atmosphere a champion of the "little guy" could flourish.

Moreover, northeastern Oklahoma has a larger concentration of Native Americans than anywhere else in the country. It was here that the "trail of tears" ended, where Indian tribes driven out of the eastern states were resettled by the federal government, and county names in the area reflect that history: Cherokee and Delaware, Ottawa and Okfuskee. Mike's populist approach won strong backing among many Native American voters and their continuing presence helps explain why the second is the only district in the state that elected a Democrat to Congress in 2000.

The other large influence on Mike Synar was his family, and particularly his father, Ed. "What made him different," says Sandy Harris, "was his streak of honesty and independence, and he got that largely from his father. That's the way he was raised." Even today Ed Synar is a force of nature, strong of arm and will, a man who made it on his own and pounded life's lessons into his three children with the force of a rancher driving fence posts with a sledgehammer. He takes vast pride in who he is and what he has done. The first time I met him, I was having dinner at his house, and he showed off the steaks before they were cooked, so the Eastern tenderfoot could fully appreciate their perfection. When I saw him again many years later the first thing he said was, "I sure cooked you a good steak, didn't I?"

Since father and son were both outspoken and hard-headed, some of their battles were legendary. The first time Mike defied his father was when he voted against giving agriculture an exemption from a gas rationing bill. The next day Ed called and Mike remembered: "He was livid with me. He told me, 'If you know what's good for you, you'll protect the farmers and ranchers.' " Things got even more testy when Mike supported a federal buyout of excess dairy herds, a move that his father feared would drive down beef prices. With considerable relish, Mike described it "as one of the greatest moments of my career." Just before the vote, Ed and his brother Steve, who were partners in the ranching business, called Mike and let him have it. "They were screaming and yelling at the top of their lungs," he recalled gleefully. "Do you know where you come from? Do you know how many cattle we have? They were very upset. But it's great."

Screaming and yelling is how Synar men often communicate. When I asked Ed if the stories about all those shouting matches with Mike were true, he replied: "Oh, yeah. They were always knock-down-drag-out kind of things. We called it skull practice. We always said there were too damn many chiefs and not enough Indians in our tribe." Mike often adopted the same high-decibel approach with corporate lobbyists and witnesses at congressional hearings, but the tactic was less effective back home at town meetings. Amy Weiss remembers a series of sessions over Bill Clinton's health care plan that Mike strongly supported. "The people in the district thought it was terrible," she recalls. "They would yell at Mike and he would yell right back. We tried to tell him that he couldn't treat constituents the way he treated lobbyists, but he kept saying, 'Goddamn it, I need to explain to them why it's the right thing to do, for them and for the country.' "

Synar reserved a special disdain for business interests that he felt were ripping off the country—miners, loggers and especially cattle grazers. He became the leading advocate for raising fees paid by ranchers to run their herds on public lands, an interesting position for a guy who mortgaged his own herd to finance his run for Congress and wore cowboy boots most of the time. "We're not Uncle Sam we're Uncle Sucker," he once said. "We're giving away our children's and grandchildren's assets." His father actually agreed with him on this one, but for a very practical reason. There were no public lands in Oklahoma available for grazing, so local ranchers like Ed and Uncle Steve had to pay full price to feed their cows, and then compete in the market with Western ranchers who enjoyed federal subsidies. "I knew he was right, but it was not a very popular issue for him to get into," the elder Synar remembers. And Ed did pay a price for his son's principles. As part of his real estate business, he sold large ranches throughout the West, and being Mike's father didn't help his client relations. "Mike Synar's name was particularly unpopular out there," Ed recalls. "They all knew who he was. They'd hear my name and the first question I'd get was, do you know Mike Synar?"

If Mike Synar was hated by his enemies, he was loved by his friends. His staff worked extremely hard and was extremely loyal. "He truly believed he was there to make a difference," says Amy Weiss. "And we all drank the Kool-Aid and were true believers, too." But his staff also knew his flaws, and relished what they called "Synarisms," his propensity for mangling the English language, particularly when he was excited. One of their favorites: "You can't have your cake and icing, too!" He used the word "orgasm" three times during a hearing when he meant "organism." Once he derided a witness for sitting there "in your expensive suit and Rolodex watch," and when his staff said the brand name was actually Rolex, he refused to believe them until he was shown the spelling in a magazine ad.

Mike dated many women but never married, and he often said the life of a congressman—staying out most weeknights in Washington, returning home most weekends—would be unfair to a family. "He would comment with regularity that so and so was having trouble at home," Sandy Harris recalls. "It would break his heart to hear other members talk that way." Toward the end of life, some friends thought that he was regretting his choice to stay single and not have children. "He encouraged me to have a kid," says Amy Weiss, and she took his advice. Her son's middle name is Michael.

Because he was "married to his job," as Sandy Harris put it, his staff became his family in Washington, and he addressed them the same way he addressed his blood relatives—loudly and lovingly. One staffer says that when he came to dinner, she stopped putting out the good crystal, because he broke too many glasses with his antics. Synar liked to host Sunday night dinners for his friends, and David Kessler, former head of the Food and Drug Administration, and his wife Paulette were drawn into Mike's circle after his defeat in 1994. Kessler describes the scene in his book, *A Question of Intent*: "Mike loved to cook, and we had dinner with him regularly. Evenings with Mike provided more than good food; they were also a theatrical experience, and everyone was expected to perform. The stage was his townhouse on Capitol Hill, the guests were his supporting cast, and he was always the star. Politics and statesmanship, conscience and cowardice, ethics and responsibility were his favorite themes."

Besides good food and pretty women, Mike also loved movies, and not highbrow movies, either. After he became sick, his friends arranged a special showing of the new James Bond movie, and his all-time favorite was *Mr. Smith Goes to Washington*, the old Jimmy Stewart flick about a courageous young lawmaker. He watched it at least three times a year, crying every time. And he never lost his farm boy habits, getting up many mornings at 5:30 to run through his Capitol Hill neighborhood. Friends say he came back one morning to find a thief leaving his house—which was always left unlocked—and Mike chased down the hapless fellow and retrieved his stolen property.

Mike's vast energy and vast ego sometimes rubbed people the wrong way. Often, in fact. A 1987 profile of him in the *National Journal* started this way: "He's aggressive, abrasive, headline-grabbing, hotheaded, crafty, a spoiled brat, a pushy fraternity kid, a vicious in-fighter. Those are descriptions from people who like him." He squabbled with reporters who covered him, especially those from the *Daily Oklahoman*, a very conservative paper in Oklahoma City and the state's largest. Allen Cromley, the paper's veteran Washington correspondent, used to tell about the time Mike came up to him and said, "Whenever you write something nice about me on Sunday, my mother makes me pancakes. And I haven't had pancakes in a long, long time." In his 1994 interview with Chris Casteel,

Cromley's successor, Synar referred to the editors of his paper as a "bunch of Neanderthals." When Mike was sick and the paper did write a nice column about him, he cracked to his friends, "Now I know I'm dying."

Within Congress, Mike had a small circle of close friends, including two former House members who are now in the Senate, Dick Durbin of Illinois and Ron Wyden of Oregon. But he was too pugnacious and outspoken to be widely popular in a place that values collegiality. Jim Myers of the *Tulsa Tribune* describes talking to Mike in his outer office after a Judiciary Committee hearing that featured some high-level officials from the Bush administration. Synar was excited about the session, and when he spotted Jack Brooks, the panel's chairman, walking past in the hallway, he shouted out, "Hey, Jack, we really got them that time." According to Myers, Brooks marched up to his young colleague, thrust his face only a few inches away, and snapped: "Synar, do you want to be an up-and-coming member of this institution, or do you want to be just another smartass?" When the startled Synar didn't answer at first, Brooks repeated the question. When Mike finally found his voice, and said of course, he wanted to be an up-and-comer, Brooks grunted and walked off.

Myers was never sure how much Brooks was joking, but Synar never fulfilled his ambitions to move up in the House leadership. He ran for a spot in the mid-eighties but was soundly beaten. "He did very poorly and did not expect to," recalls Fred Wertheimer, who worked closely with Synar on campaign finance reform. "He was not always aware of the impact he had on others. He was quite disappointed and taken aback." Synar also talked openly about running for governor or senator, but it never happened. "He was never considered an 'A' candidate for statewide office, and I think it grated on him," says Myers.

But Synar's weaknesses were also his strengths. Some lawmakers make their mark by crafting deals, forming coalitions, finding common ground. Others are gadflies, pushing and prodding their colleagues to rethink comfortable stereotypes and revisit old assumptions. They don't win Mr. Congeniality or Legislator of the Year. By their very nature, these people are irritating, even irascible. But they are also invaluable. And as Mike Synar's career unfolded, he grew more and more into the gadfly role, and even reveled in it. The bigger the fight, the stronger the enemy, the more he liked it. He was a professional David, always looking for a Goliath. Tom King, his political consultant, notes that many public officials get a thrill from risky personal behavior, with Bill Clinton being a prime example. Synar was different, his thrills were political: "He believed it was wrong to trim his sails, and he got a kick out of being a pain in the ass. He went to the edge." Adds Amy Weiss: "There was no talking him off the ledge."

So that's where he lived in Congress, on the ledge. One good example was campaign finance reform. Long before Senator John McCain took up the issue, Synar was out there, bemoaning the evil effects of big money on the political process. "Anyone who takes up that issue in Congress steps on a lot of toes and makes a lot of colleagues angry," notes Fred Wertheimer. But part of Synar's passion came from experience. He never took donations from political action committees, and mortgaged his own future to run for office. He spent $173,000 on his first campaign, and thought that was a lot of money, but when he got to Washington he was shocked to find out that many of his new colleagues had spent $500,000 or more. The price of admission to Congress kept going up, and Sandy Harris remembers Mike saying toward the end of his career: "Think about it. I have to raise a million dollars for a House seat." Added Harris: "You could see the look of weariness on his face when he thought about the prospect of doing that, year after year."

Then there was the decision to file suit against the Gramm-Rudman bill of 1985, which provided for automatic cuts in government spending if Congress failed to meet its own deficit-reduction targets. Synar's opposition grew from his well-honed philosophy that lawmakers should take responsibility for their own actions and not hide from their constituents. "I'm not an opponent of the concept of a balanced budget," he told me at the time. "But I think Gramm-Rudman is an outright abdication of our constitutional powers set forth by the Founding Fathers. They wanted us to make the tough decisions, because we were elected officials. If you turn that over to unelected bureaucrats, you basically shrink from your responsibilities."

Shrinking from anything was not Synar's style. A bunch of other lawmakers had originally agreed to join him in filing the suit but when the time came, all of them dropped away, leaving Synar to take the lead, and the heat, by himself. After he got word that the others had begged off, Synar asked the advice of his staff aide on the issue, and she said there was no question about going forward: "Your goal in life is to see how far you can push your constituents and still get re-elected." Telling the story, Synar agreed that there was "a lot of truth" in her observation. This was one more chance to play educator, to convince the voters that they were wrong and he was right: "We are out there pushing and driving, trying to move Oklahoma forward, testing and taking higher risks." Eventually he was vindicated, legally if not politically. The Supreme Court ruled the law unconstitutional.

Some of Synar's angriest exchanges came with the National Rifle Association. He was a lifelong hunter—deer, ducks, quail—and fried quail is a Synar family specialty. But he got crosswise with the NRA during his first term, when they opposed the Alaska lands bill, and his relationship continued to deteriorate. He voted for a series of measures opposed by the group: a waiting period for handgun purchases, a ban on cop-killer bullets, restrictions on assault weapons. None of these laws, in his view, threatened the rights of hunters or sportsmen, which he strongly supported. And he simply could not understand the NRA's refusal to support any gun control measures of any kind. As one former staffer put it, "I cannot tell you how much Mike despised the NRA. He thought no self-respecting hunter could support their positions. He thought they were getting crazier and crazier."

Not only was Synar a hunter in his youth, he was also a smoker, Virginia Slims to be exact. It was a brand usually favored by young women, and he came in for a lot of teasing. Finally he just quit, cold turkey. But what turned him into an activist was a young man from his district who used smokeless tobacco, or snuff, and lost part of his face to cancer. The story ignited Synar's populist furies, and as a member of the committee with jurisdiction over health and the environment, he was one of the first lawmakers to confront tobacco executives when they testified about smoking on Capitol Hill. The questioning got so heated one day that Synar told Jim Johnston, the head of RJ Reynolds, that he had given "an unacceptable answer," and that he had no "legitimate excuse" for withholding data from the panel. David Kessler, then head of the Food and Drug Administration and one of tobacco's most ardent critics, remembers thinking that "Synar needed to tone down his language."

But Synar didn't tone down anything. He filed legislation giving the FDA authority to regulate tobacco. Kessler wanted the power, but he didn't think the bill was going anywhere, and he felt he needed more evidence about the industry's manipulation of nicotine in cigarettes. In the spring of 1992, Kessler and Synar both attended a fund-raiser for the American Heart Association and found themselves—not by accident, they learned later—sitting at the same table. As Kessler recalls the scene after dinner: "I rose to mingle, but Synar collared me and we returned to our seats. He turned his chair around and straddled it like a man on a horse, his cowboy boots visible from under his tuxedo." Synar's message was as blunt as his body language: "Doc, you have to do this, you have to regulate tobacco." Kessler was taken aback: "This was before anybody else, before I was focused. He wasn't happy with me. I didn't give him the kind of commitment he wanted."

But Synar was not deterred. He became the author of the Synar amendment, virtually the only tobacco-control measure ever passed by Congress, which prods states to enforce laws against underage tobacco purchases. In a letter to Edmond Synar just days before Mike died, President Clinton called him "an American hero" and said, "It was Mike who caused us to see tobacco as a children's health threat no less menacing than the polio epidemic of the 1950s." Synar also continued to push his proposal for FDA jurisdiction over tobacco. "It was going nowhere and Mike knew it was not going anywhere," Kessler recalls. "But he understood the long pull. He understood the value of sticking with the issue and pushing, if only by inches." Then he added: "Mike was there before anybody else was, and he never left. And in some ways he still hasn't left."

Matt Myers, president of the Campaign for Tobacco-Free Kids, sees Synar's efforts on tobacco as the capstone of his career, the embodiment of what he stood for: "I increasingly saw someone who felt a special responsibility to stand up for individual citizens who couldn't fight back against corporate interests."

But the corporate interests could fight back, and they did. They spotted Synar as an endangered species—a progressive Democrat in an increasingly Republican state. The NRA said openly that defeating Mike was one of their "top priorities." Tobacco and oil interests felt the same way. And by 1990, notes Tom King, his enemies "started going after" Synar using new and sophisticated weapons. These "special interests had figured out" how to get directly involved in congressional elections, he explained, rounding up contributions for their favorite candidates but also buying their own TV commercials in selected districts. In 1992 the anti-Synar forces poured money and manpower into the campaign of Drew Edmondson, a Democrat who challenged Mike in the primary. Edmondson's name was even better known than Synar's—his father had been the congressman Mike first met as a teenager—and when the two clashed in a runoff it looked like Synar was finished. "They thought Mike was dead in 1992, they thought they had him," King remembers. "It was one of the ugliest races I've ever seen." But Synar fought back, storming through the district and relentlessly branding Edmondson as a tool of the "fat cats" who wanted to tell the good people of Oklahoma how to vote. Friends told him he looked and sounded "deranged" but the tactic paid off, and he returned to Washington for his eighth term.

In early 1994, when he sat down with Chris Casteel of the *Daily Oklahoman*, Synar sounded confident about his future. He had taken his opponents' best shot and survived: "I think after 16 years in this district they know who I am, and I know who they are, and they're willing to fight as hard for me as I am for them." He turned out to be wrong, for a wide variety of reasons. The conservative tide in Oklahoma continued to gather strength, feeding on a widespread resentment of Bill Clinton and the "weird hippie values" of the national Democratic Party, in the words of former representative Mickey Edwards. "Something settled in Oklahoma," he said, "a virulent anti-government, anti-politician idea. I'd go back to my own district and people would be really angry. It was an ill-defined anger, just a frustration with government."

That frustration was stoked and exploited by a new set of emerging political forces. Newt Gingrich and his "Contract with America" were tearing down confidence in the whole institution of Congress. Rush Limbaugh was making converts and energizing conservatives every day on the radio. The Christian Coalition joined some of Synar's older enemies on the front lines, providing fresh reinforcements and adding new issues, like abortion and gay rights, to an already long list of grievances. And Oklahoma was practically ground zero for the term limits movement, which demanded that long-serving members like Synar pledge to retire voluntarily—a pledge he never took. As Mike later told Keith White of the Gannett news service, all these groups combined "basically built up a pretty good crust that was hard to break through. They were very effective."

The groups also changed tactics, transmitting more of their messages under the radar of political reporters by using direct mail, leaflets in church parking lots, and whispering campaigns. "They did it underground in the last race" says Tom King, and one of the most damaging tactics was to suggest that since Mike was not married, he was probably gay. "He couldn't do anything about that," says King. "What could he say? I'm not a homosexual?" Another devastating issue was a handful of checks Synar had bounced at the House bank. King recalls Mike was "absolutely crestfallen" when he found out what had happened and his enemies were gleeful: "They beat the crap out of him for that."

The party of a new president often loses seats during the first midterm election, and the spectacular failure of Clinton's health care plan—which Synar ardently supported—aggravated that historical tendency. No matter how unpopular the president was in Oklahoma, Synar stood by him. He had worked hard for the party standard-bearer in 1992—even using his old training to play Ross Perot during mock debates—and he saw himself as part of the Clinton team and Clinton generation. Chris Casteel says that Mike "fell on his sword" for the president, and in his eulogy of Mike, Clinton agreed:

"When he was defeated in 1994, there was probably no person in America more responsible for it than me."

But there was another person who bore a lot of responsibility: Mike himself. All the years and all the battles had built up a lot of scar tissue and a lot of resentment. He seemed to get angrier at his critics and less tolerant of their views. His brother Alan invited him to address a gathering of doctors who peppered him with questions about the Clinton health care plan. Finally he just told the audience to go to hell, although his actual words were a bit saltier, and stormed out of the room. Amy Weiss recalls that when the campaign started polling in early 1994 Synar was getting only half the votes against any opponent: "He was basically running against himself, and losing." When Weiss tried to reinvigorate the Synar machine, she found a lot of parts missing. "She couldn't get anyone to help," says Jim Myers of the *Tulsa Tribune*, "no volunteers were showing up." Keith White adds: "When you rub enough people the wrong way over a period of time, you drive people nuts. The bad Synar beat the good Synar."

To some of his closest friends and supporters, Mike had lost his taste for the game. "He just didn't have the enthusiasm for it he'd had before," says one aide. "Sometimes we'd talk among ourselves and say, he doesn't care whether he wins or loses." Added another old friend: "He seemed to be acting out of character. I'm convinced that whatever ultimately led to his brain tumor was already affecting him. He just seemed a different person."

All these factors came together in the Democratic primary against a 71-year-old political unknown named Virgil Cooper, who spent only $17,000 on his campaign but won 52 percent of the vote. As Weiss noted, Mike Synar was basically running against himself, and he lost. In November Cooper was clobbered by a Republican, Tom Coburn, who promised to serve only three terms in Congress.

Some of Mike's friends felt that he was almost relieved by his defeat, and in post-election interviews he was decidedly upbeat. "If everybody wants me to lick my wounds or feel bad about it, they've got the wrong person," he told Keith White. "I have had the opportunity of a lifetime." David Kessler attended a farewell party in Washington for Synar and described the scene: "I worked my way through the crowd and across the dance floor to where Mike held center stage. He seemed to be dancing with three women at once, rotating from one to another. I waved to get his attention, and he smiled when he recognized me, but the band was pumping out music at a level that made conversation difficult. Raising my voice, I said whatever it is that one says to a politician who has just lost an election, and he thanked me with a grin composed half of frenzied elation and half defiance. It was not the grin of a loser."

Synar might have been relieved by his defeat, but he was bored by life outside of Congress. He disdained the usual job options for out-of-work politicians—lawyer, lobbyist, deal maker. He took a few small-bore assignments from the Clinton administration and started a nonprofit organization to work on campaign finance issues, but he had time to go to the movies in the afternoon and get more active in his church. "Anything that looked like a meeting, he joined," said one friend.

"Part of it was, he wanted to be with people. It was really kind of sad."

Meanwhile, his headaches were getting worse. When his illness was diagnosed, he saw it as another special interest to conquer. Recalls Kessler: "He kept saying, doc, I'm going to fight this, doc, we're going to win this. That was the way he approached everything." He also kept fighting on the issues he cared about. At one point when Clinton was visiting him at the National Cancer Institute, he asked Kessler to be there. A good opportunity to push the president on the tobacco issue, he said.

But the cancer was aggressive and unstoppable. So many former staff members were still so devoted that they organized round-the-clock teams to care for him. So many old girlfriends showed up at the hospital, it was a problem just keeping them apart. Kessler remembers that when Mike realized he would lose his fight, he said to his friend, "I'm at peace. I've done what I wanted to do." Few people can ever say that, and the example he set continues to echo through the lives he touched. "I think of him almost daily," says Amy Weiss. "What would Mike think about this? What would Mike say? Am I doing the right thing?"

He always said that he never wanted a long career in Washington, just a distinguished one, and he got his wish. Many words were written and spoken about Mike Synar after his death, pointing with pride and poking fun. "Now we know why Mike was always in a hurry, don't we," said Oklahoma political commentator Frosty Troy in his eulogy. And his old friend Bill Bullard joshed: "Mike believed every good thing ever said about him."

But in the end, Mike provided his own epitaph in his interview with Chris Casteel in 1994. "I have a responsibility to move my district, my state, my country forward," he said. "You've got to be looking down the road. We're trying to push the envelope to the very, very end."

Numerous people have asked, "Would you take the same course of action if you could start it all over again, or would you take a safer, less controversial stance?" My comment is always the same. "There is not one action I would change. As the chief advocate for children in my county, I carefully made each decision for the well-being and betterment of these children, and I would have to take a similar course though the consequences be many times as formidable."
—CORKIN CHERUBINI, 1996

CORKIN CHERUBINI

by Marian Wright Edelman

D R.   CORKIN   CHERUBINI , the Profile in Courage Award's sixth winner, was the newly elected superintendent of schools in rural Calhoun County, Georgia, when he noticed an alarming trend toward race-based tracking in his district's school system and decided to do something about it. At his invitation, federal civil rights officials came in to survey the county's practices and recommend changes. Blowing the whistle on a practice that had been in place since legal segregation ended in the county brought Dr. Cherubini hostile criticism, hate mail, and physical threats, and brought the community widespread tension, rumors of "race war" and riots, and white flight from the school system. The taunts and threats spread to include Dr. Cherubini's wife and young daughter, and a group of citizens filed a county injunction against him to have him recalled. But through it all, he remained committed to what was fairest and best for the children in his district.

Dr. Cherubini became the first person to win the Profile in Courage Award for actions at the local level. His award brought nationwide attention to the quietly destructive and pervasive practice of race-based tracking, and it brought Dr. Cherubini well-deserved recognition for having the courage to do the right thing.

Dr. Cherubini was born in Virginia, attended public schools in Massachusetts and New Jersey, and was educated at Troy State University in Alabama, the University of Virginia, and Auburn University. In 1970 he moved to Calhoun County, a small southwestern Georgia community of peanut and cotton farms, to teach high school English. Calhoun County's 5,000 residents were approximately 60 percent Black. Its two public schools were closer to 75 percent Black, but most residents still saw the county and schools as having a predominantly White power structure. Whites had traditionally controlled the land and large farms, the businesses and banks, and the school board.

It was during his 22 years as a teacher in the county that Dr. Cherubini began to have concerns about the achievement levels of his students. A White teacher, Dr. Cherubini noticed many of the Black students in his lower-level tenth and eleventh grade classes had only third to fifth grade reading and writing skills. He also observed that many of those same students seemed to have the ability to perform at a higher level, and just didn't have the background skills. As he said later, "When I was teaching, I would get Black kids who were potentially knockout students, but fundamentally they couldn't do anything." That was when he first began to suspect that many of the children in his classes could have done better in school if they had been expected to and helped by being placed on higher-achieving tracks in the lower grades.

But it wasn't until he became superintendent of Calhoun County schools that Dr. Cherubini got a full sense of the problem. He was elected superintendent of the 1,200-student district in 1992 by a vote of 1,137 to 922. Calhoun County schools had first been desegregated in 1970, the same year Dr. Cherubini came to the district, and 16 years after *Brown v. Board of Education*. But from the time children entered kindergarten in the county, they were "clustered" by race. Year after year there were two all-Black kindergarten classes. Two others were mixed-race but predominantly White.

Adults and school board members had always claimed this was for the children's benefit. One Calhoun County elementary principal argued that the clustering kept friends together when they started school, and that parents from both races felt "more comfortable" with this arrangement. The same clustering continued in first and second grade. By third grade, Calhoun County children were tracked into four groups by perceived ability levels—labeled "A" and "B" for the "faster" learners, and "C" and "D" for the "slower" ones. The two kindergarten classes that had been predominantly White became the A and B groups; the two all-Black classes became the C and D ones.

Once Dr. Cherubini discovered this was routinely happening, he began trying to learn why. Some school officials argued it was because students had been "tracked" by ability in the original kindergarten assignments. Dr. Cherubini discovered otherwise, and pointed out later that he didn't know of any test being given to kindergarten students that could accurately predict a five-year-old's learning ability. He also discovered that before the children left elementary school, "most students were performing—almost miraculously—at or near their arbitrarily assigned level. They had, indeed, lived up, or down, to teacher and school expectations." Once the initial groupings established in kindergarten were officially instituted in third grade, children generally stayed locked in until high school graduation. Seventy-five percent of all the Black students in Calhoun County were being tracked into lower-level classes, while most of the White students were being placed in higher-level ones. Dr. Cherubini described the situation he uncovered as "a kind of educational apartheid."

Willie James Taylor, the first Black person elected to Calhoun County's school board and the only Black member for a decade, noted that Black parents had been aware of the tracking for years, "but every time a Black parent would go over to the school and ask to have their child moved up to a higher level, they would always tell them that there was no room in the class. It was kind of like sweeping it under the rug." Earlier protests by parents to the school board had been turned away or ignored. By high school the difference between the A and B groups and the C and D ones generally meant the difference between being tracked into college preparatory or vocational classes, and so the paths that had been preselected for children when they entered kindergarten ultimately ended up leading them to very different futures. For too many Black children, racial profiling begins at birth and leads them too often to failure rather than to success and to prison rather than to Princeton and other universities.

As a teacher, Dr. Cherubini had often noted the "hopelessness and anger that dominated the minds of many youngsters" in his lower-level high school classes. He began to realize that all of this might connect back to those first arbitrary kindergarten assignments. Senator Edward Kennedy explained it this way in his remarks at Dr. Cherubini's award ceremony: "As the title of Mrs. [Hillary Rodham] Clinton's best-seller says, it takes a village to raise a child. But in Dr. Cherubini's experience, that truth was only partly true. He knew his village was raising some children—but lowering others. Calhoun County had long expected Black children to achieve less than Whites, and the expectation had become a self-fulfilling prophecy through a vicious system of racial tracking. Black children were arbitrarily put on a dead-end track in dead-end classes on the first day of kindergarten, and White children were put on a track to get real education. The tracking system was an education abomination, and Dr. Cherubini decided to blow the whistle on it, and write a new and better self-fulfilling prophecy, based on ability and achievement."

Once Dr. Cherubini understood what was happening, he said he felt immediately that he had to do something: "I don't see any real change taking place unless somebody takes the initiative to step out on a limb. Now that I'm in a position to do something, I just feel it's my moral obligation—moral, legal, and ethical." But it was at the point when Dr. Cherubini decided to fix the system that things became, in his words, "unbelievably difficult." As a teacher Dr. Cherubini had been used to occasional complaints from parents or spitballs from students, but "you don't think of an entire community, or at least the entire power structure, turning on you and becoming very hostile and threatening in many ways. Yet that's basically what happened here trying to make these needed changes."

As soon as he announced that he wanted to begin new class assignment policies that would make classes more racially balanced, starting with kindergarten and adding a grade of heterogeneously balanced classes each year, he faced stiff opposition and resistance from parts of the White community and the rest of the school system. Parents and colleagues criticized the plan in open meetings. Anonymous phone calls to his home threatened physical harm. Criticism grew worse when Dr. Cherubini also tried to address another inequity he had noticed in the school system. The high school had two girls' cheerleading teams: an all-Black basketball squad, and an all-White football squad, which received 30 times more money than the basketball squad, allowing the White cheerleaders to go to camp, receive better training, and wear better uniforms. Dr. Cherubini suggested that the cheering squads should integrate or merge. This caused school board members to tell him in an executive session that he should stay out of the schools and let the principals run them. At that point, it became very clear to Dr. Cherubini that even as superintendent his power to make change and promote just treatment for Black children in Calhoun County would be severely limited. Many would have stopped and retreated in fear, putting job ahead of justice and political safety ahead of principle. Dr. Cherubini decided to stand up and go forward by seeking additional help.

He spoke first with officials at the Georgia State Department of Education. They recommended he contact the U.S. Department of Education's Office for Civil Rights, which would be able to identify exactly whether and how Calhoun County was out of compliance with federal guidelines and would provide technical assistance and financial aid in seeking solutions. Not surprisingly, school board and community members disagreed even more strongly with Dr. Cherubini's decision to involve the federal government. There were bomb and riot threats. At one point an anonymous caller telephoned a local sewing plant to say there had been a riot at the nearby high school, sending worried parents to the school to pick up their children when in fact nothing had occurred. An anonymous flyer circulated which purportedly encouraged Black students to use the changes in tracking as the beginning of a race war on Whites:

"Support Dr. "C". We have the chance to obtain what we deserve in calhoun county! We must arm ourselves and be ready to fight for it . . . The war of the rases has started! Dr. "C" is on our side no black student will be punished for taking whatever action necessary to remove all the whites infecting our school. Dr. "C" has proven to the world that we have been mistreated and abbused in this county. We must act now to overthrow the white minority that rules this county and give it back to the majority!" [sic]

Many White parents began pulling their children from the school system. By 1996, when Dr. Cherubini won the Profile in Courage Award, many classrooms had only two or three White students left. A group called Concerned Calhoun Citizens for Education filed a county injunction to have Dr. Cherubini recalled.

Through all this enormous turmoil Dr. Cherubini courageously remained committed to his plan to ensure equal educational opportunity for his students. The Office for Civil Rights (OCR) and the Southeastern Desegregation Assistance Center, another federally funded agency that works with the OCR on desegregation challenges, agreed that Calhoun County's practices were in violation of the Civil Rights Act of 1964 and were able to offer tangible help. Consultants helped the school system with next steps: assisting school officials in reviewing alternatives to tracking; deciding on a new model that would best fit their needs; and offering workshops, conferences, and learning visits to other school districts to prepare for the transition away from race-based tracking.

Although tension and anger in the county remained high, the district began making the recommended changes. The recall attempt against Dr. Cherubini failed, largely because of support from the Black community and newly elected Black school board members. Willie James Taylor later said he told Dr. Cherubini, "When he was sticking his neck out so far, 'I have never seen a man that was brave enough to stand up to the entire country, trying to get something right for children.' " The plan to desegregate elementary classrooms went forward. The cheerleading squads were merged. And educators around the country began taking note of the Calhoun County case.

Dr. Cherubini realized that Calhoun County's story has a

larger lesson—"As 15,000 separate American school systems get ever-increasing local control, and strong national standards become less realizable, school officials must take a courageous role by not catering to the whims of special interest groups. They must make certain that millions of students not have their chances for equal opportunity nipped in the bud at a kindergarten age." He noted that Calhoun County's example "raises questions to which top school officials throughout the nation might well attend. For example, how does a school system get away with what amounts to blatant de facto segregation year after year? What improvements need to be made for monitoring and enforcing civil rights? Do we evaluate the long-range effects of our grouping practices with open minds or do we see only what we want to see? To what extent does regional politics dictate how we evaluate children? And finally, to what extent does equity in funding, within a school system as well as within a state, automatically offer some youngsters more than their share of the American dream while deferring that dream for others?"

After Calhoun County's story began receiving national exposure, Dr. Cherubini received "literally thousands of letters from people saying 'this kind of thing is going on here,' from all over the country." The story had such resonance because the questions that Dr. Cherubini raises are key ones that are still being asked over and over again today in school districts across the nation. At the time Calhoun County was receiving so much publicity, the NAACP Legal Defense Fund pointed out that "the overrepresentation of minority children in special education and the underrepresentation in gifted programs, and tracking or grouping practices in general, is a major problem for African American schoolchildren in many, many school districts." In far too many communities throughout the United States these problems continue to be widespread. Even as our nation revisits the feasibility of national standards and more accountability of schools, we still need to ask how we will make sure *all* children are expected and supported to learn and are prepared to reach the highest standards we set in place.

The Children's Defense Fund began calling attention to the disproportionate tracking of poor minority children in lower achieving tracks and special education classes decades ago. In 1974 in our first major report, *Children Out of School in America*, we documented 2 million children not enrolled in school and conducted a door-to-door survey with local community groups in 30 census tracks to find out why. Seven hundred and fifty thousand of the children the report found out of school were children with disabilities who were not being served at all. But many were students who had simply been underserved by their school districts, including many who had been inappropriately labeled slow learners and wrongly tracked.

One of the communities we visited while preparing that report was Calhoun County, where we spoke with several Black students like 11-year-old Willie. Willie had been placed in an educable mentally retarded class without his mother's knowledge or consent. The superintendent and principal of his school had told her they felt Willie had a behavior problem. No one had informed her that he was being switched to a special track. She did not recall her son ever being tested. She was certain she had never given permission for him to be tested. And she was never asked for and never gave permission for Willie's special placement.

Problems with tracking in Calhoun County and elsewhere long preceded Dr. Cherubini, and what was true in Calhoun County is still true in too much of our nation. Ninety percent of American children attend public schools, but too many are denied an equitable and quality education. Nearly five decades after *Brown v. Board of Education*, poor minority students are being disproportionately tracked for failure by low expectations, poorly trained teachers, and unequally funded schools. The achievement gap between White and minority students is unacceptably high and requires the kind of courageous leadership and action exemplified by Dr. Cherubini. Of every 100 White kindergartners today, 94 graduate from high school, 64 start college, and 34 complete 4 years of college. Of every 100 Black kindergartners, 87 graduate from high school, 53 start college, and 18 complete 4 years of college. The different outcomes for Calhoun County kindergartners that Dr. Cherubini challenged were simply a microcosm of what happens in our nation as a whole.

The Calhoun County case was a particular surprise to many people who had assumed desegregation disputes had gone away after the 1960s. Many certainly did not expect to see such a blatant example of within-school segregation. But race-based tracking and school segregation continue to persist.

A 2001 study released by the Civil Rights Project at Harvard University confirmed that much of the desegregation progress since the 1960s had been eliminated in the 1990s. A clear link exists between segregation by race and by poverty, and one of the main factors contributing to poor achievement levels for minority children is the dramatic disparity in resources provided to the poorest children. Recently a New York trial court found that New York's funding system deprived New York City students of the "sound, basic education" guaranteed by the state constitution and violated federal civil rights laws because it disproportionately hurt minority students in New York City public schools. It ordered the legislature to design a new system that adequately addresses and finances the needs of the poorest school districts. Other school districts, desperate for change as high numbers of children tracked for failure drop out of school and drop into the juvenile justice and adult criminal systems, are hoping for similar results. And partly as a result of Dr. Cherubini's courage and the publicity surrounding the Calhoun County case, many advocates and school districts are taking a long overdue closer look at racially biased tracking patterns within schools and the solutions they can implement to stop them.

Dr. Cherubini's moral courage in speaking up about the unjust tracking practices despite the opposition of his school board members and many community citizens and families needs to be replicated across the United States. As he later said, "In these small places, even now, to be vocal and outspoken is very dangerous for your livelihood, literally." But by speaking out anyway, he set an excellent example of how local education and political leaders and citizens willing to stand up for all children can build a more just society. Even before he won his Profile in Courage Award, Dr. Cherubini's actions had already ensured that no superintendent in Calhoun County would be able to get away with blatant race-based tracking that would cripple another generation of the county's minority children. And even before his actions led to change, just making the brave choice to risk his reputation and career and safety by doing what is right made him the role model all of us and all our children and youths need in school districts across America.

When he accepted his Profile in Courage Award, instead of taking all the credit, Dr. Cherubini thanked all the others in Calhoun County whose courage had bolstered his own and helped bring about the change: "Those courageous others include my wife and daughter who were at times targets of hatred and abuse, and yet they endured unfailingly, bravely. They were those teachers who invited me to visit their classes and student programs, admitting later that they would be ostracized by many of the faculty. There were board members who often made decisions based on the children's needs and well-being, knowing that they were invoking the wrath of special interest 'power' groups. Courageous media persons investigated and probed for truth, and then published or aired examples of inequities so entrenched and institutionalized, that even further exposing these inequities was often seen as a liberal attack on tradition. There were those ordinary citizens, attending town or board meetings, holding church meetings to discuss and learn and pray, or simply whispering encouragement where there seemed to be retaliation for even thinking 'improperly.' " A single teacher making the decision to extend an invitation, a single church member making the decision to attend a meeting—how powerfully all of these individual voices eventually came together for change.

Dr. Cherubini also said that years before he received the

award, his heroes had been President John F. Kennedy, Senator Robert Kennedy, and Dr. Martin Luther King, Jr.—people he had admired for their own courage. As he became an adult during the 1960s, they "were living symbols of the ideals composing my personal mosaic of American democracy. The courage these men exhibited in their efforts to ensure the rights of an overlooked segment of our society left an indelible imprint on me." Dr. Cherubini often used these three lives as examples as he taught his students. How fitting that his teaching brought him full circle to winning this honor for his courageous stand for children that celebrates President Kennedy's legacy.

As the first local leader to win the Profile in Courage Award, Dr. Cherubini was in the company of other elected officials recognized for work on a statewide or national level. But as John F. Kennedy, Jr., pointed out, "a lot of time the pressures at the local level have even more of an effect on the life of the honoree." We are all surrounded every day by people who choose courage in civic engagement in large and small ways. Like Dr. Cherubini, I hope you and I will be among them. President Kennedy, Senator Kennedy, and Dr. King are not coming back. It is up to each of us to carry on their courageous legacies as Dr. Cherubini did.

It is always the courageous acts of a few people that keep the world moving forward. In Dr. King's wise words: "Human progress is neither automatic nor inevitable. Even a superficial look at history reveals that no social advance rolls in on the wheels of inevitability. Every step towards the goal of justice requires sacrifice, suffering, and the tireless exertions and passionate concern of dedicated individuals." Similarly, John F. Kennedy pointed out in *Profiles in Courage*, "The stories of past courage . . . can teach, they can offer hope, they can provide inspiration. But they cannot supply courage itself. For this each man must look into his own soul." Dr. Corkin Cherubini looked into his own soul and made the choice to stand up for justice for all the children of Calhoun County, Georgia. Because he did, he is indeed a profile in courage. His courageous act was especially important because he stood up for *children,* who cannot vote, lobby, or speak for themselves and cannot contribute to the next campaign or turn out in the next election. I hope Dr. Cherubini's example of servant leadership will inspire all of us to care, and to serve, and to stand courageously until we become a nation where no child is left behind.

I respect people of faith, for I am one of them. As a judge, however, and as a principled human being, I will do what is legal and right. In making judicial decisions, I hope never to succumb to the political winds or to political popularity for the moment.
—CHARLES PRICE, 1997

CHARLES PRICE

by Maryanne Vollers

FEBRUARY 7, 1997, was a bright, mild winter day in Gadsden, Alabama, but when Judge Charles Price arrived at the Etowah County courthouse, the atmosphere turned ice cold. An angry crowd was waiting for him, blocking the front doors. With four stone-faced deputies on his flanks, the judge took the side entrance of the old brick building and turned down a hallway lined with more protesters. Some just glared; others shouted taunts as he passed by:

"You'll be sorry."

"Make sure you know what you're doing!"

"Atheist!"

That last epithet was a curious and painful thing to call this deeply religious man who taught Sunday school and served as steward of the St. John's African Methodist Episcopal Church. But Price wasn't surprised at his reception. Right-wing Christian activists had targeted him ever since he had been chosen at random to preside over the most controversial lawsuit to hit Alabama since the civil rights era. The case touched a raw nerve in this God-fearing region: At issue was whether or not a local judge named Roy Moore was violating the constitutional separation of church and state by displaying the Ten Commandments in his courtroom. Since it was filed in 1995, the case had become a rallying point for Bible-thumping politicians in Alabama and beyond who hoped to score points with fundamentalist voters.

Price's first ruling in November 1996 allowed Roy Moore to display the Ten Commandments, since the wooden plaques—hand-carved by Moore himself—appeared "at a distance" to be placed among several "historical, educational and/or secular symbols . . ." of the U.S. legal system. This was permissible. Judge Moore scoffed at the ruling, claiming that in fact the plaques were not educational, but *were* intended to promote Christianity. The ACLU—a party to the case—filed a motion urging Judge Price to reconsider. Price agreed, and announced he would personally visit Moore's courtroom to see how the items were displayed.

Moore's outraged supporters quickly organized a huge rally to "save the Ten Commandments." Alabama's governor, Fob James, even vowed that if Judge Price ordered the plaques removed, he would call out the National Guard to prevent it. Anonymous callers threatened the judge's life.

Price, however, was a hard man to intimidate. He was a former Green Beret and a legal pioneer who, in 1974, broke through the race barrier to become the first African American district attorney in the history of Alabama and, later, the first black circuit court judge in Montgomery County. There had been enough threats and close calls in his career to send most people looking for a new line of work. But the day he walked through the Etowah County courthouse was one of the few times Judge Price worried that someone would actually try to kill him.

The burly ex-paratrooper hid his fear as he passed through the gauntlet and into Moore's courtroom. He took his time, staring up at the large tablets hanging behind the bench. The Ten Commandments were in plain, solitary, and conspicuous view from every angle in the courtroom, including the jury box. By the time he walked back out the door, Price knew that he would have to make the most unpopular ruling of his career. The protesters were still hanging around the courthouse, shouting, singing, and praying aloud. They would not be the first—nor the last—individuals to learn that once Charles Price chose his course, there was no way to turn him around.

Charles Price was born on May 9, 1939, in Hunter Station, Alabama, a small community of 300 souls a few miles north of Montgomery. He was the fourth of six children in a family that was always struggling to make ends meet. His father, Alfred Price, was a railroad laborer, and his mother, Bessie Allen Price, worked as a housekeeper at the Greystone Hotel in Montgomery, among other jobs. Although his father completed only eight grades, and his mother had a few years of high school, both parents placed a strong emphasis on learning.

His older brothers dropped out of high school to join the military, but Charles stuck it out. Even though he was held back a year for health reasons—there had been complications following an appendectomy—he made good grades at George Washington Carver High School, particularly in subjects he liked, such as history and government. He was also a skilled debater.

"My parents demanded I get at least a high school education," Price said. In fact, he remembered that the whole community expected great things from its children. "They saw that was the only way we could close the gap between white children getting the best jobs, and our children getting any kind of job."

Like many towns in the South at that time, the white and black neighborhoods of Hunter Station were separated by a stretch of highway. The only mingling among races was at work, where blacks held the most menial jobs. Black and white students rode separate buses to segregated schools in the city.

Charles Price decided early in his life that he would study the law some day. It didn't matter that he had never actually seen an attorney: You could count the black lawyers around Montgomery on one hand.

Price came of age during the 1950s, when the Supreme Court decision in *Brown v. Board of Education* opened up the South to years of struggle over the integration of schools and other public facilities. Montgomery was an early flashpoint in the movement, when the Reverend Martin Luther King, Jr., emerged as a leader of a bus boycott to protest Jim Crow segregation laws. But Charles didn't join the civil rights marches that followed. Like many children in his time and place, he was more intent on fighting a personal revolution, one that would crack the mold of many generations. In 1959 he became the first member of his family to graduate from high school.

When he was in the eleventh grade, Charles Price met the woman he would marry. Her name was Bernice Brinson, and she was the smart, self-assured daughter of a Baptist minister.

"I admired his tenacity and his dedication," she recalls. "Besides, unlike the other boys, he would carry my books."

Bernice's parents were determined that their daughter go to college, and she enrolled at Alabama State College after high school. Charles couldn't afford to start college right away, so he joined the army as a means to continue his education. A year and a half out of high school, in January 1961, Charles and Bernice were married—after her parents extracted a promise that she would be allowed to earn her degree.

While Bernice studied to become a teacher, Charles was jumping out of airplanes in North Carolina as a paratrooper with the 82nd Airborne Division. He was later sent to Germany. It was the beginning of a long and difficult pattern of separation and mutual support in their marriage. For the next decade, one spouse would work while the other went to school, until both had completed advanced degrees.

Charles re-enlisted after his tour in Germany and joined the newly formed 8th Special Forces, a unit of the elite Green Berets. He was sent to a U.S. base in Panama where he worked as a cryptographer supporting missions in Central and South America. In 1965, he earned his discharge with the rank of sergeant (he later rose to Lt. Colonel in the Army reserves) and enrolled in Virginia Union University to get his bachelor's degree.

By this time Bernice, who had transferred to Tuskegee University to earn her degree, had taken a job teaching near Richmond, Virginia. She was also raising their daughter, Susan, who was born in 1963.

"My earliest memories were of my parents 'working things out' and taking duties with me, because someone was always in school or always working," Susan recalls. "They were both very strong disciplinarians, but very loving. Both had an incredible work ethic."

It was a hard landing into civilian life for Charles Price. "The military in those days was the closest you came to equality," he recalls. "You were making the same money as white people in the same rank—even if you were the last to be promoted! When you got that stripe you knew you really worked for it."

But the reality of being a black man without a degree in the South hit home when the only part-time job Price could find was as a night janitor in a Richmond, Virginia, clothing store.

"I had to do a lot of thinking and talking to myself," he says. "I had to convince myself that I really wanted to be a lawyer. I was making good pay in the military, and I could have made it a career. Why should I put up with this? But my answer was that I had a plan, and I had to stay the course."

Price stuck with his strategy, graduating from college within three years. He then enrolled in George Washington University Law School, finishing with honors in 1972. Price was working at the Department of Justice in Washington, D.C., when he got a call from Bill Baxley, Alabama's attorney general. Baxley had openly campaigned for black votes, and had promised to open the attorney general's office to black lawyers. Price was one of his first recruits. There were so few black lawyers in the state, and even fewer blacks in government positions, that Price couldn't resist Baxley's offer. "I always wanted to be a prosecutor, because I never thought the criminal justice system took very seriously the plight of black victims, or black folks in general," Price says. "I wanted to work from within the system to help straighten out some things."

Now that Bernice had finished graduate school in Maryland, Charles agreed to move the family back home to Montgomery.

Susan Price recalls those first days her father worked as Assistant Attorney General for the State of Alabama. "I remember him loving the law, burning the midnight oil, practicing his opening arguments on me while he drove me to school," she says. Susan Price eventually followed in his footsteps and became a lawyer herself.

It was only a year after Price took the job in the attorney general's office when a group of prominent citizens from Escambia County paid Bill Baxley a visit.

"Their district attorney was too sick to perform his duties," Baxley remembers. "They told me, 'We've got to have help! Give us your best prosecutor.' So I told them I'd send them my best prosecutor." He didn't mention whom he had in mind. But he knew it was about time for the state to get its first African American district attorney.

"Bill Baxley was brave enough to appoint me, and I was crazy enough to go down there," Charles Price recalls. In 1974 Escambia County was a rural backwater bordering the Florida panhandle. The government had always been controlled by white men, most of whom had never seen a black lawyer, let alone a prosecutor. So when Charles Price parked his state vehicle in front of the county courthouse, walked into the clerk's office, and announced, "Hi! I'm the new D.A.," he might as well have been announcing a Martian takeover.

"I thought that clerk was going to fall over and die!" Price recalls.

Back in Montgomery, the attorney general's phone was

ringing. "Someone from that delegation called me and told me I'd never get another vote in Escambia County if I didn't remove Price," says Baxley. "I told him, 'All right, I'll have to do without the votes.' "

Luckily, the circuit judge and county sheriff were broadminded men and quickly gave Price their support. He returned their confidence by aggressively prosecuting murders and other serious felonies that had been going unpunished for years. It was an exhilarating but dangerous time in Price's life. One day a white businessman who had also been in the military came to his office and warned the young D.A. not to accept any invitations for dinner out in the county. Then he gave him a .25 automatic for protection.

"I never thought about the fear, to be honest with you," says Price. But he took the precaution of always leaving the county before dark, and driving an hour and a half to and from Montgomery morning and night.

In the end, Price did such a good job as prosecutor that, when Baxley called him back to the capital for another assignment, he got an angry petition from a familiar committee. "They said, 'If you take Charles Price away from us you'll never get another vote in Escambia County!' " Baxley says with a laugh. "And I told them, 'Well all right, I reckon I'll have to do without you.' "

In 1975 Price became deputy district attorney for Montgomery County under another progressive white prosecutor, Jimmy Evans. Next year, the Prices' second child, Charles II, arrived. Soon after, Price entered into private practice. In 1982 he was appointed to an assistant municipal judgeship for the city of Montgomery by a tough Republican mayor, Eddie Fol-

mar. On April 4, 1983, Price was given his historic appointment as the first black circuit court judge in Montgomery
County by George C. Wallace himself, the Alabama governor
who once pronounced "Segregation Forever!" He had recently
repented his racist politics, and was elected to a third term
with the help of black voters. Wallace was also paralyzed, often
hospitalized, and in constant pain since a would-be assassin
shot him in 1972. The governor summoned Price to his hospital room, and talked to him cordially for most of an hour
before signing the papers making him judge. "You didn't think
I was ever gonna sign, did you?" the governor said.

"He was still the old George Wallace to me," says Price,
"but I had no hatred in my heart when I was sitting there,
talking to him. In fact I felt sorry for him."

Since then, Judge Price has been elected to the position,
unopposed, for three consecutive six-year terms. He is up for
reelection in 2002. In those years Price has handled many controversial cases. He has tried drug cases, Klan cases, and gang-
ster killings, where witnesses and jurists alike were threatened.
As a circuit judge in the state capital, he has had to subpoena
the governor's testimony and preside over huge civil cases,
such as tobacco company lawsuits. There were five circuit
judges in Montgomery County who might have been picked
to decide *Alabama v. ACLU,* but a computer in the clerk's office
chose Charles Price.

The case had a long and tortuous history even before it
landed in Price's courtroom. It began in federal court in 1995,
when the ACLU of Alabama sued Roy Moore on behalf of
several residents of his judicial circuit who were members of
a group called the Freethought Society. They sought to stop

him from imposing his religious values in a government court-room. Judge Moore, a West Point graduate with political ambitions and fundamentalist beliefs, not only hung the Ten Commandments above his bench, but he opened his court sessions with Christian prayers.

The federal judge dismissed the case on the grounds that the plaintiffs did not have standing to file a lawsuit because they had been never compelled to appear before Judge Moore and be subjected to his religious proselytizing.

At this point, the ACLU dropped the case. Then, in a highly unusual move, Judge Moore met with then-governor Fob James and Jeff Sessions, Alabama's attorney general, to try to force the issue through the courts and get a solid ruling. The state countersued the original plaintiffs along with Judge Roy Moore in a "declaratory complaint" that asked the question whether or not the courtroom procedures Moore followed were constitutional. The case was filed in Montgomery County circuit court, where it eventually landed on Judge Price's bench.

A different kind of judge could have punted the case straight into a higher court and rid himself of any political consequences. "The easiest thing for me to do would be to have said that the court finds there is nothing impermissible about prayer and the Ten Commandments, and taken the view: 'Let the appellate courts decide it,'" Price says. "That would have been what a lot of judges would do in tough cases. But I couldn't do that."

There was no state law to guide him in his ruling, so Price turned to the federal courts and the U.S. Supreme Court to find precedents. In his judgment, rendered on November 22, 1996, Judge Price cited *Larson v. Valente*, 456 U.S. 228 (1982), among other cases, to rule that "state-sponsored prayers that demonstrate a denominational preference are proscribed by the Establishment Clause of the United States Constitution." Since Judge Moore's prayers were strictly Christian, and imposed on people who did not choose to attend his court, Judge Price found him in violation of the First and Fourteenth Amendments of the U.S. Constitution and Articles 1 and 3 of the Alabama Constitution, which prohibits state-sponsored religion.

Price ordered Moore to cease and desist the courtroom prayer sessions. But in a split ruling, he allowed the display of the Ten Commandments, citing *Harvey v. Cobb County, Georgia*, 811 F. Supp. 669, 678 (N.D. Ga. 1993). In the Georgia case, the court found that the Ten Commandments could be legally displayed in government buildings only if they were placed in a historical, educational, or secular context, and not in a manner that promotes religion.

Nobody was completely satisfied with this mixed decision. But when Judge Price made the extraordinary move to reconsider his ruling, a highly organized pro–Ten Commandments movement swung into action. At the head of the pack was an ultraconservative Christian fund-raiser and political operative named Dean Young, founder of the Gadsden-based Christian Family Association. The one-time head of Moore's legal defense team, Young began organizing rallies to support his former client. He bused in church groups to meet Judge Charles Price at the Etowah County courthouse. The crowd was stirred up by some strong rhetoric, particularly some words Governor Fob James had told a Baptist gathering a day earlier. "The only way those Ten Commandments and prayer would be stripped from that courtroom is with the force of arms!" James had declared.

Those words were running through Charles Price's head as he made his way past angry faces in the crowd surrounding the Etowah County courthouse after he inspected Judge Moore's courtroom. But the attack he was waiting for never came and he made it safely to his car for the long drive back to Montgomery. The incident was so unsettling because it reminded Price of the days of segregation.

"I could see the history repeating itself with the governor threatening to call out the National Guard," says Price. "It reminded me of Little Rock (when the Arkansas Guard was called out to prevent the integration of a high school), and the march from Selma to Montgomery. It was a flashback to the old Wallace times."

After returning home to Montgomery, Judge Price took the weekend to formulate his ruling. Before long, he experienced another flashback to the civil rights struggle. "I sat at the desk and thought: What would Judge Frank Johnson do?" he says. Frank M. Johnson was a hero to Price and a whole generation of Americans who valued tolerance and equal rights. He served as a U.S. district judge in the Middle District of Alabama, and on the eleventh circuit, where many groundbreaking civil rights cases were decided. Johnson's rulings on voting rights and school desegregation changed America forever. They also caused him to be denounced as "the most hated man in Alabama." He attracted so many death threats that he was under federal protection from 1961 to 1975.

"For a few seconds, I reflected on Judge Johnson, and wondered if I would be ostracized as he was," Price admits. "He was blocked from entering his church and never went back. He almost lived a reclusive life. But he is the one federal judge that all others look to, because under difficult situations, he never blinked. He would never have hesitated to make this decision. So I just sat down at the desk and did what I should have done the first time around."

On Monday, February 10, 1997, Judge Charles Price reversed part of his original ruling in *Alabama v. ACLU* and ordered Judge Moore to either place the Ten Commandments in a historical or educational setting, in accordance with *Harvey v. Cobb County, Georgia*, or remove them from his courtroom.

In his decision, Price echoed the Georgia decision by stating "to those who have asked the Court by phone calls, individual and multiple signature letters, and postcards to 'save the Ten Commandments,' all of whom the court respects, that the Ten Commandments are not in peril. They are neither stained, tarnished nor thrashed. They may be displayed in every church, synagogue, temple, mosque, home and storefront. They may be displayed in cars, on lawns and in corporate boardrooms. Where this precious gift cannot and should not be displayed as an obvious religious text or to promote religion is on government property (particularly in a courtroom)."

James A. Tucker, a lawyer for the ACLU of Alabama, applauded Judge Price's decision as a "victory for the Constitution and the rule of law." He also praised the judge's fortitude in making it. "In light of recent threats by the governor to topple the rule of law, Judge Price's ruling demonstrates extraordinary courage in the face of sheer demagoguery."

"My decision had nothing to do with religion," says Price. "It had nothing to do with the Ten Commandments. It was about following the law. But clearly some people thought that I was passing judgment on the Ten Commandments themselves."

As expected, Price's ruling was condemned by right-wing fundamentalists. Even though the Alabama Supreme Court stepped in and stayed the decision until appeals could be heard (eliminating the need to mobilize the National Guard to "protect" the Ten Commandments from the courts), the furor only grew in the following weeks.

Judge Price was denounced in opinion columns and letters to the editor in newspapers across the state. The governor's office was logging in 700 letters a day, almost all in support of Roy Moore. Dean Young collected 215,000 signatures in favor of the Ten Commandments, which he displayed at a publicity event. "We think the Lord has chosen Gadsden, Alabama, as a war ground to determine if America does have its trust in God," Young told reporters.

The frenzy spread as far as the U.S. Congress when Alabama Representative Robert Aderholt introduced a nonbinding resolution in the House honoring Judge Roy Moore and supporting the display of the Ten Commandments in courthouses and other government buildings. Although the resolution did not carry the weight of law, Christian political activists threatened to target members of Congress who opposed it. It passed 295 to 195. The Alabama legislative adopted a similar resolution.

Most frightening to Price and his family was a massive rally at the state capitol attended by Governor Fob James, Roy Moore, and conservative politician Ralph Reed. Twenty-five thousand people poured into Montgomery to "Save the Ten Commandments." There was no doubt about from whom.

Around the time of the rally the sheriff's department supplied Price and his family with round-the-clock security. There had been threats, including one caller who reached the judge on his home telephone to tell him, "You're not a Christian, and we're gonna get you off the bench. You'll be dead before the Ten Commandments come off the wall."

Susan was in Seattle, working as an government attorney; Charles II—Chuck—was attending Morehouse College but had come home for Easter break. The whole family was in shock over the sudden change in their lives. "We were apprehensive and angry," recalls Bernice Price, now an assistant professor of humanities at Alabama State University. "Being guarded is like being held hostage. You can't go to the store, you can't go to church, you can't go any place without security. And the presence of security drives the point home that something devastating could happen. I was afraid for him."

There was never, however, a discussion of whether the judge should change his mind, or his job. "My husband does not quit," says Bernice Price. "He brings his formal training in the law together with the wisdom of experience. And he does not allow anything to deter him."

Luckily for Judge Price, the one place where he might have been vulnerable—St. John's AME Church—became a sanctuary for him. "I'm a person of deep, deep faith," says Price. "My pastors and fellow church members knew my decision had nothing to do with religion or my belief in the Ten Commandments."

A few other voices also rose in his defense. Some exasperated editorial writers expressed anger at the politicians who were taking advantage of the heated atmosphere: The *Montgomery Advertiser* admonished the governor for threatening to employ "total resistance" to the rule of the courts, calling

James's remarks "appalling." It went on to say, "Judge Moore, like Governor James and every other American, is free to practice his religion as he chooses, but not free to impose his religion on anyone else in his official capacity. If he cannot separate his private spiritual life from the secular duties of a judge . . . [then] he should in good conscience leave his office."

As it turned out, Judge Moore did not leave his office, and he did not cease and desist from praying in the courthouse. Nor did he remove the hand-carved plaques behind his desk until he left his job as circuit court judge to assume his new role as chief justice of the Alabama Supreme Court. Moore ran for the seat on his fame as the "Ten Commandments Judge" and was swept into office in the Republican landslide in Alabama in 2000. Justice Roy Moore chose not to display the Ten Commandments in the supreme court, but has hung them, legally and properly, on a wall in his chambers. The still-defiant Moore has, however, recently installed a granite monument of the Commandments in the supreme court rotunda.

The case of *Alabama v. ACLU* eventually died out with a whimper, not a bang. As expected, it was appealed to Alabama Supreme Court, which, in 1998, dismissed it on a technicality. The high court found that the plaintiffs did not have standing in the case, since there was never any controversy between the governor, the attorney general, and the defendant, Roy Moore, since they had colluded to file the lawsuit.

"The Alabama Supreme Court found the easy way out," says Judge Price. "If they had done the right thing, they would have written to the issues, and let the case go to the Supreme Court."

Judge Charles Price continues to preside over cases in Montgomery County, and plans to run for another term in 2002. He's not worried about losing his seat. "People in Montgomery County know what type of judge I am," he says. "Everybody knows the ruling was correct. The governor, the judge, and the attorney general were playing a game. They knew what the law was, and still is, but it was a good issue that they all could ride on."

While Price now downplays the political and personal risks he took, Maurice Bell, an old friend and, at 78, still a practicing attorney, sees the decision for what it was: "There's a church on every corner here in the Bible Belt," says Bell, "and it took a lot of courage to rule the way he did."

In the months following his decision to remove the Ten Commandments from Roy Moore's courtroom, Judge Price had ample cause to reflect on the meaning of courage. He spoke to the subject during a commencement speech at Tuskegee University in May 1997.

"Courage cannot be taught to you," Judge Price told the crowd of new graduates. "Instead it emanates from your principles, your values, and your moral and ethical beliefs . . . It takes courage to rebuke popularly held opinions. It takes courage to choose the road less traveled. The courage of one protects the rights of all those who are affected, particularly in America."

When Charles Price is asked if he has any regrets about the difficult and historic case that tossed him, for a time, into a political tempest, he says, "The only regret I had was that I didn't make the ruling in the beginning. But I was trying to be fair."

Until you have to fight for your government you tend to take it for granted. . . .

As a prosecutor I am not sure I did anything in this situation that any other prosecutor in America would not have done. Every day all across this country men and women in law enforcement put their lives on the line to enforce the law so that the rest of us can live in peace. They are the true unsung heroes. . . .
—NICKOLAS C. MURNION, 1998

Nickolas C. Murnion

by Ron Suskind

J UST AHEAD, ACROSS a moonlit prairie of buttes, scrub grass, and jagged gulches is tiny Jordan, Montana—a town *Life* magazine once called "The Loneliest Town in America." It's home to *The Law Man*.

He's a part of this landscape: a stock character in the drama of how an angry, unruly land was tamed in the mythic movement west . . . though, looking left and right, no one seems to have won any victories over this lonely piece of earth. The struggle to franchise civilization on a million-acre vacant lot called Eastern Montana is, in fact, an ongoing war of attrition—of man versus the elements—turning, each day, on whether a survival kit of basic American principles is used wisely and well and with hard-eyed vigilance. The vigilance of a band of isolated settlers—their designation still, like a century ago—among whom is a quiet, solitary man, a loner, who stands tall for justice. If it ever came down to chaos and lawlessness on the open plains, he wouldn't back down, for any reason. *You'd have to kill him.* It's a comforting myth that there are men like that, somewhere. Makes us feel safe, everywhere. And that's why, on principle, we love Nick Murnion. We love the idea of him.

The basic facts are now commonly known. Nickolas C. Murnion, the prosecuting attorney of Garfield County, took on a band of homegrown terrorists, the anarchic, coherently livid, armed-to-the-teeth "Freemen," better organized heirs of Ruby Ridge and Waco, and took 'em down. It was 1994 and he placed their prairie rants about onerous taxes, unjust federal regulations—their live free or die fighting, property rights for all! whoop—up against the bulwark principle: Rule of Law. *You boys are breaking the law and we're hauling you in . . .* The Freemen laughed—*you and what army!*—and put a million-dollar bounty on Nick's head and the heads of a handful of officials who stood up to be counted. Undaunted, Nick Murnion went on the attack, filed charges, and called the FBI, the hated *feds*—part of a cabal villainized by every rural Montanan including scoundrels at the Interior Department's Bureau of Land Management or Fish and Wildlife or any one of a dozen distant, arrogant alphabet agencies. He told the FBI he needed some backup . . . *no one could deny that.* What followed were seiges and standoffs and arrests, with daily broadcasts on the national news, until the whole snarling bunch was in jail. And Nick Murnion's strong jaw and steady gaze was recognized—far and wide—as a profile of courage.

The sirens are deafening, the shrill cry of mayhem. I leap from my bed at Jordan's Garfield Motel and a moment later, have on my jeans. I can make out several sirens, closing in. *Disaster! Close by.* The mind races. This, after all, is Garfield County—an area the size of Connecticut with just 1,406 residents—and the heart of "Freemen Territory." Just yesterday, a guy was arrested nearby for passing counterfeit "Freemen" checks. A few hours west of here in Lincoln was where the Unabomber hid out. And there've been some stirrings of late—read about it in the eastern papers—with a rise in militia activity matching a downdraft in the rural economy, the worst since the 1930s, with wheat at $2 a bushel and farms closing on this parched terrain where only frustration seems to grow.

Just out the front door of the motel, two ambulances, a school bus, and a fire engine pass by in a line. Everyone within earshot is spilling onto Main Street, wide-eyed, necks craning, pointing.

And waving.

Waving?

From the school bus's windows, high school girls are waving back on their way to the state volleyball championship. It's a parade, Jordan-style. Brief and to the point—a creep-along of shiny, never-used disaster vehicles and a busload of smiling girls.

A few minutes later, men in caps and hunting jackets are crowded into two booths at the Jordan Drugstore, shoulder-to-shoulder in the murmuring aroma of close bodies, mildewed denim, and fresh coffee. Tucked among them is Nick Murnion.

"Come on in—water's fine," he says, holding up a white porcelain cup as brims all around dip in silent affirmation and soon I have a cup and the din resumes—choice, lean cuts of comment—about the chances of Jordan (now named Garfield County District) High's Lady Wolverines in the state tourney ("the lead ambulance in that parade cost $90,000—they better win"), the last time there was a blaring vehicular send-off for a team going to a state championship (the boys class B 1966 basketball team, everyone agrees), and onward to how depressed wheat prices hardly even matter considering the thinness of this year's crop. "If it rained forty days and forty nights, we'd get a quarter-inch here in Jordan," says Karen Fitzgerald, owner of Jordan Drugstore (her husband's the druggist), filling everyone up at 50 cents a cup. "Ain't that right, Father?"

Father Leo, a young circuit-riding priest for three tiny cities across 200 miles—a white collar under a feed company cap, nods—"the Lord has a dry sense of humor . . ." and everyone chuckles before lurching into how those "greenie weenies" are protecting coyotes and replenishing the wolf population on the prairie so the big, clever canines "can have lunch on our sheep." That's George Hageman talking. He's a garrulous friend of Nick's, a Vietnam vet and proprietor of the Pioneer Garage, like his father and grandfather—who asks "what about that Freeman they just arrested in Wolf Point [Montana] for the bad checks?" And everyone turns to Nick—his unparalleled expertise meriting a moment, but just a moment, of deference—who says, "Well, they're still out there, but it's isolated

and unorganized . . . don't think we'll have any more trouble."
Brims tip all around.

I ask if people in Jordan think Nick's a hero for standing
up to the Freemen. Embarrassed laughs all around are ended
by George. "We don't use words like 'hero' around here." The
question itself—the notion of status being determined by
some special talent, noteworthy act, or conferred notoriety—
seems to burn away the booth's equanimity and, soon, everyone casually saunters off to start their day, leaving just me and
Nick.

"You'll get some debate, even now, about what happened
back then," he says, quietly, shaking his head, balding and
gray now at 47. "You commit yourself to doing the right thing,
but it's never as simple as you think. Oh no, never quite that
simple."

Nick Murnion has lived two lives, a before and an after. That's
a particularly rare feat in a small town, where you pretty much
get to live out the one life everyone expects . . . considering
that they knew you in third grade or were "real close" with
your mom, dad, grandma, grandpa, uncle Herbie, aunt Rose,
or cousin Charlie who served in Korea ("don't think he saw
action, though . . ."). In a town like Jordan, population 365
(down from 498 in the 1990 census), personal histories are
so densely interwoven they create a blanket of expectations
that can be comforting, but has been known to suffocate.

Few families around here have a history as wide and deep
as the Murnions. John Murnion came over from Ireland in

1912, when Garfield wasn't even a county. The lore, in this case, is instructive. He was due to make the crossing on the maiden voyage of a spanking new vessel with an extraordinary reputation: unsinkable due to the latest technology in airtight compartments. He had a ticket for steerage. But he hesitated. "Ain't never proved itself," he's said to have told his mother, "and a Murnion trusts nothing that hasn't proved itself." So John—after crossing to New York on a boat *other than the Titanic*—signed up for a 320-acre plot of land in Montana as part of a federal homesteading program, supported by the railroad lobby, which wanted this godforsaken country to be settled along its newly laid tracks. There were brochures of lovely vistas and breezy texts—promoted by the government—about the miracles of "dry farming" on what was reputed to be some of America's most fertile, though underappreciated, soil.

Again, the bubble reputation burst. John and the other settlers learned some hard truths. The tracks never came through Jordan. What passed through, instead, were biblical plagues—drought, heat, dust, grasshoppers, and bone-shattering winters—that swept most homesteaders off this land in just a few years. Small log cabins, with bowed roofs, still dot hilltops here and there. Temperatures in the winter can drop to 50 degrees below zero and the rainfall averages about 12 inches a year, the bottom fringe of what can support most crops. What's left: thin harvests and the raising of cattle and sheep, which fight, each day, for enough to eat across vast tracts of land.

The human struggle to secure basic human services out here is no less daunting. Jordan has one of the nation's only public school systems with dormitories, once housing up to

150 students during the week, a daily journey home being simply too far. After decades of failed attempts to lure a doctor to town—one was a drunk; another, Gregory Hemingway, Ernest's son, had some personal problems and simply vanished one night—the town finally managed to build a small medical center manned by a physician's assistant.

In this spare environment, the Murnions—along with a dozen or so other original families—stuck it out. Over decades, they were rewarded. The extended family now owns more than 100,000 acres of pastureland, most of it stretching 30 miles north of Jordan to the edge of the Missouri Breaks—a series of majestic caverns and lakes that mark early turns of the Missouri River.

That's where Nick grew up, fishing, hunting, and working on the family farm. There was, however, a presumption of high achievement. The Murnions were more educated than most and Nick, like many of his siblings, was Jordan High School's valedictorian. If anyone would go off to college, it'd be him. So, after giving the Jordan High School commencement address in 1971, he went off to Montana State University at Bozeman—a city a hundred times the size of Jordan; then to law school at the University of Montana at Missoula, a conventionally progressive college town that is viewed from pursed-lipped Garfield County as a den of libertine iniquity.

The few people from Jordan who ever make such a journey—attaining professional credentials and nourishing exposure—almost never return. Which is why in 1978, Nick's last year of law school, the then–Garfield County attorney was *the only lawyer in the county.*

"I thought about going to a big firm, or continuing my

journey away from Jordan with some other job, but the land, and my family's history on it, just seemed to draw me back," he says, in a rare episode of reflection. "It's not as though I didn't like what I saw in the bigger world; I just felt like I belonged in Garfield County. I felt this strange tug." So, in his last semester of law school, Nick filled out various forms—registering as a Democrat and a candidate for county attorney—and mailed the envelope to the Jordan Post Office. The incumbent was a newcomer to town (there only three years) and, as a Murnion, Nick had a distinct advantage. On a Tuesday in June, Nick won the post—a half-time job paying $18,000 a year; that Saturday, he graduated from law school.

What's a 24-year-old prosecutor, with no courtroom experience, to do?

Whatever comes up. Most of it small and rather intimate. There's really no zone of privacy in this county. Practically everyone's related to everyone else, by blood or marriage—a sprawling, feuding, ornery cousins' club. In this mix, young Murnion quickly acted like the last guy you'd invite to the family picnic. His philosophy: *Sure, I've known you my whole life, but the law's the law.* In the early 1980s, he prosecuted the then-venerable sheriff for insurance fraud. And, in the late eighties, he did the same favor for the county treasurer, who skimmed a few hundred dollars in auto licensing fees to help her through some tough financial straits. Considering how a half dozen or so public officials run the whole county, this is a little like siccing the IRS on your bridge club. What's amazing is not only that both were driven from their offices in disgrace; it's that soon thereafter Nick would see both of them on the street and everyone was cordial. In a community with more respect for bloodlines than bloodless statute, he somehow managed to enforce the law as though it were the only thing that mattered. *And still get re-elected.*

Acts of courage, it is said, often emerge from some underlying architecture of character. Drawing hard, neat lines, visible to all, on a grid of right and wrong—of legal and otherwise—was a first, public rendering of Nick Murnion's character. The forthright prosecution of colleagues and cousins was something folks in the county took a while to get used to, but eventually recognized as a thing of value. Then, they didn't even notice it anymore—they just noticed him. While this bridging of person and principle was professionally valuable—eventually making Nick politically unchallengeable as county attorney—it would have to carry a weight, an almost diabolical pressure, that he couldn't have imagined. Upon this bridge of person and principle, everything soon would rest.

How do these things ever start? It's a refrain as open-minded as a shrug, a conversation starter about how you never know a starting point until it's thickly overgrown and hard to dig out. Nick Murnion can't afford such imprecision. He's a prosecutor. He deals in causation.

So he fixes the point of origin at a moment in January 1993, when Ralph Clark and Dan Peterson were standing in his office on Main Street in Jordan—really the only street in Jordan—making demands.

They were angry men in fleece-lined jackets and feed-company hats, with easy access to firearms—a designation that applies to much of Garfield County and the core of Nick Murnion's constituency. People feel powerless against blunt, blind forces—whether it's a spring freeze or some distant regulator—and they want to lash out. On this morning, the men were directing their frustration at the Farmers Home Administration, the FmHA, which provides a financial infrastructure for the lives of many distressed farmers and ranchers. It lends them money, generally at low interest, holds the lien on their properties, offers relief when needed, and demands—according to certain legal strictures—a modicum of cooperation. Eventually, you have to make payments on your loan; at some point, the money actually runs out. Mind you, the FmHA isn't benign, nor is it malignant. It's expressionless, with no discernible pulse, like the referee calling fouls in a close game. Just doing his job, he gives everyone someone to howl at.

Ralph and his adviser, Dan, are members of a home team on a long losing streak—farmers too deep in debt to get bank loans, who have borrowed heavily from the FmHA to survive. Once seated, they howled at Nick about wanting to sue the FmHA because it's an illegitimate agency, loaning them money that, they asserted, has been worthless since the United States went off the gold standard. Nick, in his capacity as county attorney, took notes as he listened to men he has known his whole life—constituents, after all. He told them that he was sympathetic to their plight but had no jurisdiction to criminally prosecute a federal agency. They left, murmuring curses.

A few days later, a document was delivered. It was a "Confession of Judgment" against Nickolas C. Murnion, stating that he is "liable for $500 million in minted silver," for fraud, malfeasance, dereliction of duty, and other infractions linked to not prosecuting the FmHA.

He read it over three or four times, not sure what to make of it. It was like a legal document written by an irate, creative eleventh grader.

"Don't think I can write a check for this one," he told his secretary. "Know where I can pick up a load of minted silver?"

It was just the start. A flurry of similar, legal-sounding lien documents piled up through the spring and summer, as an "us" versus "them" intensity began to collect around Jordan like heat vapor. In April, the U.S. Fish and Wildlife Service raided the property of some elderly ranchers who they thought were poisoning eagles, *with CNN cameras in tow*. Ranchers love the national symbol as much as the next American, except when they kill lambs—which the majestic birds do with relish. No local authorities—including Nick or local law enforcement—were warned about the raid; no hard evidence was found. The incident resulted in the doddering couple being splayed across national TV and admitting to possession of an unregistered pesticide.

In this whipped-up atmosphere against malicious outsiders, a midsummer meeting by something called the National Federal Lands Conference—a right-wing, antigovernment group—drew more than 200 attendees to the Veterans of Foreign Wars Hall in Jordan. A county prosecutor from New Mexico, a man whose job is almost identical to Nick's, shared the dais with some antitax activists and described how to thwart federal regulations by running them through the approval process of county planning boards.

And on it went, with Nick laughing off the strange liens while he carefully monitored the simmering discontent. When, in January 1994, 26 local men and a few women moved to take over the Garfield County Courthouse for a meeting of the "Supreme Court of Garfield County, Comitatus"—their own self-styled legal arm—Nick told them they were not a legitimate entity and tried to stop them. He called for backup from his buddy Sheriff Charles Phipps and Charles's lone deputy, Darrell, but the trio was outnumbered. All they could do was videotape their angry, strident neighbors and friends as they issued writs to attach the property of local judges. The mob was suddenly self-sustaining, nourishing itself on notions of empowerment, righteous rage, and rebellion that, on most days, made them feel like Minutemen farmers attacking British redcoats. They started calling themselves Freemen. Just loved saying the name.

One morning a month later, the town woke up to handbills plastered everywhere: BOUNTY OF $1 MILLION FOR THE ARREST OF NICHOLAS MURNION. Other handbills called for the arrest of Sheriff Charles Phipps and a few more for various county officials.

Nick and Charles sat in Nick's office, as each looked at his wanted poster. What to do?

Anyone wishing to act on the request, the posters stated, should call the Freemen's newly appointed constable, William Stanton, whose phone number was printed in bold. Like the Murnions and the Phippses, the Stantons are also one of Garfield County's old families, and Bill Stanton—known as a tough, no-nonsense, says-what-he-means rancher—also happens to be the uncle of Charlotte Stanton Herbold, the county treasurer and clerk of court, whom Nick works with almost every day.

"Let's just call Bill up," Nick suggested, and pulled out a taping device. "See what he says."

Charles, whose land is just a few miles from Bill's, dialed.

"Hey, Bill. This is Charles . . . Nick and I are here and I see that you've put a bounty out on us." He winked at Nick, trying to keep it light and neighborly. "Could I turn myself in and collect it?"

"You could," Bill said, icily. "But you probably wouldn't live to enjoy it."

"Why's that?" Charles responded, his voice getting tentative.

"Because," said Bill, all business now, "you'd be tried and you'd be hung."

"What, you gonna build a gallows on Main Street?"

"No we wouldn't want to waste the taxpayers' money. We'll just throw some rope over the bridge and hang the bunch of ya."

A minute later, the phones were returned to their cradles.

Nick and Charles looked at each other, feeling disembodied.

"We've got a problem," Nick said finally. "A big problem."

That day, that night, and the next day and night, Nick dug through law books, tissue paper pages of the federal and state code, as he looked desperately for citations about treason, anarchy, revolution. The concept of rule of law—that the full complexity of human interactions can be effectively officiated by these volumes of logjammed legal prose—is as much an article of faith as of fact. You've got to believe that the statute—though a secondhand rendering of public will, often drafted by legislators whose motives may only loosely configure to a law's "spirit"—is somehow sacred; that, despite imperfections, in the end it may be all we have to keep us from the darkness. Nick believes it. It's something he dare not talk about at the drugstore over coffee, how his faith in the letter of the law has sent him, time and again, into his beloved statute books to adjudicate countless gray-shaded disputes in the life of the community. The problem now was that the Freemen weren't so much attacking specific laws but rather the premise upon which the whole structure is built: the very concept of rule of law. For the few men who upheld the law in this county, they were presenting a choice: your belief in this principle, or your life.

Nick, the politician, knew that he couldn't counter discontent from people's losing farms by debating abstract principles; these folks would end up haranguing forever, as Garfield County's incarnation of constitutional government ground to a halt. No, he'd need to trust the law and let it work, by showing that the Freemen were *currently acting illegally* and then commence prosecution.

Finally, it was staring right at him: an ugly, one-eyed orphan of the state's criminal code, the Montana Criminal Syndicalism Act. The act defines syndicalism as the advocacy of "crime, violence, force, arson, destruction of property, sabotage and other unlawful acts or methods" as a means of achieving industrial or political revolution. It's a felony.

The conception and birth of this act in 1918 is not a thing of pride. Montana's newspapers, largely controlled back then by the huge Anaconda Mining Co., had been demanding that Governor Sam Stewart call for a special session to punish radical labor unionists, also called the "wobblies," that had been plaguing the company. The session was called and, on cue, the act was passed as a means to prosecute advocates of a then-nascent principle: the general strike.

Nick, the lawyer, scratched his head. My oh my, this would be tricky. That a law passed to prosecute opponents of unchecked corporate power—activists who are considered pioneers of America's labor movement—would be revived to indict Freemen would seem perfectly logical to many antigovernment sympathizers in Garfield County. Big companies and big government are seen from this outpost as brethren in mendacity. What's more, it seems no labor activist was ever actually prosecuted under the act.

But syndicalism was all Nick Murnion could extract from his long shelves of dusty volumes. He would have to carry it into legal battle and claim it as holy writ.

If sober self-interest is the most common calculation of political figures, Nick was doing the opposite: staking out a position that would leave him conspicuous, vulnerable, and without ready means of self-defense.

Soon, felony indictments were filed; any convictions would carry serious consequences. A line had been drawn in the red clay of Eastern Montana that seemed to scrape across American bedrock.

And Nick Murnion's old life officially ended.

A light morning rain, a blessing in any season in Eastern Montana, has stopped and Nick slips out the front door to his office, then ducks next door to "The New U" to see if his wife,

LeAnn, is ready. He could have gone another way: straight back from his desk, past an old safe (Nick's office was once a storefront bank), and through a little shared hallway that smells of lacquers and aerosols.

The two establishments share more than the hall. LeAnn's the town beautician, after all. They work side by side, gathering clients and gossip, exchanging notes, grabbing a bite and a beer. Soon enough, LeAnn the stylist and Nick the lawyer are settled across the street at the Hell Creek Bar, one of two bars in this one street town; this being the big one with its sprawl of round tables by a long bar, a room in back with pool tables, a couple slot machines whose lights shine garishly.

They order beef strips on rolls and talk about nothing, like married couples do. They and their children—Trevor, 10, and Erin, 14—live about 500 yards away in a modest ranch house with untended grass, a boat on a trailer out back, and a dog in a pen. LeAnn says that "this town is like a giant family, sometimes a giant feuding family, and we try to stay above the fray, but that's just not possible." She is eight years younger than her husband and grew up on a small ranch near the Missouri Breaks, chasing steer through rough canyons. Nick earnestly toiled on the debate team; LeAnn, the most popular of girls, starred on the high school rodeo team and was a cheerleader.

Where Nick is often judicious in what he says—befitting a man who knows so much about people's business—LeAnn, every bit as current on the affairs of the town, is unfettered.

"Part of being happy in Jordan is not thinking too much

about what it'd be like somewhere else," she says, polishing off her beef strips sandwich and downing a beer. "Sure, Nick's a lawyer, and I run the beauty shop, but there's no upper or lower class, here. This place humbles you, everyone's equal, just trying the best they can to make a good life out here—which isn't easy for *anyone*! That struggle, I guess, is what all we share . . . maybe the only thing."

Nick, not wanting to talk about struggle, grabs his non-alcoholic O'Doul's—no beer for lunch—and strikes it up with some folks at a nearby table. He asks Frank, a huge man in a parka and muddy boots, to tell the story about when he went to the Freemen compound for his indoctrination. Frank obliges, saying, "They thought I'd be interested in being a Free-man 'cause my farm was taken in a foreclosure, like a lot of places. So I went."

He tells how he entered a trailer at the compound and saw a noose of thick rope with a 50mm gun—a shoulder-cannon, really—hanging from it.

"They talked about the rights of people to live free, and how the government was illegitimate and on from there. They said they'd had about all they were going to take. I just listened. After an hour, I said, 'If you fellas want to come back with me, I'll drive you over to the authorities and you can make your case to them. If they agree that what you're saying makes sense, then I'll join you.' "

That's not what the Freemen wanted to hear and, after a little glaring and posturing, Frank was escorted out. Nick, listening intently, nods along. He likes that story; it indicates that plenty of others were with him—even those, like Frank, who felt they were wronged by the federal government—and that any sensible person would see the Freemen as a bunch of crazies.

Duly sated, he gets up to walk back to the office—has some papers to file on an estate dispute—and LeAnn, seeing some ladies waiting out front of "The New U," follows him.

Sitting at a nearby table is a wide-faced, top-heavy man in a cowboy hat. His name is John Murnion. He and big Frank are chummy and, once Nick's gone, John, who also lost his farm a few years back, joins in to tell about his Freemen connections. Yes, he was considered a friend of many of those involved. And, of course, everyone knew he was Nick's first cousin.

"You've got to understand that many people in this county agreed with what the Freemen were saying, the stance they were taking. It was maybe their methods that caused the problems."

Maybe their methods? Like hoarding weapons, setting up an armed camp, and threatening public officials? "Well, you have to remember that most everyone around here is armed, and maybe a little wary, living out on their ranches or whatever. And they'll fight to protect what they believe in. But no one will do anything to anyone who's part of this community. It's the people who enforce federal laws that make no sense and hurt people from around here . . . they're the enemy."

Like your first cousin.

"No, no Nick's a good man. It's just that he made us choose, I suppose. You know, which side are you on . . . and that can cause some real divisions."

Charlotte Stanton Herbold, Bill Stanton's niece, saunters

over. She resigned as county treasurer in the early stages of the Freemen's challenge and now runs the Hell Creek Bar with her husband. She listens for a bit as John Murnion distills the issue. "The problem is that the Freemen are our friends," he says. "And here, friendship isn't given easily or given up easily. Out here, we feel we're kind of all in this together, backing each other up, and that's something that goes beyond laws." Indeed. The community's take-care-of-our-own interdependency—of people who are isolated and bonded tightly to one another by history, blood, and the challenges they face each day—creates a fabric of shared interest as nuanced and varied as any set of laws. Beneath that canopy, you can do almost anything you want.

Charlotte, measuring her words, puts a bow on it. "We've got something right here that no one else can buy, for any amount of money."

Everyone turns to her, wondering what that is.

"Freedom."

When this ancient, raw brand of freedom collided with civilization's duly constituted laws, it could have gone either way.

Nick knew that as he filed the indictments. But he also knew that he had one small, precious advantage: he was from here, he was *of here*. With his diverse experiences and legal training in Missoula, he had a foot in the bigger world, but he was also one of them—a Jordanite to his core. It would have been different had he been an outsider yelling "you can't, you won't, the rules are the rules"—as was typical. It wouldn't have been a contest. The community would have attacked the interloping authority, probably rallying around the Freemen, digging in. Simply put, it needed to be someone from the inside to stand up for the broader principle: a nation ruled by laws, not men.

So, a few weeks after the bounty posters were hung—and the day Nick filed his indictments—a meeting of the "Sheriff's Posse" was called. One hundred and fifty men, most of them carrying guns, crowded into VFW hall. Nick stood before them and said that he was outraged. This time they weren't threatening some tax-collector or bureaucrat from Washington. No, this time it was him, *Nick, for Christsake!*

With so much on the line, he'd present his odd profile of being *of here, but not*—a thing he'd managed to successfully conceal, over years, in his "aw shucks" daily interactions—for public judgment. An up or down vote, and that's that. He and Charles couldn't be outgunned again, as they had been that day with their video camera at the courthouse. They were rapidly losing authority. It was the edge of the abyss.

"I grew up here," he said that night. "I know everyone in this room. These Freemen don't represent what we're all about. We don't threaten each other in this community. We stick together, but we also stand up for what's right. And, Goddammit—you can disagree with it or not, but the law is the law. This is the form of government that you chose in 1919 when Garfield County was formed. You're seeing an attack on that government, your government. You have a choice with us— with me and Charles—you can elect us or turn us out of office. With them, you have no choice. Now, we need to know, right now, who is with us, and who is not." A few men applauded, tenatively, looking this way and that, and then everyone joined in, and it was thunderous. A resolution condemning the Freemen's actions was passed, and 85 men signed up for the sheriff's posse.

Looking back, that was a moment when courage was mustered at the darkest hour. Nick straddled the divide—recklessly trying to turn his *of here, but not* liability into a strength—and convinced his constituents that Garfield County was, in fact, part of the wider world, just like Nick Murnion—something they'd never been forced to face and publicly admit. But they did. It felt fine. And that's why the balance of power shifted and the rule of law was restored to this hard land.

A few months later, William Stanton was arrested in Billings. He was tried, convicted and sentenced to 10 years in prison, the first man ever convicted under the Montana State Syndicalism Act of 1918.

Nick is driving his Chevy pickup truck toward the Missouri Breaks, where the land becomes hilly and verdant as it approaches the beginnings of the big river. He had to probate a will this morning, then handle a drunk driving charge, and it all went pretty quickly so he took the afternoon off. With winters so hard here, spring feels like a blessing from God—and the hills are carpeted in green.

We pass ranches owned by his brothers, who've tethered their lives to this land and have struggled, just as his father and grandfather, to make it yield a reasonable living.

"It's not been easy on any of them. Even with a lot of land, it's a hard life. You can have land worth a few million, but be underwater on what you can make from wheat and beef. It's not tenable to say, 'Sell out to pay your bills'," he says, as the truck bumps along. "My life has gone in a very different direction from life on these farms. Far afield from what I would have figured."

Far afield, in this instance, would refer to awards from bar association groups and prosecutorial agencies around the country, invitations to speak, and scores of entreaties from people who simply want to meet him. It was in 1998 that Nick won the Profile in Courage Award from the John F. Kennedy Library Foundation. Before the big trip East, LeAnn, committing crimes against Jordan's no frills code, quietly slipped off to Billings and spent $300 on a dress; Nick bought a tuxedo. Soon they were off to a distant planet: Nick and his family waiting in the lobby of the plush Boston Harbor Hotel when Caroline, John Jr., and Ted came by to pick them up for the formal awards dinner at the Kennedy Library. "There they were, and we were just kind of stunned. You know, you feel like you've known them forever, though you've never met them. And Ted walks up to my children, like some kind of grandfather, and says, 'You kids need to come see the ships in Boston Habaaaaah,' and off they went. It was one of those 'just plain folks' moments you never forget." And on it went— photos curbside at the Kennedy Library "like at the Oscars," Nick glowingly recalls; a whirl of tuxedoed governors and senators offering congratulations; a slap on the back from the owner of the Red Sox; LeAnn holding tightly, throughout, to Nick's arm.

And then they were on a plane for home. The next day,

newspapers around the country published feature stories with photos; the *Jordan Gazette* ran a small item.

Which is fitting and probably for the best. This sort of recognition can create some real "so now you think you're better than us" friction in Jordan. Meanwhile, the outside world keeps beckoning—there have been calls recently for Nick to run for lieutenant governor of Montana, or attorney general. He has gracefully declined, even while he wonders, more than he might like, about life outside of Jordan.

When he feels that tug, he jumps in the truck and drives. Bumping along out here, far from the cluttered little office on Main Street and the neck-deep minutiae of human affairs in a tiny town, he can think about wider ambitions as he takes in the landscape, with its hard edges and soft valleys, red clay, and resilient wheat. It's a complex transaction: the sweeping land spurs his expansive thoughts, and then the sight of it all, endless but so familiar, settles him. By the end of the drive, any drive, he assures himself that he won't be leaving this demanding, majestic place anytime soon. Maybe not ever.

Today, Nick takes a few detours, and ends up near a place he hasn't been in years: a road leading to what was once the Freemen compound. Memory and sage grass have obscured some reference points, and he squints to try to recall what was where; the FBI roadblocks, the trailer command posts, the nest of network news satellite trucks.

The escalation of events built steadily, if slowly, once Nick began his prosecutions in 1994. He started to dig up connections between various militia groups in Montana and neighboring states, trying to convince authorities in Washington of the potential for a brushfire of antigovernment activity. Then, in April 1995, Timothy McVeigh blew up the Alfred P. Murrah Federal Building in Oklahoma City, killing 168 people in the worst terrorist attack on U.S. soil at the time. Suddenly, patterns Nick had been outlining started to take on national import. What spurred on McVeigh might compel others. Like him, extremist groups across the Great Plains were outraged at the fiery finale in Waco, Texas, where 80 Branch Davidians died in 1993 after an FBI seige. Congressional inquiries into that incident, along with an inquiry into the FBI's shooting of Randy Weaver's wife and son at Ruby Ridge, were under way in Washington, generating headlines.

And now, another armed camp was growing steadily in Montana. Freemen from across the area gathered about 30 miles northwest of Jordan at the farm of Ralph Clark, the man who had come into Nick's office two years earlier.

They called it "Justus Township," with its own court, financial instruments, and set of public officials. Incidents with increasingly violent overtones increased through the fall and winter of 1995. Meanwhile, the Freemen accelerated the filing of liens against property, against individuals, against states and federal agencies—adding up to more than a billion dollars in claims—and gumming up parts of the country's financial and legal machinery. In that such liens were sometimes temporarily booked as assets by financial institutions, the Freemen would write checks or money orders withdrawing cash before back offices realized the error. In all, they illegally obtained $1.8 million through this scheme. Meanwhile, antigovernment rhetoric of relying on natural law rather than man-made law found increasingly willing audiences. Farmers drowning in debt would come to weeklong Freemen classes conducted at the headquarters and, in some cases, used bogus "Freemen checks" to clear away their obligations.

For nearly a year, Nick collected information on all these activities, filed criminal indictments, and implored the FBI to take action. In the spring of 1996, a few FBI agents arrested two of the group's leaders in a sting near the farm. The remaining 20 or so, with a few children, holed up on the farm. The backup that Nick and others had been calling for—an army of FBI agents and specialists—finally arrived. The stage was set.

The siege went on for 81 days. Jordan was overrun with FBI agents, news teams, and curiosity seekers; a circus of a particularly modern American cast. Celebrities of the antigovernment movements, including Randy Weaver, showed up. People spent money at the bars, the Garfield Hotel, and the town's one supermarket. FBI agents love haircuts and LeAnn's business boomed. The locals were quoted each day. And on it went. Instructions from Washington were clear: Don't let this turn into another Waco. So, in a state of readiness, guns poised, everyone waited.

It might have ended in a bloody battle, Nick says, had it not been for a twist "where the rules of how we live out here finally took hold in middle of all the craziness." As his pickup begins to ascend a dirt road near the Clark farm, Nick explains how the financial problems that drove Ralph Clark to his office in 1993 ended in the foreclosure of the family farm, and his grand-nephew, Dean, bought up some acreage at the bankruptcy auction.

As the pickup clears the crest of a hill, we can see a cluster of houses where the Freemen holed up and Nick can just make out what's left of a neglected fence line. "Over there's where they came up, Dean and some of his friends on their tractors. The FBI didn't really consult us through the long siege, they didn't care much about what we thought, so this was the moment the local folks finally just stepped in. A few lawyers from this part of Montana and me and Charles all got together to help Dean get a court order from our local district judge— saying he had a right to get to his land—and then use it to get past the FBI roadblocks and start working on that wheat field right over there. Now, there was no love lost between Dean and the other Clarks, who were the core of the Freemen. He didn't agree with what they were doing, a split like you found all across the community. But, it was already June and if the fields weren't planted soon there'd be no crop come fall. So that's what he and his friends did. They dug the field for planting."

When the Freemen heard the tractors, they burst out of the Clark house and poised their guns to fire. It was a crossroads moment, just like when Nick made his speech saying that he's not some outsider, that he's *of this town*, but that this town is part of something bigger, part of a country, an ideal. This time, they looked at one another across a fence, people who had known one another forever, who had played together on the high school football team, who had drank warm beer at the Hell Creek Bar on nights colder than any you can imagine, and who had married one another's little sisters. Suddenly, the glamorous rhetoric about freedom burned off like a mist, and then the gun barrels drooped and the tractors kept rolling. Time to plant some new seeds.

Next day, the whole thing ended, when the Freemen surrendered.

The FBI agents congratulated one another on how they ended the siege with their unyielding enforcement of the law, some even received citations, but Nick understands how delicate the conversation really was—between the rule of law and complex human interactions, between our lesser and our better angels—and how it is ongoing.

He parks the pickup and knocks on the door of a house, once the epicenter of a national struggle—now a chicken coop.

"Anyone in there?!" he yells, trying to look inside through a tear in the screen. Inside, there are squawks and flutters, as chickens roam near a pen for ring-necked pheasants—formerly the house's screened porch. After a moment, Barb Clark, Dean's wife—a young blonde in mud-caked, rubber boots—emerges with her towheaded toddler. Nick and she chat cordially for a few minutes about local goings-on, how she and Dean are managing on the farm, and how her son, who's now climbing on Nick's bumper, asked a few weeks back "why Grandpa" (that'd be Dean's father, Richard, Ralph's nephew and one of the most virulent of the Freemen) "can't come home and play."

"We explained that Grandpa did a bad thing and won't be coming home for a few years." Then tough Nick Murnion, who started a chain of events that landed "Grandpa" in prison for that 10-year sentence, did something odd and lovely. "So, Barb, how's Richard doing?" he asks, tenderly. "How are his spirits?"

And she smiles. "Well, he's okay Nick. Quieted down, and

all. But he'll be just fine in the end." She pauses. "I'll tell him you asked after him."

In the end, that empathy is the rarest display of courage, the kind that heals.

Not that Barb, or anyone around here, knows what it was really like for Nick in the darkest moment. It's something he never talks about, and tries to think about as little as possible. But driving back to Jordan a few hours later as night fell, across long empty stretches of unmarked roads, an ugly memory creeps up on him. How, one night in 1995, as he was pressing his prosecutions and friends—even fellow prosecutors—were saying back off, he got a call. It was the day after he won the conviction of Bill Stanton and the Freemen were stunned and outraged. A bunch of them were caught driving north from the mid-Montana town of Roundup toward Jordan. They had a stash of weapons in their truck, along with an odd assortment of items. There was rope, duct tape, flashlights, video equipment, handcuffs, blindfolds, $60,000 in gold and silver, and a map. It took the sheriff's deputies from Roundup a bit to realize it was a map of Jordan. There were two marks: one was an office on Main Street; the other was a house with a boat in the backyard. They were on their way to kidnap Nick Murnion.

In the weeks that followed, driving alone for hours between tiny towns, Nick was afraid. It was a new sensation, fear, and it stunned him. He realized that standing up for the law in this time and place made him a target, with danger always nearby. And that he might very well have to die for a principle. And that he was ready to make that sacrifice.

It was then that Nickolas C. Murnion, a lonely figure racing across the darkened prairie, actually became *The Law Man* of our shared imagination.

And it is a comfort, truly, to the grand, unfinished American experiment that he's out there, still.

[W]hen you champion your own community, they may well back you. And when you accept the challenge of leadership of your own community, they may follow you. But when you accept the challenge of confronting your own community, you risk rejection and alienation.

But it is, nevertheless, the height of courage.

—LORD JOHN ALDERDICE, LEADER OF THE ALLIANCE PARTY OF NORTHERN IRELAND, 1998

The most significant thing that happened wasn't the agreement, in my view, but was that the people of the island of Ireland voted for the charter of change that the agreement is.

So it isn't for us; it's for my children and grandchildren . . . It's for the future. It's for a new beginning. It's the promise of peace, and freedom, and justice, for the people of the small island of Ireland.

—GERRY ADAMS, PRESIDENT OF SINN FEIN, 1998

[F]or most of us involved with the party talks, we took [a crucial] decision when we entered into the Belfast agreement on that Good Friday, at Stormont. And now, of course, we're engaged in less dramatic, but more important, hard work of carrying the agreement into fruition, getting it implemented, getting the arrangements there, coping with the difficulties that arise—and there have been and there will continue to be some difficulties.

But I think we can cope with them, and we will be able to work them through. . . .

—DAVID TRIMBLE, NOBEL LAUREATE, LEADER OF THE ULSTER UNIONIST PARTY, 1998

And as we move now to the new century, let us move to our new beginning. Let us leave our past—and it was a terrible past—let us leave it behind us. Let history judge it. But let's now lay the foundations, as we are doing, for that new beginning, and let's begin to work together in the new century. . . .

And let us have the first century in our island history in which we will not have killings of human beings on our streets, and in which we will not have emigration of young people to other lands to earn a living. And as we work together to achieve that, and particularly to use our energies to build rather than to destroy, I have no doubt that we will transform that little island.

—JOHN HUME, NOBEL LAUREATE, LEADER OF THE SOCIAL
DEMOCRATIC AND LABOR PARTY, 1998

THE IRISH PEACEMAKERS

by Michael Daly

THE 2,368TH PERSON killed during the Troubles in Northern Ireland was an off-duty Protestant policeman and poet named Sandy Stewart, who was shot in 1981 when two masked IRA gunmen burst from a rainy night into his Catholic fiancée's seaside pub.

At the funeral, the eulogist cited a poem that Stewart had published a thousand violent deaths before, in 1975. He had titled the poem "A Breath of Hope for Ulster."

Give us Grace to see a brighter dawn
The hope that could inspire our needs
Strange there seems to be a chance
Time has not left us destitute . . .
Or is it only wisdom come to be
Made by the motion of history.

A lone piper led the way from the Ballee Non-Subscribing Presbyterian Church to the adjoining graveyard. The fiancée, Ann Boal, then returned to running her pub in the coastal village of Killough. Boal called the small pebbledash snug the Ann Boal Inn in a fanciful play on the name of Henry VIII's ill-fated second wife. Boal had intended no allusion to the schism that accompanied the sixteenth century English king's decision to defy the tenets of the Catholic Church by divorcing his first wife and marrying Ann Boleyn.

That long-ago marriage had led to Henry VIII's splitting with Rome and founding his own Church of England. He also declared himself king of Ireland and head of his new Church of Ireland in a further effort to subjugate the stubbornly Roman Catholic and rebellious land that England had first invaded three centuries before. He closed monasteries and confiscated land and spent three years stomping out an uprising in which Irish nationalism was now further inflamed by religious outrage.

This twinned suppression of nationhood and faith became only more onerous with each ensuing rebellion and evolved over the generations into a legacy of intolerance and massacre and famine. The grievances of centuries had stormed into the pub with those two masked gunmen and made a target of an unarmed and defenseless cop who himself cared so little about religious difference that he planned to make Ann Boal his first and only wife come Easter.

The bride-to-be had been only a few feet away as Stewart slumped with gunshot wounds to his head and back. The memory awaited her each day she opened the Ann Boal Inn and was ever poised to overwhelm her at any undistracted moment.

When the pub closed for the night and the patrons went off to their families she was left with only the senselessness of her loss and the insensibility offered by the drink stocked behind the bar. The drink may have helped send her to an early grave in 1986, but everyone knew that she really died from the bullets fired that rainy night five years before.

The Ann Boal Inn was bought by Malachi Curran, the retired head of the Northern Ireland civil servants' union. He is a Catholic and he had suffered the stings of discrimination, but he had also been a longtime friend of Stewart as well as of Boal. He had only to look over at the cozy spot by the fire where Stewart had died to be reminded that Irish history was ultimately a story told one death at a time, each eclipsing all the others in the hearts of those left behind.

"You can't sit in a room 20 feet from where your friend was shot dead and not feel it," Curran says. "You ask yourself why . . . what has it been for, the deaths and murder?"

More people asked this question with each new killing, and in 1996 a massive IRA bombing in London prompted the British government to announce elections to a Forum for Peace and Reconciliation in Northern Ireland. The sheer number of parties demonstrated the complexity of the conflict.

The vast majority of nationalists were aligned with either the moderate Social Democratic and Labour Party (SDLP) or Sinn Fein, the IRA's political wing. The unionists were more fractured, answering the IRA with a jumble of their own three-letter acronyms. The majority party was the relatively moderate

Ulster Unionist Party, the UUP. Right behind and gaining was the less tolerant Democratic Unionist Party, the DUP.

The Protestant paramilitaries fell into two main groups. One was the Ulster Defense Association, the UDA. Its political wing was the Ulster Democratic Party, the UDP. The other was the Ulster Volunteer Force, the UVF. Its political wing was the Progressive Unionist Party, the PUP.

The Protestant paramilitaries commanded few votes, but more than enough bullets and bombs to wreck any peace agreement in which they had no say. The British contrived to guarantee their inclusion by declaring that the top 10 political parties in the Forum elections would also be included in talks aimed at finally ending the killing.

Curran and several former comrades saw this "top 10" provision as an opportunity to resurrect the spirit of the defunct Northern Ireland Labour Party, which until the Troubles had polled up to a third of the electorate. Curran still smiled at the memory of Catholics and Protestants banded together with the common purpose of improving the lot of working people. He could summarize with a single word what caused the party to disintegrate.

"Fear."

At the Forum elections, the Labour party again appeared on a ballot and it chalked up exactly 0.83 percent of the vote, just enough to come in tenth and thereby earn a place at the talks. Curran had remained active over the years in County Down's district council despite the dangers attendant on playing even a minor role in Northern Ireland's public life, and this made him as close to a statesman as his ghost of a party could offer. He was chosen to lead Labour into talks whose very existence marked a triumph of true courage.

For the next two years, Curran commuted between the Ann Boal Inn and a drably modern office block outside Belfast officially known as Castle Building B. He kept daily company with people who had reached the table only at great political risk and, in many cases, the direst mortal danger.

The bravest people of this long war proved to be those who sought to end it. Their physical grit was outdone only by their moral valor as they pursued agreement rather than retribution. One participant negotiated with the chief representative of an organization that had murdered his father, the father having once conspired to murder that same representative.

When the participants finally reached what became known as the Good Friday Agreement, they assembled before the television cameras in a room whose "salmon-pink" décor seemed to have been selected as one hue that carried no hint of either unionist orange or republican green. They went around the table in order of size, each party endorsing the document, with even the most incidental participants being accorded a particular place in Irish history.

"It was a big moment," Curran says. "The last word."

You Can't Eat a Flag

WHAT MIGHT BE considered the first word had been spoken by Sam Hume of Derry a half century before the talks were convened. Hume was an unemployed clerk and shipyard riveter whose renowned penmanship enabled him to cadge the odd coin or pack of cigarettes by serving as a scribe for the city's poor. The letters and forms more often than not concerned difficulties with unemployment benefits or housing. They imparted to Hume a particular perspective when he came upon his son, John, at a rally of tricolor-waving nationalists.

"He just put his hand on my shoulder and he said, 'Don't you get involved in that stuff, son,' " John Hume remembers. "I said, 'Why is that, da?' He said, 'Because you can't eat a flag.' "

Sam's son became a schoolteacher and a community activist and finally the leader of what would become the majority party among Catholics, the Social Democratic and Labour Party, the SDLP. He stuck to a political philosophy grounded in his father's pragmatism.

"Real politics are about jobs and houses, providing people with decent living standards," John Hume says.

The younger Hume's other great influence was Martin Luther King, who inspired a civil rights movement that swept Northern Ireland in the late 1960s. Words that would become world-famous were painted at the end of the block of houses where Hume's mother was born.

"You Are Now Entering Free Derry."

The North of Ireland became much like the American South as Catholics marched and Protestant working people played the role of white rednecks and the police acted too much like their counterparts in Alabama. Hume joined in singing "We Shall Overcome" and stayed true to King's philosophy of nonviolence even after British troops shot and killed 13 unarmed demonstrators in Derry in 1972.

"My view was that it should strengthen the determination of everyone to solve our problems so that something like that would never happen again," Hume says.

The central problem seemed too clear to elude anyone.

"We are a divided people. And violence deepens divisions."

This simple truth became more tragically apparent as the killing escalated on all sides. Not even the worst atrocities shook Hume from the belief that the only way out of the madness was what he termed "just ordinary common sense."

"Difference is an accident of birth, so why fight about it?" Hume says.

He had a standard response to talk of revenge.

"The doctrine of an eye for an eye leaves everybody blind," he would say.

Such sentiments caused Hume's house to be attacked twice. He was warned on numerous occasions that he was on somebody's assassination list. He was in Belfast Airport with a fellow SDLP member when a man pulled a gun on them. A pair of cops tackled the gunman before he could fire. One of the cops afterward seemed less shaken by the gun than the prospect of his Unionist relatives finding out he had saved the two SDLP men.

"I'll never be able to go back home again," the cop reportedly said.

Hume and his comrade flew on to London and continued their efforts to serve as intermediaries between the IRA and the British government. The British had only succeeded in further inciting rebellion by instituting internment without trial. Quiet dialogue proved more persuasive than all the barbed wire in the province and the IRA agreed to a cease-fire.

An IRA delegation made its own flight to England for a secret meeting. They presented demands that British officials deemed impossible and the encounter ended after only 90 minutes.

Twelve days later, the IRA rocked Belfast with 20 bombs in less than 90 minutes in what became known as Bloody Friday. The British responded by sending troops into Catholic "no-go" areas, most notably Hume's "Free Derry." He continued to follow what seemed only common sense and endorsed a British proposal to create a democratically elected government with executive positions guaranteed to Catholics. There were also to be links to the Irish Republic.

The scheme foundered on the issue of policing and was abandoned in the face of a Protestant work stoppage. The more extreme loyalists bombed the Republic, killing thirty-three. The IRA bombed pubs in the British city of Birmingham, killing twenty-one.

Hume went international, seeking economic investment from America and successfully running for a seat on the European Union in Strasbourg. He strode onto the bridge that crosses from France to Germany and considered what would have happened if he had stood there at the end of World War II and predicted after 25 million deaths that in less than a lifetime all of Europe would band together with a common purpose.

"If I'd said, 'We'll all be together and the French will still be French and the Germans will still be German, I would have been sent to a psychiatrist," Hume would later say.

The secret was precisely what he had been advocating back

home; respecting differences, and working together in everyone's common interest.

"As we do that together rather than waving flags and calling names we will break down the barriers of centuries," Hume would add. "Better to spill sweat than blood."

THE BULLET AND THE BALLOT

BACK IN NORTHERN Ireland, Bobby Sands went on a hunger strike in the "H-Block" at the Maze prison to protest the treatment of IRA inmates as criminals rather than as political prisoners. He began a diary the first day he refused food.

"I am standing on the threshold of another trembling world."

Those opening words proved more prophetic than anyone anticipated after an Ulster representative to the British parliament suffered a fatal heart attack. Sands declared himself a candidate for the vacancy and Hume's SDLP declined to oppose a man who was running from a prison hospital bed. Sands won by a majority of 1,446.

He died as Bobby Sands, M.P., and a newborn notion stirred even as nine fellow hunger strikers followed him to the grave. The notion was that Republicans could fight with the ballot box as well as the bullet, and nobody seemed to understand the potential more clearly than Gerry Adams of the IRA's political wing, Sinn Fein.

"The peace process began with Bobby Sands," Adams says.

Adams was from Ballymurphy, a small Belfast neighborhood where the British Army conducted as many as 1,500 house searches a night, rousting some families from their beds a half dozen times. He was the son and nephew of IRA men, his father having been wounded in a shoot-out with the Royal Irish Constabulary in 1942.

The younger Adams had been an apprentice barman when he was swept up in the most recent convulsion of what he had viewed since childhood as a historic struggle against a foreign oppressor. He was beaten and jailed without trial and otherwise encouraged to play his part.

Even Adams's foes recognized early on that he was politically astute and strategically brilliant. He was just 25 years old when he was freed from interment to participate in that 90-minute secret meeting with the British. He told one official that what he really wanted to do was get a university degree. The official asked why he did not do exactly that.

"Well, I've got to help get you British out of Ireland first," Adams supposedly said.

By the end of the hunger strike, the struggle had taken 2,361 lives. The bullet claimed Sandy Stewart as Adams pursued the ballot box, successfully running for Parliament in 1982 even though Sinn Fein had a policy against actually sitting in Westminster.

In 1984, Gerry Adams, M.P., nearly became the 2,623rd fatality, when he was shot five times in an assassination attempt by the Protestant paramilitary Ulster Defense Association, the UDA. He was still pushing the ballot box three years later, when a mistimed IRA bomb in Enniskillen killed 10 manifestly innocent Protestants.

The Republic observed a minute's silence, the televisions there going mute as the screens showed only a white dove. The news reported Adams's saying, "I do not try to justify yesterday's bombing."

"There is no military solution," Adams was subsequently quoted saying. "Military solutions by either of the two main protagonists only mean more tragedies."

These words did not escape the attention of John Hume, who had been asked by a Belfast priest, Father Alec Reid, if he would be willing to sit down with Adams. The bombing greatly increased the physical and political dangers of doing so, but Hume understood that the dove of peace would never become more than a TV image until the IRA was ready to suspend the violence.

"If I can save one human life . . . it was my duty to do it," Hume says.

In a series of meetings, Hume sought to convince Adams that the British had effectively disavowed any strategic or economic stake in Ireland, thereby removing the IRA's justification for violence.

"The traditional reasoning was the British were in Ireland defending their interests using force, therefore the people had the right to put them out by force," Hume says.

Hume's argument was not helped when plainclothes British soldiers summarily executed three unarmed IRA volunteers on Gibraltar. Their funeral was attacked by a lone loyalist gunman who had come hoping to avenge Enniskillen by assassinating Adams, but settled for killing three mourners.

At one of those funerals, a pair of plainclothed British corporals in a civilian car chanced into the procession and were beaten to death. Fr. Reid administered the last rites.

"Our parish is seen as dripping in the blood of the murders," he said afterward.

In such circumstances, nobody should have been surprised that the talks between Hume and Adams were publicly declared to have ended without agreement. A close listen to Adams did afford some hope.

"Neither John Hume nor I has been contaminated by our contract with each other," Adams was quoted saying. "Dialogue for consenting adults may actually be good for us.... There can be life after dialogue."

The body count in Northern Ireland had passed 3,000 when news came that the Berlin Wall had tumbled. Hume flew to Germany to deliver a speech and he gave Chancellor Willy Brandt a chunk of the "Peace Wall" that still stood between Catholic and Protestant communities in Belfast.

"I was conscious that, as the Berlin Wall was falling, the Belfast walls were rising," Hume was later quoted saying.

From South Africa came equally startling news that the man Adams calls "the first citizen of this planet" had been freed. Nelson Mandela's release after nearly three decades in prison added to a sense that the world was entering a time of change.

"As Willie Shakespeare said, there's a tide in the affairs of men," Adams says.

The top British official in Northern Ireland publicly declared that his government harbored "no selfish or strategic economic interest" there, but the Troubles raged on. The loyalist paramilitaries began outkilling the IRA. The IRA mortared 10 Downing Street and exploded its biggest bomb yet in England, causing $1 billion in damage to the City of London financial center. A smaller bomb in Warrington killed two youngsters aged three and twelve, and there was a renewed wave of revulsion at IRA violence just as a neighbor spotted Adams leaving Hume's house in Derry.

The neighbor called a reporter, who broke the news that Hume and Adams had been continuing to meet clandestinely. Hume was widely vilified for allowing himself to become a "pawn" of the IRA.

"I was heavily attacked from all sides," Hume recalls.

Hume and Adams had been working on what they hoped to persuade the British and Irish governments to issue as a joint declaration. Hume had written the first draft in the fine handwriting he had inherited along with his father's wisdom. Adams had replied with his own version and it had gone back and forth.

The ninth draft of the "Hume-Adams initiative" was passed to the Irish government in an envelope, but the hopes sealed in with it dimmed after an IRA bomb intended for the UDA exploded prematurely in a Shankill Road fish shop, killing nine Protestant innocents.

Adams condemned the attack as inexcusable. He also served as pallbearer at the bomber's funeral, signaling to hardliners that he still quite literally stood by the IRA.

Hume attended the funeral of the seven innocents killed in retaliation by two UDA gunmen who burst into a Greysteel pub in Halloween masks, shouting, "Trick or treat!" The daughter of one victim approached Hume.

"Mr. Hume, we've just buried my father," she was quoted saying. "My family wants you to know that when we said the rosary around my daddy's coffin, we prayed for you, for what you're trying to do to bring peace."

Hume was photographed turning away in tears, but the lasting image of those days was of Adams shouldering the bomber's coffin. British officials responded by reinstating an order excluding him from the mainland.

"I will not talk to people who murder indiscriminately," Prime Minister John Major declared.

Major wrote to his Irish counterpart that he was not about to entertain an initiative that had even a whiff of Adams.

"Association with Hume-Adams is a kiss of death," Major stated.

Major called for a new approach that would not involve Sinn Fein, but within hours he found himself in an impossibly hypocritical position. The news broke that the British had been in secret talks with the IRA for three years.

A month later, in December 1993, the embarrassed British joined the Irish government in issuing a joint "Downing Street Declaration" based in significant part on the envelope that Hume and Adams had passed on.

"It is for the people of the island of Ireland alone, by agreement between the two parts respectively, to exercise their right of self-determination," the declaration stated.

One of the two authors of the initiative behind this declaration had been hospitalized with exhaustion. The 1,168 people who sent John Hume get-well cards and letters ranged from the sister of a dead hunger striker to an "ex-member of the security forces."

The other author of the Hume-Adams initiative was still excluded not only from Britain, but from the United States. The British objected strenuously when they learned Adams was seeking a visa to visit America. President Clinton, who has ancestors from Enniskillen, went ahead and granted Adams a 48-hour visa to attend a peace conference in New York. Nobody was more surprised than Adams when he was welcomed like a kind of pop star.

"You almost have an out-of-body experience," he remembers. "It isn't really you."

The man the British had sought to demonize as a criminal caused the *New York Times* to gush.

"An articulate and enigmatic leader in a centuries-old struggle," the paper stated.

Numerous observers remarked on his calm.

"I was actually very jet-lagged," he says. "I was asleep for the forty-eight-hour period."

Adams returned home having established a new legitimacy for himself and therefore Sinn Fein. He had begun to ponder why the struggle by "valiant and brilliant" Republicans had continued for centuries without having "vanquished the oppressor."

"Maybe the lesson of history is not that we have to keep fighting but that we have to try another way," Adams says.

LET'S NOT BE FOOLS ANY LONGER

AFTER THE FISH shop bombing and the trick-or-treat massacre, a silhouetted figure had appeared on television as a spokesman for the Protestant paramilitary Ulster Volunteer Force, the UVF. He had a message for the IRA.

"Please lay down your weapons," he said. "The Loyalist paramilitaries have said they will lay down theirs. Call their bluff. Let our people move on together."

The silhouette was David Ervine. He was born in East Belfast, quite literally in the shadow of the Harland & Wolff shipyard, where the *Titanic* was built. He had been 18 years old on the bloody Friday in 1972 when the IRA bombs rocked Belfast. The dead happened to include another 18-year-old named William Irvine from a few streets away, and the name and age were so close to Ervine's that many people thought he was the one who had been killed.

"Then I thought it might have been me," Ervine remembers. "Or mine . . ."

Ervine saw himself becoming the protector of his family and his community when he joined the UVF. His political and military philosophy was two syllables deep: "Hit back."

In 1974, Ervine was arrested for having a bomb in a stolen car. He was sentenced to 11 years and he was welcomed by the prison's UVF commander, Gusty Spence.

Spence had been the prime suspect in the first killing of the Troubles, the 1966 sectarian murder of John Patrick Scullion as he walked home to his blind and widowed father. Spence was subsequently convicted of the Trouble's second killing and he had undergone a sort of jailhouse conversion, calling for a universal cease-fire in 1977. He proclaimed that the paramilitaries should ignore "bigoted Unionist politicians" such as Ian Paisley, who inflamed prejudices and let others die. He met each new UVF prisoner with a question.

"He asked me, 'Why are you here?' " Ervine recalls. "I said, 'Possession of explosives with intent.' He said, 'No, *why* are you here?' I thought, 'Arrogant bastard,' but the question didn't leave me."

Ervine ever so slowly, ever so painfully achieved a new perspective on the passions that had put him in prison.

"Shibboleths that allow you to kill someone you've never known," he says.

He decided that intolerance had been fostered by the powers-that-be so working-class Protestants would keep their Catholic counterparts in line.

"The Catholics weren't second-class citizens," Ervine says. "They were third-class citizens. *We* were second-class citizens."

After five and a half years, Ervine was freed. He declared his own personal cease-fire and went to work as a milkman, but he continued to ask himself questions and he kept getting swept up in political discussions in the pub. He demonstrated such acumen in what he calls "barroom debate, if you like" that in 1984 his old outfit recruited him to return not as a solider, but a strategic analyst.

"I was headhunted by the UVF," Ervine says. "They craved analysis . . . 'Where does this lead? Where do we go?' "

In 1991, the UVF joined the UDA in declaring a cease-fire to signal their support for talks the Northern Ireland secretary of state had initiated among the bigger political parties, Sinn Fein not included. The talks quickly dissolved as Unionist politicians once again proved their favorite words were "No! No! No!"

The violence resumed with unprecedented ferocity, and the security forces notified Ervine that he was the target of various assassination plots. He spent many nights sleeping away from home, living out of plastic garbage bags.

Ervine was not alone in feeling that the politicians had squandered the opportunity offered by the cease-fire, once again leaving the paramilitaries to suffer the consequences. The UVF decided to chart its own course with its fledgling political wing, the Progressive Unionist Party, the PUP.

"Maybe it was time to remove the saber from the saber rattlers," Ervine says.

Ervine became the PUP's counterpart to Adams. A half mile and the other side of a war from Sinn Fein headquarters, Ervine studied a book of Adams's writings, seeking clues to current Republican thinking.

"I used to sit and think, 'What does that bearded bastard really mean?'" Ervine remembers. "There was clear evidence that new ideas were being thought."

He eventually risked a secret meeting with the man many Loyalists considered to be the devil himself. Here was a mission of peace as dangerous as any of war, and he fully understood the likely consequences if he were spotted anywhere near Adams.

Ervine decided that Adams shared his view that the war was a stalemate and that a futile war is an immoral war. Ervine would cite the old Irish truism that you can't kill an aspiration.

"If I don't want them to have the aspiration, that doesn't mean they're not going to have it," Ervine says.

Peace began to seem truly possible after Adams's other secret meetings with Hume led to the Downing Street Declaration. Ervine had by then begun a years-long, ever dangerous effort to convince his own hard-liners. He applied his particular brand of common sense.

"When you're in a hole, stop digging," he would say.

Then, the splinter Republican group the INLA shot three men outside Ervine's offices, including a senior UVF commander. The payback came two days later, when UVF gunmen shot six Catholics to death in a Loughinisland pub as they watched Ireland play the United States in the World Cup.

"It was one of the worst days of my life," Ervine says. "I thought the chance was gone."

More killings followed on both sides, but Willie Shakespeare's tide continued to carry Republicans and Loyalists along. The IRA declared a complete cessation of all military activity in August, and Ervine's comrades put a Belfast-style spin on it by painting a message on the Shankill Road.

ON BEHALF OF THE LOYALIST PEOPLE ON THE SHANKILL ROAD WE ACCEPT THE UNCONDITIONAL SURRENDER OF THE IRA—SIGNED UVF.

The Loyalists declared their own cease-fire two months later. The formal announcement was made by the man suspected of the killing that started it all, Gusty Spence. He offered an apology.

"In all sincerity, we offer to the loved ones of all innocent victims over the past twenty-five years abject and true remorse," he was quoted saying.

A silhouette no longer, Ervine evoked the "thousands of people dead, most of them working class."

"We've been fools," Ervine was quoted saying. "Let's not be fools any longer. All elements must be comfortable within Northern Ireland."

Ervine then uttered precisely the same words that Sam Hume had spoken to his son more than a half century before. "You can't eat a flag."

HIS FATHER'S SON

NOT EVEN THE enlightened David Ervine was willing to accept an invitation to join Gerry Adams on a trip to Washington, D.C., the following St. Patrick's Day. The sole unionist leader who did go had the most compelling personal reason to refuse.

Back on December 22, 1987, a note was passed to the Stiff Little Fingers during a rock concert at Ulster Hall in Belfast. The lead singer announced that a Gary McMichael should call home.

"Right then, I knew what had happened," McMichael says.

McMichael's father, John, had become the Troubles' 2,899th fatality. John McMichael had been targeted by the IRA because he was second in command of the UDA, which after all had tried to kill Adams two years before. McMichael's killers had not been dissuaded by the treatise he had just issued titled "Common Sense" after the document of the same name by the American revolutionary Thomas Paine. This modern version contended that the Loyalists would have to sit down with Sinn Fein and accept a power sharing arrangement much like the one that would be set forth in the Good Friday agreement.

John McMichael had met with Hume and the Irish-American human rights activist Paul O'Dwyer, as well as Roman Catholic Cardinal Thomas O' Fiaich, who declared him a man of peace. The cardinal praised McMichael's efforts to cross the religious divide.

All that had ended with a bomb placed in the elder McMichael's car. The younger McMichael felt compelled to take up the quest even though he suspected that was not what his father would have desired.

"I don't think he wanted me to find myself in the same position he did," Gary McMichael says. "I felt I had no other choice . . . There was something too important to lose."

A young man who had never entertained thoughts of going into politics became leader of the UDA's new political voice, the Ulster Democratic Party, the UDP. The war was still on and the IRA continued to target his father's associates, killing three in the weeks leading up to its cease-fire.

The police warned Gary McMichael that he himself was the target of an imminent assassination plot. He accepted this as "part of the job."

"Until the cease-fire, there was business as usual," McMichael says. "It's just one of those things."

McMichael proved himself his father's son six months later, when he bucked the consensus of the other unionist leaders that the Washington, D.C., trip would only increase Adams's newfound legitimacy.

"If he's going to talk in their right ear, they're going to hear me in their left ear," McMichael says.

In Washington, McMichael found himself in rooms festooned with shamrocks and tricolors. He was treated as a curiosity as rare as if he had landed from another planet.

"Like a Martian; 'This is a *unionist!*' " McMichael recalls.

At the White House, McMichael discovered that the East Room can be a very small chamber when you share it with a man who represents the organization that killed your father.

"It's not easy . . ." McMichael says.

McMichael did not forget that his father's organization had tried to kill Adams.

" . . . It was right peculiar indeed. But, if you let emotion get in the way, you're not going to get anywhere."

Hume brought Paul Newman over to meet an actual unionist, but what caught the media's attention was when the actor asked Gerry Adams for an autograph. The media also reported the stirring moment when Hume paused while singing the Derry anthem "The Town I Love So Well."

"Come on up here, Gerry, and join us," Hume was reported to have said.

Adams did indeed join in, and the nationalist sing-song could not have improved McMichael's reception when he got home, where the major Unionist parties were continuing to inflame passions rather than offer solutions.

"I came back to many problems," McMichael says. "I really did."

I HAD BEEN CALLED A LOT WORSE

SINN FEIN'S LEADER was meanwhile having increasing difficulty restraining the IRA's hard-liners, who had expected the British to initiate all-party talks immediately after the cease-fire. The British had instead insisted that the IRA first disarm, or "decommission," its weapons. The anniversary of the cease-fire also marked a year of impasse, and at a Belfast rally Adams offered a public reminder about the IRA.

"They haven't gone away, you know."

In November, Bill Clinton became the first U.S. president to visit Northern Ireland. He met with Paisley and Trimble and stood with Hume before a cheering crowd in Derry. He publicly shook hands with Adams, but also offered a comeback to the old IRA battle cry "Tiocfaidh ar La," Our Day Will Come.

"You must say to those who still would use violence for political objectives: You are the past: your day is over," Clinton said in a speech outside Belfast City Hall.

Clinton had brought along George J. Mitchell, the former U.S. senator from Maine. Mitchell's father, George K. Mitchell, had Irish roots, but had never known his parents. George K. had been transplanted into another culture when a Lebanese-born couple adopted him from a group of orphans lined up in a Maine church.

"Never in my life do I remember him mentioning Ireland," Mitchell says.

George J. Mitchell's parents had both worked in a textile mill, and whatever his ethnicity, he possessed a Humeian pragmatism that made him the ideal candidate to head a new international commission on the unresolved question of disarmament. He knew the right question to ask Hugh Annesley, the chief constable of the RUC.

"When I asked him whether, if Gerry Adams wanted to, he could persuade the IRA to decommission prior to negotiations, Annesley replied flatly, 'No, he couldn't do it even if he wanted to,'" Mitchell would write.

The Republic's security experts agreed, and Mitchell concluded that the British plan for prior decommissioning was "unworkable," just as Hume had been saying from the start. The British were hardly pleased, having expected Mitchell simply to endorse what they presented as a matter of principle but was in fact more a question of politics.

Mitchell met British pressure with simple logic; weapons could always be replaced anyway, and the real issue was whether the parties intended to use them. The commission promulgated a set of principles to which any group seeking to join the talks should first consent. These "Mitchell Principles" mandated total renunciation of the bullet and unqualified commitment to the ballot box.

"What is really needed is a decommissioning of the mindsets in Northern Ireland," Mitchell wrote.

As Mitchell headed back to America, he taped an interview with David Frost in which he noted that 18 months had elapsed since the cease-fire and still no talks had been scheduled. He suggested that the IRA's patience must have limits.

Six days later, the Docklands section of London was devastated by a 3,000-pound bomb of fertilizer and confectioners' sugar crammed into a car transporter.

A year and a half after the cease-fire and just three weeks after the bombing, the British and Irish governments set a date for talks. There was first to be a special election that would accord the top 10 parties a seat at the table.

Ervine's PUP and McMichael's UDP came in seventh and eighth, far behind the fourth place finisher, Sinn Fein, which garnered 15.5 percent of the vote, its highest Ulster-wide total ever. Sinn Fein was nevertheless excluded because all participants had to affirm the Mitchell Principles. A reminder of the IRA's current stance came four days later, when it set off its biggest bomb yet, devastating the center of Manchester.

Even with Sinn Fein absent, the more recalcitrant unionists managed to make the talks contentious and tortuous. They declared that Mitchell was not the chairman they wanted and they likely would have seized his chair had a British official not physically occupied it until he arrived. Mitchell was welcomed by bellows of "No! No! No!" from the DUP's Paisley, whom many historians credit with getting all the killing going in 1966 with his anti-Catholic agitation. Paisley then stormed out.

Mitchell had never encountered anything like this in American politics, and he likely would have quit then and there had he not feared the whole process might collapse. He remained in his seat, addressing the group as if nothing had happened.

The next day, Paisley and the others returned and formally accepted the Mitchell Principles, if not Mitchell. Several refused to address him as "Mr. Chairman," addressing him instead as "Senator."

"I had been called a lot worse," Mitchell says.

The first weeks were spent arguing the ground rules. Debates stretched deep into the night on matters such as "does the chairman have more or less authority if he makes a decision after 'consulting with' the participants, or 'having regard' to their views or having 'due regard' to their views?"

"I didn't know the answer before the lengthy discussion, and I didn't know it after," Mitchell writes.

Mitchell did develop unshakable respect for some of the participants, later saying that Hume would be remembered as one of the great figures of history. Mitchell termed Ervine a paragon of redemption, taking particular note of an exchange between the former bomber and a Unionist politician who objected to calling the talks part of a "peace process."

Politician: "If this is peace, let us have war."

Ervine: "That's easy for you to say, safe as you and your family are in the suburbs. But, if there's war, it's we and our sons who'll do the fighting and the dying. We want this process because it's the only hope for peace."

As the vote on the rules neared, Mitchell learned that his older brother was dying back in Maine. Mitchell knew the talks could unravel if he left at such a crucial moment, and the doctor informed him that his brother would most likely hold on for several weeks. Mitchell headed for the airport the moment the rules were approved, but his brother had died by the time he arrived home.

Mitchell had two consolations, one that the peace process was still alive, the other that his wife, Heather, was pregnant. He returned to the talks in Belfast feeling the "reaffirmation of life" only to hurry home when his wife called to say she was ill. She miscarried and he spent several days consoling her. They were walking by the fountain at Lincoln Center when she told him that he had to go back to Belfast.

"She said, 'If you don't go back and try, you'll never forgive yourself,' and it was true," he says.

Mitchell rejoined talks that took four months just to decide on an agenda. He continued to demonstrate such patience and cool that some would deem him the most sainted man to visit Ulster since St. Patrick himself.

"This sounds corny, but it's not; If you really believe in what you're doing, you can tolerate almost anything in order to achieve it," Mitchell says.

The violence raged on and IRA gunmen attempted to kill the deputy secretary of Paisley's party as he visited his critically ill son in the intensive care unit at the Royal Children's Hospital. One bullet pierced an incubator, fortunately missing the child inside, but reminding everyone that the talks were only talk unless there was a reckoning with the IRA.

McMichael later summed up the absurdity of seeking to negotiate the end of the war without including the group that was also known as the Provos in reference to the IRA's split years before into the Provisional and Official wings.

"You've heard of the expression 'Waiting for Godot'?" McMichael says. "We used to call it 'Waiting for Provo.' "

THERE IS NO SUCH PLACE AS NOWHERE

IN ITS EXILE, Sinn Fein was periodically briefed on the talks' progress by the leader of a party that by one measure was bigger than only Curran's tiny Labour group, but by another represented half the population, Catholic and Protestant.

Monica McWilliams is the daughter of a cattle dealer and she was raised in the town of Kilrea, which was just big enough to have a separate doctor, pharmacist, grocer, and butcher for Protestants and Catholics. She could see the local Orange Hall out her back window and she would watch youngsters her age going in for a dance on Saturday nights.

"I always wanted to go, but I never could because it was

Protestant," she remembers. "This is how I was brought up and I never met a Protestant until I was eighteen years of age."

In her teens, McWilliams joined the Northern Ireland Civil Rights Association, marching under signs reading ONE MAN, ONE VOTE as the peaceful protestors were met with truncheons, rubber bullets, and CS gas.

The escalation of the Troubles saw her home repeatedly rocked by IRA bombs intended for nearby targets. Her aunt dove under her bed after one deafening roar.

"We said, 'You can come out now . . . It was a bomb,' " McWilliams recalls. "She said, 'Thanks be to God. I thought it was that awful thunder.' "

McWilliams became the first member of her family to attend college. She says of her days at Queens University in Belfast, "My memories are of many firebombs and people being shot in front of me."

On weekends, she and her friends would hitchhike home. Her best friend, an economics student named Micky Mallon, was returning home from Toomebridge one night in 1973 when he was beaten and shot to death by the UDA. His chair was empty at the next exam.

"The invigilator came down the line and said, 'Where is this guy?' " Monica remembers. "I said, 'He's dead and his funeral was yesterday.' [The invigilator] said, 'Here's your paper, get on with it.' "

McWilliams later studied urban planning at the University of Michigan. She returned to Belfast as a teacher and later became a professor of Women's Studies. She had realized that "one man, one vote" was only half the equation.

McWilliams remained a nationalist, but she had documented instances when the IRA shrugged at domestic abuse committed by one of its own. She had also seen RUC officers place themselves at grave risk by responding to domestic abuse complaints in nationalist areas.

"So, the conflict needed a more sophisticated analysis," McWilliams says.

At the news of the talks, McWilliams and several compatriots decided that women should have a voice extending beyond religious differences. The first matter at hand was what to call their party of Catholics and Protestants.

"I thought, 'What about Women's Coalition?,' but then I realized 'WC' would not look good on a ballot," McWilliams says.

The question of who would lead the Northern Ireland Women's Coalition (NIWC) was still not settled when McWilliams flew off to a conference in Australia. The papers had to be filed in her absence, and she only learned of her compatriots' choice when her husband met her at the airport on her return.

"He said, 'You're the leader of a political party?' " McWilliams remembers. "I said, 'God, am I?' He said, 'You're trying to tell me you didn't know this?' "

The NIWC campaigned with the slogan, "Say Goodbye to Dinosaurs," which particularly galled some established politicians. McWilliams recalls, "Paisley said the only table we would ever be at is the table we'd be polishing."

A Paisley deputy declared, "These women came out of nowhere and they should get back to nowhere."

The NIWC replied, "There is no such place as nowhere."

The NIWC reckoned that if just 100 women garnered just 100 votes each, then the party would make the top 10. They placed ninth, and just six weeks after its inception, the NIWC officially became part of the peace process. Unionists such as Paisley greeted them with moos and boos and cries of "stupid women."

"They couldn't abide that women were suddenly finding their voice and taking attention away from them," McWilliams says.

One Unionist who welcomed the NIWC was David Ervine, who in McWilliams' words, "represented people who murdered people I knew." Ervine now became her defender.

"He said, 'Just point out to me who's giving you a rough time,' " McWilliams says. "I realized who was the gentleman and who were the humiliating terrorists."

The balanced representation of Catholics and Protestants in NIWC did not keep Paisley and his ilk from branding the women "Sinn Fein in skirts." Paisley would have been apoplectic if he knew McWilliams and her colleagues were secretly meeting with Sinn Fein in pubs and hotels.

"Once in a car," McWilliams says.

McWilliams would encourage Sinn Fein to join the peace process and end the wait for "Provo." She would then return home to her husband and two young sons in their tidy house at the edge of a loyalist area that was seized each year by a paroxysm of intolerance. Graffiti demanding "All Taigs Out of Here" would go up on walls and a Catholic would be burned in effigy at a big bonfire.

"One year it was Gerry Adams, but most years it's the Pope," McWilliams says.

In May of 1997, all the parties, including Sinn Fein, gathered at a remote location in South Africa that had once served as a missile testing site. The establishment Unionists agreed to go only if they were "hermetically sealed off" from Sinn Fein with separate transportation, lodging, and dining facilities.

"We brought apartheid to South Africa again," McWilliams says.

One-time opponents from both sides of the South African conflict teamed up to counsel the visitors that negotiations are about give and take and that if you seek to get everything you will get nothing. The most powerful lesson was the sight of a former African National Congress leader chatting with a former South African Defense Force general.

"They were laughing and clapping each other's back," McWilliams says. "Guys who had shot and killed each other. They said combatants are the first to seek an agreement because they'll be the ones who get killed if it breaks."

Nelson Mandela himself walked in and joked with his ANC comrade.

"He said, 'Why are you talking to that white general?' and then he laughed," McWilliams recalls.

On the last night, the South Africans hosted a barbecue. A prominent Paisleyite began chatting up a young lass and seemed delighted with himself until he was told she was not only with Sinn Fein, but was the most wanted woman in Northern Ireland.

"[He] nearly burned his bum trying to jump over the fire to get away from her," McWilliams says.

By midnight, McWilliams had retired with the rest of the delegation to a bar. Ervine entered and strode up to a senior

Sinn Fein man, saying with East Belfast flip, "You can have a united Ireland, but you can't have my place at the bar."

The two ended up singing "*Memories of the way we were . . .*," which Ervine later described as "what I thought was appropriate for the moment." Others joined them and even one of the more recalcitrant unionists drifted in. McWilliams remembers going into the bathroom at the end of the conference and pausing at the sink after she washed her hands.

"I was standing, looking in the mirror saying, 'This is it,' " she recalls.

Playing Safe Was Not an Option

O N J U L Y 2 0, 1997, the IRA reinstated the cease-fire and Sinn Fein was admitted to the talks. Paisley's DUP and a like-minded smaller party immediately withdrew. Mitchell was not sorry to see these untiringly fractious elements depart.

"If they had stayed, there would have been no agreement," Mitchell says.

The big question was whether the largest of the Unionist parties, David Trimble's UUP, would stay. Trimble is descended from Scotch Presbyterians that the British transplanted to Northern Ireland as a way of both ridding themselves of an irksome minority and keeping the Irish in line. His ancestors were among those who defended Derry against King James's army of Catholics in 1689, shouting what would remain the bywords of Unionism.

"No surrender!"

Trimble took up that cry in the early 1970s when he joined

the right-wing, quasi-paramilitary Vanguard Party. His leader and mentor was Bill Craig, who as Northern Ireland minister of home affairs had directed or abetted much of the police violence against the civil rights marchers. Craig once predicted that the time might come to "liquidate the enemy."

But, as the Troubles intensified and the enemy fought back, Craig suddenly decided to negotiate a power-sharing deal with Hume and the SDLP. His fellow Unionists denounced him as a "Lundy," as in long-ago Mayor Lundy of Derry, who had dared to negotiate a surrender during the famous siege 300 years before. Craig was cast from political life, his protégé Trimble along with him.

"Ten years in the wilderness," Trimble says.

When an MP from the Ulster Unionist Party died of throat cancer in 1990, Trimble managed to sidle into the vacancy. He proved he understood the power of a photo op in 1995, after a traditional Protestant march was allowed to pass through a Catholic street in Garvaghy.

Paisley was waiting to welcome the marchers on the other side when the relatively obscure Trimble stepped up and hoisted the icon's hand with his own in triumph. The image presented Trimble as Paisley's equal and nobody's Lundy and helped make him the UUP's new leader.

Trimble also became Paisley's main rival. Paisley was apparently seeking to make himself the bigger man at the talks by bellowing the loudest challenge to Mitchell's chairmanship.

"[Paisley] had the greater experience and thought he would be the dominant figure," Trimble says. "It was a very difficult time."

Trimble declined to go along and a Paisley cohort heckled him as if from the walls of old Derry: "Ulster is not for sale!"

Trimble now faced the more explosive question of whether to remain in talks that included Sinn Fein. A quiet poll indicated that more than 80 percent of his party's executive favored staying, but the rank and file were more dubious.

Trimble was aware that he would be betting his political career on any agreement being acceptable to a significant majority of Unionists. He also knew that if he joined Paisley's walkout he would be a follower, not a leader, and that he would be triggering the collapse of the peace process.

"You can't just walk away from this," Trimble says. "You have to reassure yourself and other people you did the right thing."

Trimble resolved to remain even if he risked being cast back into the wilderness. He was not ready to directly address Sinn Fein and he would only negotiate with them through an intermediary. But he would sit under the same roof.

"I know my own leadership was at risk the whole way through, but it wasn't a situation where you could play it safe," he says. "Playing safe was not an option."

When he arrived at the talks, Trimble was flanked by Ervine and McMichael. The paramilitary representatives had not for a moment considered joining Paisley's boycott.

"What we used to say about Paisley is that he was prepared to fight to the last drop of everyone else's blood," McMichael says.

McMichael's constituents had learned firsthand that the tongue can be as dangerous as the gun.

"They understood that one word a person might say on the TV might decide if somebody dies that night," McMichael says.

These men had no need to posture or rail.

"They had nothing to prove," McMichael says. "They had proven themselves."

Some of those who had been the most violent in the past were now the most anxious to see the violence ended.

"People who have been closest to the conflict can be the most open-minded," McMichael says. "They sounded like the peace people to me."

Even so, McMichael and Ervine as well as Adams all had some hard-line constituents who viewed compromise as surrender. The danger of assassination by the fringe was ever present as they sought to explain each new twist in the face of the naysayers.

"When somebody says, 'You're selling us out,' it takes two seconds to say and an hour to refute," Ervine says. "It's very hard to fight the simplicity of populist argument."

Ervine had to interpret for the UVF "every word uttered by the other side."

"Explain, explain, explain," Ervine says.

At one point, some of Ervine's constituents decided that he had deliberately failed to apprise them of an important development. He arrived at his office to see graffiti on the surrounding buildings reading, "Who does Ervine think he speaks for?" He later learned that one senior UVF man wanted to have him killed.

"But, the others said no," Ervine says. "A very dodgy time."

Ervine's mantra through such moments was a sentiment

that was shared by all the participants and kept the talks on keel through the most difficult moments.

"I don't want my children and my grandchildren to go though what we've gone through."

A fortnight after substantive negotiations commenced, Mitchell flew home to New York for the birth of his son, Andrew MacLachlan Mitchell. The new father thought of other new parents back in that place of bullets and bombs and he telephoned his staff in Northern Ireland, asking how many babies had been born there that same day. The answer was 61.

Mitchell went over to where his son was sleeping. He picked the child up and held him close.

"He couldn't hear me, but I told him that for him and for his 61 friends in Northern Ireland I was somehow going to get this job done, and when I did I would refer to it as Andrew's peace," Mitchell writes.

Mitchell flew back to Belfast with renewed resolve, but the grown-ups in Northern Ireland were no closer to an agreement at the Christmas break. He would write that all the parties were "deeply frustrated and discouraged."

The year ended with the breakaway Republican INLA killing the leader of the breakaway Loyalist LVF in prison. The LVF retaliated by killing five Catholic innocents. These included Adams's nephew, Terry Enright, a community worker who became fatality 3,574 while moonlighting as a doorman at a nightclub that happened to be owned by Ervine's sister-in-law.

The murdered man's one-year-old was reported to have

pointed at a photo of him, said "da," then clutched it as she slept.

"The child can't even talk and you think this isn't registering, but it really goes into the kids' hearts," the grandfather Terry Enright, Sr., was quoted saying. "There's no doubt about that."

Terry Sr. placed the blame on not just the actual gunmen, but on those politicians who were "condemning the killing and then deliberately blocking any sort of meaningful discussion."

"I believe that all the people in Northern Ireland want peace and want a settlement and they believe themselves that a settlement can be reached," Terry Sr. said.

The funeral was the biggest in Belfast since the hunger strike. A prominent member of Trimble's UUP offered his condolences to Adams.

But, back at the talks, the UUP stuck to its refusal to directly address Sinn Fein. The other parties ceased segregating themselves into the "orange" and "green" sectors of the cafeteria at mealtime, but the UUP continued to eat separately. A UUP man who encountered Adams in the men's room locked himself in a toilet stall.

"That's what I call a siege mentality," Adams was quoted saying.

On repeated occasions, Trimble vowed never to shake Adams's hand.

"I ask him to give me a hug instead," Adams would quip. Such shenanigans would have been only a laugh were it not for the specter of more violence. Mitchell finally decided to set a deadline for an accord, the Thursday before Easter, only three weeks away.

"The earth was moving," Ervine recalls. "The choice was for you to go with it or not."

On the Sunday before the deadline, the British and Irish governments presented Mitchell with a draft of the "strand" concerning the relationship between Northern Ireland and Ireland. The governments asked Mitchell not to change so much as a word. They also requested him to claim the draft as his own.

Mitchell understood that to do otherwise might trigger a rupture between the two governments and jeopardize the talks. He also correctly surmised that the draft was more "green" than the unionist side could accept.

"It was unsellable," Ervine says. "I thought I was in trouble."

SOMEBODY HAS TO WORK IN THE DESERT

THE ONLY APPARENT solution was voiced to the television cameras outside Castle Building B by the leader of the small, cross-community Alliance Party.

Lord Alderdice had been deputy head boy at Ballymeana Academy and he had trained as a psychiatrist at Queens University. He had been raised to peerage in 1996 and accorded a seat in the House of Lords, which he noted was originally a gathering of barons who had private armies not so different from paramilitaries.

His constituency at the peace table most prominently included his three children.

"If we don't reach the Promised Land until the next generation, so be it," he says, "Somebody has to work in the desert."

Now, only two days before the deadline, he addressed the media with the title of Lord, the concern of a father, and the insight of a shrink who, in his words, had been seeing "Ulster on a couch." He called on British Prime Minister Tony Blair and the Irish Toiseach Bertie Ahern to come to Belfast.

"If the prime minister wants a deal, he had better get here fast," Alderdice said.

Blair arrived that very evening.

"I feel the hand of history on our shoulder," Blair said.

At 7 A.M. the next day, Blair huddled with Ahern over breakfast. The two subsequently met with Trimble and by the next day they had made the strand of contention less "green."

Sinn Fein began making noises that Trimble was winning too many concessions and that the agreement was no longer green enough. The talks drew so close to either collapse or breakthrough that the Thursday deadline passed almost unnoticed.

With a little more green here and a touch more orange there, the situation brightened. President Clinton worked the phones, reassuring Adams of continued American involvement. Adams finally said that Sinn Fein was prepared to accept the agreement.

"You know we've been asked to swallow an awful lot," Adams was later quoted saying.

In the UUP office, Trimble seemed to be feeling much the

same. Several lesser UUP members felt it was too much to swallow and balked. Trimble went ahead and telephoned Mitchell, saying he also was prepared to approve the agreement.

"Ready to do business," Trimble was quoted saying.

Mitchell had learned in the U.S. Senate not to wait when you had the votes. He notified the other parties that there would be a formal vote in 15 minutes.

At 5 P.M. on Good Friday, the group convened in the big salmon pink room. The voting went around the table. Trimble ended centuries of unionist "No! No! No!" with a single syllable.

"Yes."

Hume's SDLP voted the same, as did Adams's Sinn Fein, subject to consultation with its membership. Alderdice's Alliance and Ervine's PUP and McMichael's UDP were all in favor, as was the smallest party.

"Agree," Malachi Curran said.

A woman's voice sounded amongst the men.

"For the agreement," Monica McWilliams said.

Mitchell declared that the parties had reached an agreement that would now be presented in a referendum to the entire island of Ireland. He praised all those at the table for their true valor.

"It doesn't take courage to shoot a policeman in the back of the head, or to murder an unarmed taxi driver," he said. "What takes courage is to compete in the arena of democracy, where the tools are persuasion, fairness, and common decency."

Blair said, "Courage has triumphed!"

Hume said, "For all of our people Good Friday will be a very good Friday."

Ervine said, "This is absolutely historic!" and added, "Now I'm going down to the pub."

McWilliams headed home to her two sons and said, "We did it! We really did it!"

The eleven-year-old said, "Yeah, I'll believe it when I see it."

The eight-year-old asked, "Mom, does that mean all the murders will stop?"

McWilliams said, "No, unfortunately, it doesn't . . . We've made a deal and now we're going to have to build it and building is going to be harder than making it."

Adams still had to convince his constituents. He arranged for ANC members to fly in and impart to IRA volunteers the lessons of South Africa. He also convinced the British to release "the Balcombe Street gang," four men who had served 24 years in prison for bringing the war to London. They strode triumphant into a Sinn Fein ardfheis, or gathering, and tears welled in the eyes of some of the hardest hard-liners. The delegates overwhelmingly approved the agreement.

"I think a lot of Sinn Fein delegates may have woken up the next morning and said, 'What have we done?' " Adams says.

The agreement still had to be voted on by the peoples of Northern Ireland and Ireland. The polls showed that support among Protestants was dropping from 85 percent to just 55 percent, with the biggest group of undecideds among the 18–24 age group. The SDLP proposed a pro-agreement concert that would bring U2 into the realm of the UUP, UDP, PUP, and DUP. The band's lead singer, Bono, agreed.

"Who's Bono?" Trimble asked.

Onstage, Bono stood with Trimble on one side and Hume on the other. The world-famous singer hoisted their hands just as Trimble had hoisted Paisley's hand three years before. This image helped propel the agreement to approval by a vote of 676,966 to 274,879.

The final count was completed just as Hume was ordering an egg and onion sandwich in the Kings Head Pub in Belfast. He dashed off without eating to hear the results. The crowd in the pub grabbed one another's arms and began singing "We Shall Overcome."

The simple common sense that Hume had been championing for three nerve-fraying, health-wracking decades seemed to have finally prevailed. The death toll stood at 3,592.

A crazed few on both sides continued the violence and a Loyalist firebomb killed three young Catholic boys in Antrim. Breakaway Republicans killed 28 innocents with a car bomb in Omagh. But the peace held.

"And that can't be anything but wonderful," Ervine says.

At the Ann Boal Inn, Curran hung framed photos of himself with Nelson Mandela and Bill Clinton. Curran had only to look around the pub to remember Ann Boal and Sandy Stewart, who would have celebrated their seventeenth wedding anniversary on the Easter after the Good Friday agreement that was imparting the breath of hope for Ulster the policeman had imagined in verse.

"It's a good poem," Curran says.

Until we abolish soft money, Americans will never have a government that works as hard for them as it does for the special interests. That is a sad, but undeniable fact of contemporary politics.

I believe public service is an honorable profession. I believed that when I entered the Naval Academy at seventeen and I believe it still. I am an old man now, and I should be content with a life that has been more blessed than I deserve. But the people whom I serve believe that the means by which I came to office corrupt me. That shames me. That shames me. Their contempt is a stain upon my honor, and I cannot live with it.

—JOHN MCCAIN, 1999

I'm holding in my hand my own original thirty-five-cent copy of Profiles in Courage *that I read as a young teenager. I loved it. It fueled my not very well hidden interest in going into politics and maybe even becoming a U.S. Senator. But its influence was not simply to make me want to be a senator. Rather, this thin little book spoke volumes about what kind of a senator it is worthwhile to be. What* Profiles in Courage *illustrates is the role risk and sacrifice can or should play in a career in public service.*

—RUSSELL FEINGOLD, 1999

JOHN MCCAIN AND
RUSSELL FEINGOLD

by Albert R. Hunt

JOHN MCCAIN IS no stranger to unfriendly fire.

During the Vietnam War, the young naval aviator flew 23 bombing missions over North Vietnam; on the twenty-third, he was shot down, captured, and, for five and a half years, with frequent and brutal torturing, was a prisoner of war. Before this ordeal, he was victimized by "friendly fire": Aboard the USS aircraft carrier *Forrestal*, McCain was sitting in his plane when it was accidentally blasted by a six-foot Zuni missile. Encircled by flames, his flight suit on fire, he crawled away from the burning aircraft. Wounded, with shrapnel in his chest and legs, McCain helped control the carnage and assisted others before getting help for himself.

This prepared him for the carnage of 2000, otherwise known as the South Carolina primary. In February 2000, Senator John McCain had scored a huge upset in the New Hampshire primary; with a win in South Carolina, he would be on his way to the Republican presidential nomination. That sent chills down the spines of the Arizona Republican's many adversaries.

In South Carolina the big guns trained on him. A self-styled leader of an obscure veterans' group appeared with the GOP establishment's candidate, George W. Bush—sometime member of the Texas Air National Guard during the Vietnam War—publicly accusing Mr. McCain of not caring about veterans. This was mild compared to the stuff below the radar screen. A professor at fundamentalist Bob Jones University sent out an e-mail alleging John McCain had sired two illegitimate kids. (In fact he had adopted his first wife's two kids.) There were vicious fliers about the candidate's current wife's drug habits and, in the Bible Belt precincts, charges that he has a black daughter. (His wife years ago had an addiction to pain medication, which she acknowledged and has overcome, and the McCains have an adopted daughter from Bangladesh.)

"South Carolina may have been meaner than Vietnam," the senator says, only half in jest, a year later.

The successful Palmetto State jihad against McCain was orchestrated by Pat Robertson and the religious right, with the knowledge and subtle assistance of some party leaders. The overarching theme was he's immoral, left-wing, and represents anti-American values. Yet McCain throughout his 18-year congressional career always voted against abortion, for the death penalty, and compiled voting records in the 80 percent to 90 percent approval range from conservative groups on national security and economic issues.

Why the vitriolic opposition? Money, which Jesse Unruh, the late speaker of the California assembly, dubbed the

"Mother's milk" of American politics. John McCain is the architect of the McCain-Feingold measure, which seeks to clean up campaign financing of national elections and reduce the flow of special interest money. This is a system under which most incumbent politicians and interest groups—ranging from the oil industry to labor unions to the religious right—flourish; any effort to change it is a threat.

That's what the South Carolina campaign was about. Immediately after the Arizona Republican clobbered George W. Bush in the initial New Hampshire primary, Julie Finley, one of the Republicans' top money people, at a session of big soft-money donors, worried that if McCain won the presidency, "we're out of business."

The link between money and politics is pervasive throughout American history; in *Profiles in Courage*, John F. Kennedy noted that the great Daniel Webster was on the take. Periodically, reforms clean up the worst offenses and then new loopholes and techniques are discovered; like any reform, campaign finance changes are an ongoing process.

The most contemporary version followed the Watergate scandals. Despite a Supreme Court decision that undercut some of the congressionally enacted reforms, the subsequent presidential elections—one won by Jimmy Carter and two by Ronald Reagan—were as clean as any in modern history. Then, aided by an inept Federal Elections Commission, soft, or unregulated, money started to creep into the system. This spending from most every imaginable interest group soared more than five-and-a-half-fold, from $86 million in 1992 to $487 million in 2000. It became a major source of funding and a narcotic for both parties. For the first time, overall spending on House and Senate races in 2000 topped $1 billion, or a quarter billion more than only 10 years earlier.

McCain's junior partner in the mission to alter this system, Senator Russell Feingold, faced his baptism by fire under different electoral circumstances. The Wisconsin Democrat was running for reelection in 1998, after a single term. He started off a decided favorite. In January, pollster Geoff Garin told him he was above 50 percent and running 15 points ahead of his challenger, Republican Representative Mark Neumann. His independent progressive political persona was popular in Wisconsin and the indefatigable then-44-year-old political veteran would outwork any opponent. Democrats felt confident.

But Russ Feingold decided to make it harder; he was co-sponsor of the McCain-Feingold legislation to limit spending by congressional candidates and to ban soft money—the unregulated and unlimited contributions from wealthy individuals and vested interest groups—and he was going to abide by it . . . period. It's not rare for a candidate to pledge spending or contribution limits *if* his or her opponent does likewise. But Russ Feingold wasn't insisting on a level playing field; he would shun soft money, much of which is funneled through the political parties, and limit his own spending irrespective of what his opponent did; and Representative Neumann had no intention of spurning this cash cow. This was unilateral disarmament.

Over the summer the Republican Party soft money machine and supportive interest groups—right-to-lifers, the gun lobby, and the Christian Coalition—poured it on, attacking the incumbent for his opposition to a ban on late-term abortions and a constitutional amendment to prohibit flag burning, and depicting him as a big-spending liberal. At the same time Senator Feingold was rejecting Democratic soft money and writing letters to friendly interest groups—labor, environmental, and pro-choice votes—instructing them not to spend any money on his behalf.

The results were predictable. By Labor Day, Mr. Garin found the Feingold lead had slipped to six points; this was a danger sign. The opposition money machine continued and by early October Garin polls found the race tied. It is almost axiomatic in politics that any incumbent running dead even a month prior to the election—especially one that doesn't enjoy the usual financial advantage of incumbency—is a goner.

With his Boy Scout optimism, Feingold insisted that Badger State voters couldn't be bought. On October 16, 1998, two and a half weeks before polling day, even he began to worry, however. He had just debated Representative Neumann and was out having a drink with friends and staff when his campaign manager called with the latest survey: "We're down two." The senator had a sleepless night. Senator Mitch McConnell, the leading opponent of campaign finance reform and Senate Republican campaign chief, was ecstatic: To defeat the chief Democratic sponsor would be the death knell of McCain-Feingold.

In Washington, Democratic Senate leaders Tom Daschle and Bob Kerrey feared McConnell was right; desperate to save this seat, they tried to funnel soft money into Wisconsin over the candidate's objections. Feingold went ballistic and made them pull the ads. Smaller contributions, or hard-money donations, chiefly from Wisconsin residents, were pouring into the campaign, but Feingold had vowed not to spend more than $3.8 million. It was evident he would have much more than that to spend in a race where he trailed.

Geoff Garin, a pollster with an unsurpassed reputation for candor and integrity, told his Wisconsin client: "You're going to win or lose by a point and you have a lot of (unspent) money which could determine the race." Feingold stuck to his pledge. "Russ never flinched," Garin recalls. By election day, spending on behalf of the Neumann campaign, including well over $3 million in party soft money—versus none for Feingold—exceeded $11.5 million. That was more than twice as much as spent on behalf of Russ Feingold. About $1 million of soft money or so-called "issue advocacy ads" were spent by labor and environmental groups to boost the Democrat's chances, against his wishes; but this was less than a third of what interest groups on the right spent against him.

Russ Feingold's optimism prevailed. On election day he won by two points, or less than 38,000 votes. In his victory speech, he warned: "Senator McConnell, I'm coming your way."

Senators McCain and Feingold, inextricably linked by the issue, are an unlikely duo, a real political odd couple. John McCain is a war hero, an Episcopalian, son and grandson of famous admirals. He boasts that he graduated fifth from the bottom of his 1958 class at the U.S. Naval Academy (first in that class was John Poindexter, Ronald Reagan's national security adviser, who was disgraced by the Iran/Contra scandal). Russ Feingold is the grandson of Jewish immigrants, a non-veteran, a graduate of Harvard Law School, and a Rhodes scholar. John McCain still revels in stories about his wild youth; Marie, the Flame of Florida, was an early girlfriend. Russ Feingold was born a straight arrow; jaywalking would be a stroll on the wild side. Both have pronounced independent streaks, yet on most matters Russ Feingold is a liberal and John McCain a conservative; the establishments on both these ideological sides mistrust their supposed ally.

McCain is wound tightly and has a volcanic temper. When his presidential campaign momentarily took off, Senate Republican Leader Trent Lott, among others, privately told associates he wasn't temperamentally suited "to have his finger on the [nuclear] trigger." There was a not-so-subtle and ugly suggestion that McCain had been psychologically decimated by the POW experience. (More than any other candidate he revealed his entire medical history, which lent no credence to that charge.)

Over lunch a year after South Carolina, John McCain still bridles at the tone of his Republican colleagues. "Lott said some of the most malicious things I've ever heard," he declares, as did Arkansas Senator Tim Hutchinson, "who I'd probably exchanged ten words with." Yet the usually blunt and media accessible Arizonan continues to agitate colleagues.

He infuriates many of his fellow senators with persistent battles against wasteful pork-barrel spending; examples abound, ranging from $14 million to study the aurora borealis to unnecessary military depots to a $350 million aircraft carrier, to be built in Pascagula, Mississippi, that the navy doesn't want. He reveals that a disproportionate number of these projects are located in Mississippi, courtesy of his rival, Senate Majority Leader Trent Lott, a prince of pork.

Russ Feingold is more diplomatic, although he's widely viewed as a holier-than-thou moralist. When the huge Watergate class of reformers reached Congress in 1975, a grizzled

Massachusetts lawmaker, James A. Burke, complained, "They think this place is on the level." Russ Feingold still thinks the place is on the level.

But without this intensity and conviction—and willingness to pay a price—McCain-Feingold never would have gotten on the radar screen, much less passed the United States Senate. These two disparate politicians displayed exceptional courage, though with different models from John F. Kennedy's original work. McCain's willingness to take on his own party, at enormous personal and political cost, is reminiscent of John Quincy Adams. When Senator Adams stood up to British intimidation in 1807, JFK chronicled, the Federalists, interested only in Massachusetts's commercial interests, disparaged him as a "popularity seeker," or a "party scavenger." Flash forward almost 200 years and that's how more than a few Republicans view John McCain.

Russ Feingold's courage was more like Edmund Ross, the obscure senator from Kansas, who in opposing the impeachment of President Andrew Johnson said he "looked down into my open grave." In the fall of 1998, Russ Feingold, adhering to his principles, similarly could see his own political grave. But Feingold eventually won while Ross was never reelected.

Of the odd couple, McCain is the dominant presence. Indeed Feingold borders on idolatry in describing his colleague: "He's an authentic American hero. It's a thrill for me to know somebody like that. I would have been happy just to read his biography . . . but I got to be close to somebody who's such a great man."

The hero is indispensable to the McCain persona. Peter Kann, publisher of the *Wall Street Journal*—whose conservative editorial pages have not been kind to Senator McCain—wrote that when "it comes to character, conviction and courage," John McCain "stands as an oak among saplings." You cannot understand John McCain without visiting his Vietnam ordeal and the perspective it provided for his life. It is no coincidence that Hemingway is his favorite author; what may seem a huge risk to ordinary politicians is tame stuff for McCain.

As the son of a top admiral he was a trophy prisoner; that made it even harder. In his autobiography, *Faith of My Fathers*, he describes one of the low points: "On the third night, I lay in my own blood and waste, so tired and hurt that I could not move. The Prick [the North Vietnamese chief guard] came in with two other guards, lifted me to my feet and gave me the worst beating I had yet experienced. At one point, he slammed his fist into my face and knocked me across the room toward the waste bucket. I fell on the bucket, hitting it with my left arm and breaking it again. They left me lying on the floor, moaning from the stabbing pain in my refractured arm . . . I tried to take my own life. I doubt I really intended to kill myself."

But when the North Vietnamese offered to release him early for propaganda reasons, McCain, adhering to military procedure, insisted he wouldn't leave until more senior POWs were released. Robert Timberg, in his marvelous book *The Nightingale's Song*, describes the reaction of one of McCain's fellow prisoners, Jack Van Loan, as North Vietnamese dignitaries entered the cell: McCain cut loose with "some of the most colorful profanity that you would ever hope to hear. He was calling them every name in the book and telling them that he was not going home early, that he was not going to ask for amnesty and not to ask him that again and to get out and, furthermore, screw you and the horse you rode in on . . . They would have lugged him out of there that day and let him go. And here's a guy that's all crippled up, busted up, and he doesn't know if he's going to live to the next day, and he literally blew them out of there with a verbal assault. You can't imagine the example John set for the rest of the camp."

Most men would be bitter, vengeful. Yet despite this inhuman treatment, Senator John McCain led the effort to normalize relations with Vietnam. In 1993 he privately told Bill Clinton, the leader of the other party and whose evasion of the draft during the Vietnam War infuriated more than a few veterans, that "I'll provide any cover you want for Vietnam." When President Clinton first journeyed to the Vietnam Memorial he was accompanied by John McCain.

Equally remarkable is the story of David Ifshin, who in 1970 led a group of antiwar students to Hanoi where their anti-American protests were piped into McCain's prison cell. Years later, the two would reach out to each other. "David didn't feel good about what he had done," says his wife, Gail, "and found John McCain so honorable and so open that they developed a real friendship." When Ifshin tragically was struck with terminal cancer, few were more supportive than McCain. "When David was really sick, John came over and spent a beautiful afternoon with him; it meant so much to us," recalls his widow. "Since David's death, John has been so attentive to me and our kids."

The sweet side of John McCain's nature resides with the combative side. McCain credited the legendary Democratic Representative Morris K. Udall with helping him enormously when he was a young Republican House member. Mo Udall was one of the funniest, most revered, and respected men in American politics. But in the 1990s when he lay in a veterans hospital in Washington, ravaged by Parkinson's disease, unable to recognize anyone and barely conscious, a regular visitor—one of the very few—was Republican Senator John McCain, who would talk and read to him. Mo Udall died in 1998 but his son, Representative Mark Udall, says of John McCain: "He went to see my dad when no one else did. He did it out of affection."

It was the confrontational McCain who first engaged Russ Feingold in 1994 in an oft-told story. The Wisconsin Democrat was leading an unsuccessful fight to cut funding for an aircraft carrier. Suddenly, John McCain appeared on the Senate floor and with intensity demanded to know if Feingold had ever been on a carrier. When Feingold acknowledged he hadn't, McCain snapped: "Then learn about it."

Feingold, politicking in Wisconsin later that year, was more than a little surprised when McCain called to see if the two could work together on reform issues; as this partnership developed, it led to banning senators from taking gifts from vested interests, more disclosure rules, a crackdown on the revolving door between government and private interests and, most significant, campaign finance reform. McCain saw that Feingold, whatever his inexperience with aircraft carriers, was a very able, independent-minded, principled politician—a desirable ally.

The Democratic lawmaker is very much a product of the independent and progressive tradition of Wisconsin; McCain calls him a "man of unusual integrity and honor . . . a combination of Proxmire and LaFollette," two predecessors from Wisconsin in the United States Senate. In this culture, money and special interests are sublimated to ideas and people. He was first elected to the state senate in 1982, when at 29 he faced an 83-year-old GOP incumbent in a Republican district. He raised a total of $17,500 and the state matched it. That was all that could be spent. Election night young Feingold actually conceded but by early the next morning had scored an upset, winning by 31 votes.

Russ Feingold may be a do-gooder but he's an ambitious one. On election night in 1986 he was winning reelection, as was Republican Senator Bob Kasten. When Kasten appeared on television, Feingold told his sister Dena, a rabbi, "I'm going to spend the next five years organizing a grassroots campaign to defeat Kasten." Although outspent 3 to 1, Feingold comfortably defeated the GOP incumbent in 1992.

And he has consistently opted for principle over party, to the dismay of more than a few Democrats. He was one of a handful of Democratic senators to vote for John Ashcroft for attorney general, although they disagree on practically every important issue facing the Justice Department. Senator Feingold insists presidents should have leeway to pick their own cabinet, a flexibility that Democrats will want when they occupy the White House, and the standards for executive branch and judicial appointments are quite different. Some liberals remain furious over the Ashcroft vote. But few who know Feingold, even those who disagree, question his sincerity.

But a month after the worst terrorism in American history struck on September 11 Russ Feingold was the sole member of the United States Senate to vote against an anti-terrorism bill. Others shared his concern about the legislation's broad-reaching provisions that seemed to sanction unfettered surveillance and virtually unlimited detention in the name of fighting terrorism. But public opinion overwhelmingly supported anything labeled "anti-terrorism" and the Wisconsin Democrat alone opposed the measure.

This was consistent with a trademark Feingold independence; nowhere was it more in evidence than during the impeachment of Bill Clinton. The early procedural considerations took on a very partisan coloration. On an important issue—whether witnesses should be called before the Senate or whether they should proceed immediately to closing arguments—Senator Feingold was the one Democrat to vote with the Republicans. "I thought, how can you vote not to hear the evidence and say you're doing impartial justice?" he explained later.

Senator Feingold concluded that Mr. Clinton did not commit impeachable acts. It's no surprise, however, that their relationship was never close. Russ Feingold genuinely believes in a Chinese Wall between campaign contributions and governance; Bill Clinton sees campaigning, fund-raising, and governance as a seamless web. "I took Clinton seriously at his first inaugural that his would be the cleanest and most ethical presidency ever," Feingold recalls. He subsequently was shocked at the Clinton fund-raising abuses and called for an independent counsel to look into allegations of wrongdoing. He blames Bill Clinton's 1996 campaign for the final destruction of the soft-money system: "Bill Clinton said to his lawyers that he didn't have to follow the understanding that you can't use soft money for TV ads. That was the moment that a bullet was put in the head of the system." ("The White House is like a sub-way," 1996 Democratic fund-raiser Johnny Chung declared. "You have to put in coins to open the gates.")

But the 1996 fund-raising scandals failed to embarrass most politicians in either party. The 2000 political conventions turned into special interest solicitation orgies. In Los Angeles, Senate Democratic Campaign Chairman Bob Torricelli instructed all Democratic lawmakers they were to attend 25 specially arranged fund-raising events; the battle for the Senate, he warned, was tight and this was essential to grease the way for Democratic hopes in the fall. There was one objector: Russ Feingold, who went to a counter convention, blasted his colleagues, and said this made him "ashamed" to be a Democrat. Then he spoke to the Democratic convention and, to the dismay of party leaders, specifically chastised the party for allowing soft money to "become so much a part of this convention."

While not the red flag that McCain is to fellow Republicans, this is illustrative of Feingold's willingness to rub the sores of his fellow Democrats on the issue of money and politics. Several years ago, stealing a page from Wisconsin's Bob LaFollette, Feingold began a "calling of the bankroll" when major measures reached the House floor. He would chronicle how much the special interests involved in the legislation had forked over to the parties and senators. When bankruptcy reform, for example, came before the Senate, Russ Feingold, on the floor, noted that: the credit card companies had given $4.5 million to the parties and candidates; on the very day the House cleared the legislation one affected company, MBNA Corporation, gave $200,000 of soft-money contributions to the Republican Senate Campaign Committee.

Colleagues considered this sanctimonious. When he called the bank roll on an oil bill, that resentment exploded. Republican Senator Kay Bailey Hutchison and Democratic Senator Mary Landrieu, both supporters of the oil industry, sought to get Feingold's remarks ruled out of order on the grounds they were a "personal attack," prohibited by Senate rules. They didn't succeed.

Unlike Feingold, McCain learned about the evils of big money in politics the hard way; he got burned. As an Arizona House member and then Senator, he was attracted by the support of Charles Keating, owner of Lincoln Savings and Loan. In the 1980s Keating and his associates contributed more than $150,000 to McCain campaigns and the lawmaker and his family vacationed at the Keating home in the Bahamas.

When the savings-and-loan scandal exploded, the poster villain was Charles Keating; his failed company cost taxpayers some $3 billion and stories surfaced about senators he financially supported bringing illicit pressure on regulators in his behalf. This was the infamous Keating 5.

There was a lengthy and public inquiry, which tarred McCain. The outside counsel to the Senate investigating committee, Robert Bennett—later to become Bill Clinton's lawyer—concluded that John McCain had displayed poor judgment but, unlike three of the other Senators, had not engaged in any illegal or wrongful activity.

McCain was deeply embarrassed, but curiously, it whetted his appetite for reforming the system. This was to be a tortuously slow process in which the objectives and legislative agenda of McCain and his fellow reformers changed repeatedly.

To be sure, there are genuine reservations about the

agenda. Some First Amendment proponents contend any limitation on spending and contributions is a violation of free speech. Some claim what is needed is more, not less, money in the system. Moreover, critics charge, McCain-Feingold would be an incumbent-protection act.

If that were so, incumbents would have enacted it a long time ago. In fact, it is the current system, with the avalanche of soft money in national elections and the unlimited spending permitted in congressional races, that impedes competition in congressional elections. During the politically turbulent past decade, over 95 percent of House incumbents were successfully reelected as were almost 90 percent of Senate incumbents. Not coincidentally, in all but a few cases, incumbents enjoyed a huge financial advantage.

When vacancies do occur there's a familiar scene in most congressional elections around the country. A candidate sits in a small room with a desk, a telephone, and a Rolodex full of top potential contributors and dials for dollars for hours and hours almost every day. Candidates from both parties complain this often takes more time than discussing issues with experts or dealing with the real-life problems of constituents. If successful, these lawmakers come to the nation's capital and, often before taking the oath of office for the first time, launch into another familiar ritual: the Washington fund-raiser. Lobbyists and other interests can pay $1,000 for cocktails and hors d'oeuvres—or if they're lucky, dinner—to welcome new lawmakers from Pocatello or Portland or Phoenix whom they've never met before. Money and fund-raising are central to the Washington culture today.

Campaign solicitations usually get easier for politicians as they build seniority, but the scam rarely ceases. "We have become part-time Senators and full-time fund-raisers," former senator David Boren, currently the president of the University of Oklahoma, complained. "Even the schedule of the Senate itself is now arranged around the need to raise money for the next political campaign, rather than around the need to solve the nation's problems and do the people's business."

McCain-Feingold would alter, not revolutionize, the connection between politics and money. But it would reduce the reliance on money in elections and minimize the huge advantage enjoyed by incumbents in a system that gives comparatively little to challengers. That's why it produces such fury in the cloakrooms of both parties; several years ago Mitch McConnell, the head of the Senate Republican Campaign Committee, and Bob Kerrey, his Democratic counterpart, both told their respective caucuses in the same week that McCain-Feingold would cost them the Senate. Both cannot be true, but both men believed it; in campaigns, money is a narcotic.

For years congressional leaders, especially Republicans in the Senate, used every possible tactic—refusing to schedule the legislation, employing procedural roadblocks and filibusters—to kill McCain-Feingold. It was a testament to the extraordinary patience and toughness of this political odd couple that it wouldn't go away. If Russ Feingold's 1998 gamble had lost, it may well have. But when it became the signature issue for John McCain's remarkable though unsuccessful presidential run in 2000, the dynamics shifted.

Trent Lott and Mitch McConnell took solace that the presidential election of George W. Bush, a foe of overhauling campaign finance laws, might be lethal for reformers. But McCain and Feingold insisted they would tie up the Senate unless they got a vote; any possibility of delay ended when conservative Mississippi Republican Senator Thad Cochran joined their ranks at the start of the 107th Congress.

The odds still were tough. Before the measure reached the floor John McCain and Russ Feingold created a critical private pact; they would vote together on any measure, thereby making any partisan effort to sandbag the bill harder.

This reflected the genuine closeness and camaraderie that had developed over the past seven years between them. There were strains, with McCain once storming out of a meeting with Feingold. The next day however they struck a compromise. After the 2000 campaign they traveled around the country touting their reform, developing a mutual respect and affection not common in the Senate.

The Senate took up the battle in March 2001. McCain was both the leader and the enforcer. No politician in Washington was more of a magnet for media attention; he was accessible, quotable, candid, and articulate. Senator McConnell vehemently complained to news organizations that there was a decided McCain bias. There was, but it wasn't ideological. It was simply he was a more forceful and attractive presence. In the highly visible two-week debate McCain-Feingold foes thought they had a secret weapon: McCain's temper. They were determined to provoke him. The Republican maverick, however, was aware of that tactic and studiously avoided any outbursts.

If John McCain was Mr. Outsider, Russ Feingold was Mr. Insider. He too had his lapses; the Wisconsin Democrat was convinced his party leader, Tom Daschle, was selling them out, especially when Mr. Daschle's outside campaign finance counsel, Robert Bauer, sought to drum up opposition from Democrats. In fact, Tom Daschle—as McCain predicted—helped deliver the crucial votes for McCain-Feingold.

Fred Wertheimer, former president of Common Cause and a longtime campaign finance reform advocate, thinks there was a critical moment when Feingold's determination and nerve saved the day. In exchange for banning soft, or unregulated, money there was a proposal to triple the hard money ceilings to $6,000 per individual for each election cycle. There was a case for that trade-off. Yet as Wertheimer notes, it might have alienated enough Democratic supporters that "it would have killed the bill." Feingold insisted to McCain they hold tough. They did, striking an eventual compromise halfway between, that was accepted by a solid majority of senators.

Both men knew that however this particular struggle ended it was only a battle in the long war. The issue would not go away; they would be there to wage it over the next few years. They would make it much more difficult for entrenched politicians to perpetuate this system. They realized reform was an ongoing process, evasions quickly would be discovered, and it was critical to keep the pressure on. But for the foreseeable future, because of their persistence and courage, the landscape would not be the same.

On April 2 the Senate passed McCain-Feingold, 59 to 41. Immediately after the vote, on the same floor where they'd clashed in their initial encounter over an aircraft carrier, the charismatic, kinetic war hero from Arizona and the sober, studious Rhodes scholar from Wisconsin embraced.

Justice is not available to all equally; it is something that many of us must struggle to achieve. As an elected official, I know that fighting for what is just is not always popular but it is necessary; that is the real challenge that public servants face and it is where courage counts the most. Without courage, our action or inaction results in suffering of the few and injustice for all. . . .

Women often face multiple barriers in their professional life, like racism, sexism, and discrimination. As we overcome these barriers, my belief in democracy, equal protection under our Constitution and liberty for all is reinforced. It gives me great hope to see women of all races and backgrounds, not only breaking the glass ceiling, but shattering it.

—HILDA SOLIS, 2000

HILDA SOLIS

by Anthony Walton

IN WESTERN LOS Angeles County, the zip code of 90210 is demarcated to the north by Mulholland Drive, to the south by Wilshire Boulevard, and to the east and the west by two canyons, Laurel and Coldwater. Inside this zip code, and in the immediate vicinity, for that matter, there are exactly zero landfills, no gravel pits, and no power or chemical plants. Roughly nine miles away, following traffic-clogged Interstate 10 across the Los Angeles River into eastern Los Angeles County, is postal zip code 91706, bounded to the west by Peck Road, to the east by Sunset Avenue, and to the north and south, respectively, by the Foothill and San Bernadino freeways. Inside and abutting this zip code are a water table so polluted it has been a Superfund site for twenty years, power plants, chemical factories, seventeen gravel pits, and five land-fills, including Puente Hills, twenty-two stories high and the largest west of the Mississippi River.

That 90210 is the fabled postal description for Beverly Hills, and 91706 the appellation for several working-class towns and unincorporated areas in the unsung San Gabriel Valley, may or may not be accidental; most Americans would find the aforementioned geographic distribution of waste and mining facilities unsurprising, perhaps not even worthy of note. Corporations and municipalities do not, it is assumed, target lower-income and minority areas for such facilities; in this view, held by many all across the political spectrum, it is simply that people with money move away. Those left behind are unfortunate, but hardly the victims of an intended or deliberate injustice.

Inadvertent or otherwise, these sorts of environmental disparities weighed heavily on the mind of California State Senator Hilda Solis in the middle and late 1990s as she canvassed for votes while working Senate Bill 115 through the state assembly. SB 115, as it came to be known, was designed to implement new legal guidelines in the identification and mitigation of the negative environmental and health effects of pollution and waste-disposal facilities on low-income and minority populations. Residents of Solis's district in eastern Los Angeles County daily encountered such nuisances and hazards as a grammar school with the Puente Hills landfill literally in its backyard; the poisoning of the San Gabriel Reservoir from perchlorate (a rocket fuel additive) contamination, which led to the closing of all wells over a wide area; and, in Irwindale and neighboring municipalities, a landscape so scarred by mines and quarries—craggy, runoff-filled, hundred-foot-deep holes in the ground—that it resembled the postapocalyptic battlefields of science fiction epics.

In the late 1990s, this region would become a battlefield not only in appearance but also in fact—over the proposed Senate Bill 115. Hilda Solis was working at the forefront of something new in American politics, the emerging environmental justice movement, which concerns itself with what has been called "the intersection of race and space" in American society. "There are laws to protect endangered species," Solis has stated, "but no laws to protect less powerful and less protected communities from becoming environmental dumping grounds." In championing this cause Solis would face intense opposition from entrenched and monied corporate interests, as well as from California's powerful conservative governor, Pete Wilson, who argued that the state's environmental laws should remain "color-blind"—ignoring the already-present inequities this stance would lock in place. But the issue seems clear-cut, and the conflicts engendered by it nearly Solomonic: as Solis has stated, "Don't we all want the same things for our children? Clean air, clean water, open space?"

Solis would later describe her political fight for the bill as "nerve-wracking," even disheartening. The challenge would test most of what she had learned in school, in work, and in life, and would cause her to question some of her deepest beliefs about the possibilities inherent in the Constitution and our political system. But in choosing to push for environmental justice, a new articulation of the benefits and costs of the most mundane aspects of day-to-day life in America, Hilda Solis was a politician finding her own voice, as well as part of a larger surge of leaders helping an entire community enter the American mainstream. If it is true that California is at the forefront of most changes, good and bad, in America, then the fight over SB 115 is indicative of the new kinds of civic battles that will be fought all across the country in the not-too-distant future, as demographics change and new concerns come to the fore. New times require new leaders; yet these concerns were anything but new to Solis, as battles for equal opportunity, equal treatment, and equal consideration under the law had shaped her earliest personal experiences and political awareness, and had come to be defining themes of her life.

The state of California is known for its valleys, with place-names that have accrued meanings that extend beyond mere geographical denotation into myth. There is, for example, the Owens Valley of Los Angeles water acquisition (or *Chinatown*) fame; the San Joaquin and Imperial valleys, where so much of the nation's produce is grown; the Napa, with its vineyards; and, it almost goes without saying, the San Fernando, with its endless miles of suburbia and legendary teenage girls. According to the United States Geological Survey, the final arbiter in such matters, there is strictly speaking no such landform as the San Gabriel Valley; for our purposes it can be thought of as the area south of the San Gabriel Mountains, extending to the south and east of the city of Pasadena and including among many others the municipalities of Covina, El Monte, Alhambra, Rosemead, and Temple City.

Novelist James Ellroy grew up in the San Gabriel Valley and could be considered its unofficial poet laureate; his memoir, *My Dark Places*, paints the landscape as flat and nondescript, the climate as unrelentingly hot and plagued with smog, and the population as substantially white and lower-middle class. The only aspect of that description that has altered since Ellroy's childhood in the 1950s is the population, now predominantly Latino, an indication of larger demographic shifts in the state of California as a whole. To drive the numberless streets of the San Gabriel Valley, past the strip malls and small bungalows and franchise restaurants, retail stores and repair shops, is to experience the other half of Los Angeles County—never more than 20 miles away from the glamour and vast privilege of Brentwood, Bel Air, and Santa Monica, but eons away in temperament and expectation.

Hilda Solis was born October 20, 1957, in the San Gabriel Valley town of La Puente, the third child and oldest daughter of first-generation immigrant parents Raul and Juana Solis. Solis's mother, to escape grinding poverty in her native Nicaragua, had entered the United States through the port of New Orleans; her father, Mexican by birth, had entered through Arizona and worked his way through Texas and Colorado as a laborer, farmworker, and railroad worker before settling in southern California, where he would work in factories, ending his career as a Teamsters shop steward. Solis's parents met in a citizenship class in Los Angeles in the early fifties, and began together the difficult struggle of raising a family and making a place for themselves in their adopted country.

Solis has described her childhood as "very traditional, very quiet. Centered around our family, and often involving me staying around the house to help care for the younger children." She attended Temple Academy in La Puente, a public school that, like her neighborhood, was then principally Anglo, during a time when the town was known more for citrus trees than housing tracts. The Solises were proud of the fact that they were able, through work and saving, to purchase their home, the first new house in their part of town. This ethic of sacrifice for the greater benefit was something both parents passed on to the children: "We had a big family and my mother had to work, which resulted in some of us having to take on chores and help the family at a very early age." As she got older, Solis began to work outside the home as well. "I worked in the student store in high school, selling school supplies, candy, the usual."

At La Puente High School, her life began to change. La Puente was a large school with a more ethnically diverse student body than those of her grammar and middle schools. Solis did not participate in student government but did get a job through the federally sponsored Neighborhood Youth Corps, which paid her to work after school in the town library. This was the first of several government programs that would begin to widen her horizons. "I could make thirty dollars a week there, and that meant every couple of weeks I got a paycheck of sixty dollars. It meant so much to me." She was also becoming aware of the social and civic turmoil of the day: "I started high school in 1972, the beginning of the end of the Vietnam War. I recall very vividly some of the images I saw on television, the walkouts in East L.A., the fact that so many of the young people who were killed in the war—a disproportionate number—were from our area. There was a lot of discord. There were walkouts at our school. I think young people were wanting to express themselves, to say, 'No, we don't agree with the establishment, there are different opinions here, and if we're a democracy we ought to be able to respect that.' I remember that as something that I always knew would be a part of me."

It was also at La Puente that a significant mentor entered Solis's life. Robert Sanchez had been Solis's social studies teacher in junior high school; she would, from time to time, engage him in spirited but serious arguments over the Constitution and issues of the day, a Solis family tradition. "My father always said to question everything; don't just accept other people's opinions. There were several times I'd be pressing [Sanchez] in class on some topic and the bell would ring and everybody would stay to hear us keep going." When he later became her high school guidance counselor, Sanchez was the first person to suggest to her that she could go to college. "No one in my family had ever attended college. I was dubious, and not only for financial reasons. I wasn't in the college curriculum, I hadn't been groomed for college admission. There were certain injustices that I saw, which students, for example, were selected to go to college. Who got promoted by teachers to be in a position to do more. There was tracking at our school, it was already the haves and have-nots."

Solis considers her own career to have been something of an accident. "It just so happens I ran into somebody who convinced me I could go to college because there were programs that existed, I could get financial aid, and it wouldn't be a hardship on my family. My parents were working class and they didn't have the money. If I hadn't known about these programs, I wouldn't have been able to achieve what I have." Sanchez also made Solis aware of the history and larger social significance of these opportunities: "They were the result of the civil rights movement and the empowering of communities, disadvantaged communities, communities of color."

Reflecting on this experience leads Solis to a very personal defense of affirmative action. "Bob Sanchez was tenacious. He had me fill out college applications, had me meet with recruiters. The recruiters took me to the schools and showed me all the opportunities that were available. They wanted to have minority students attend their campuses. I thought, 'Wow! This is my way to improve my life, to do something.' " Solis's parents were wary at first, as many members of minority groups are, of disclosing the necessary personal and financial records, but after a brief trip to reconnoiter the dorms and "make sure it was legitimate," they became enthusiastic supporters of their daughter. In 1975, Solis enrolled in California Polytechnic University's Pomona campus as the first member of her family to pursue a higher education.

It is important to pause here and note that Hilda Solis's life and career represent, in several senses, something much larger than herself. Her education and career in politics, the methods she has used while campaigning for and serving in office, and the causes she has chosen to champion are the fruition of the lives and careers of her early heroes and the examples they set. The work thus far of Hilda Solis evidences a younger American who has, working within the system, taken up the causes, and more importantly the spirit, of leaders like Martin Luther King, Jr., Robert F. Kennedy, and, in particular, Cesar Chavez and his associate Dolores Huerta.

At the time of Solis's birth, migrant workers from Mexico

and Central America were regularly cheated by labor contractors, indifferently exposed to pesticides, terrorized by law enforcement, deprived of rights of assembly and free speech, and subject to high rates of disease and infant mortality. Cesar Chavez and the United Farm Workers of America initiated a vast educational and organizing effort to better these conditions. The UFW utilized the grassroots strategies of Saul Alinsky and the tactics of nonviolent resistance exemplified by Gandhi and Martin Luther King, Jr.; the union also drew on the Latino culture's strong emphasis on community to build a support base among Latino families. In a series of strikes and boycotts, the UFW drew media attention to the plight of migrant workers and directly confronted the power structures of local and state government, corporate agriculture, and consumers unaware of the realities of food production.

Solis, by virtue of her growing up in the industrial landscape of suburban Los Angeles, had only a secondhand knowledge of these struggles; but in her youth, in the sixties and early seventies, a sense of Mexican American empowerment was in the air. The successes of Chavez and the UFW helped galvanize this rising Chicano movement, which called for ethnic pride, access to higher education, and the elimination of racial stereotypes in the media. Chicano student groups staged walkouts at high schools and universities to focus attention on their concerns (activities in which Solis participated), and in 1970 staged the Chicano Moratorium March against the war in Vietnam.

One leader of the farmworkers' movement in particular caught the eye of young Solis: Dolores Huerta. Born in 1930, Huerta played a huge role in the development of the UFW:

helping to plan strategy; lobbying for the union in Sacramento and Washington, D.C.; exhorting workers and standing on the front lines from the first strikes in the San Joaquin Valley in the 1960s through the strawberry-pickers' strikes in the nineties. As a woman assuming a leadership role in a traditional, patriarchal community, Huerta at first faced some opposition from within as well as without: at times when she showed up in the field to conduct UFW meetings, the startled male workers wouldn't speak to her. But Huerta's life and work would make her a role model for a whole generation of younger Latinas. Hilda Solis says simply, "Seeing Huerta's personal sacrifices inspired me, the personal sacrifices she made in her career to champion the causes of working people striving to be treated fairly and given just payment for their labor."

At California State Polytechnic University in Pomona, Solis began her long and difficult rise to office and influence. She decided, after trying several fields of study, to major in political science. The university's Pomona campus was centered on engineering, but "this made poli sci a small enough program, twelve to thirteen in a class, that I received real quality time and attention from professors who encouraged me to continue to grow and challenge myself." This nurturing atmosphere played an instrumental role in her intellectual development, as it was in several political science seminars at Cal Poly–Pomona that Solis began to feel an affinity for the subject.

Her world was widening. At school she met students from other parts of California and the United States, as well as the Philippines and India, "places I had never heard of or didn't know much about. That was very educational for me, meeting new people was essential." Solis had been admitted to Cal Poly–Pomona through the federally subsidized Educational Opportunity Program (EOP), which provided minority students with mentors from similar backgrounds and orientation sessions to help them acclimate to university life. "It provided a warm, family atmosphere that helped me adjust and figure out what my priorities should be. Without it I might have fallen through the cracks—other students did. It was a good support group."

Her first job on campus was working for EOP as a recruiter, reprising in many ways, for others, the role that Robert Sanchez had played in her life. She went back to La Puente High School and was able to inspire a record number of minority students to apply to college. "I was able to get twenty to twenty-five students to attend Cal Poly—that was the first time they'd ever seen that number of minority students from La Puente. It was so incredible for me to be able to help that many people out, to be able to show them how the process works." Solis was becoming an activist, working with several student organizations. The Mexican-American Student Association to which she belonged raised money to bring lower-income African American and Latino students from Pomona to the campus. "We would pay for their bus ride, spend the afternoon with them, talk to them. We wanted to try to get them to see that they too had choices, that they could go to college and have a better life."

Solis graduated from Cal Poly–Pomona in 1979 and, on the advice and encouragement of a professor who taught at the University of Southern California as well as Cal Poly, headed to USC for graduate work in public administration. She had earlier intended, as an undergraduate, to prepare to go to law school, but a bad experience with another professor had discouraged her from this goal. A professor of constitutional law at Pomona had a reputation "for being rough on students, and on students of color in particular. He was unrelenting on me, and I was demoralized. I was pretty stupid to let someone get to me like that. I started thinking the law wasn't for me. Now I'm writing laws anyway. I like to tell this story to students, especially students who don't think they can do it, that they can become lawyers, or congressmen, or CEOs. If that professor did that to me, imagine how many other students he affected in a negative way. Who made him the gatekeeper?"

At USC, Solis entered the Intergovernmental Management Program (IMP), a master's curriculum designed to groom students for careers in public service. IMP allowed students, as a part of their studies, to work in government offices at the state, local, and federal levels, in Los Angeles, Sacramento, and Washington, D.C. She spent her first semester in Los Angeles, working at California State–Los Angeles with a nonprofit group studying the collective bargaining agreements of municipalities and public agencies. Students were responsible for finding their own internships for the remainder of the program, and Solis wrote more than a hundred query letters. She was pleasantly shocked to receive a response to her longest shot, a letter she'd written on a lark at the suggestion of a friend: she was offered an internship at the White House with the Office of the Chief of Staff.

Solis became a staff assistant, writing the White House Hispanic Affairs newsletter under the direction of Esteban Torres, a Carter administration staffer and later a congressman from California. She finished her academic work in Washington, a rewarding if busy time: "It was a very intensive program. I had to do my classes as well as my job, be ready for all of that. I was always working." After Jimmy Carter lost the 1980 presidential election and she received her degree, Solis was offered a position with the federal Office of Management and Budget. But she spent only a year at this post before deciding to return to California. "It was quite an interesting experience," she says, "because many of the programs I'd been working to defend the previous year under Carter were now being ripped apart. It didn't feel good."

But the California to which Solis was returning was itself undergoing a sharp rift. The split between Republicans and Democrats, conservatives and progressives, is probably more extreme in California than in any other state in the nation. The years of Solis's childhood and adolescence had witnessed a conservative ascendancy that propelled Ronald Reagan into the governor's office and that—just four years after the election of the ultraliberal Jerry Brown—passed the famous (or infamous) Proposition 13, the voter-initiative referendum that dramatically cut property taxes and essentially led to the defunding of municipalities and the state's once-unparalleled educational system. As governor, Reagan spoke for "law and order" and what were perceived to be the interests of suburban "taxpayers." Pete Wilson, another avatar of the state's conservative movement, would be elected governor in 1990 and would push the Republican agenda further, lending vocal support to a number of initiatives that further cut state funds and programs, among them Proposition 209, which ended affirmative action in the university system, and Proposition 187, which denied health care education benefits to illegal immigrants.

Solis's political consciousness and future would be shaped by the crucible of California. Solis herself had benefited from the state's higher educational system at its peak, and from several state as well as federal affirmative action programs—EOP, Grants, and Work/Study among them. "Much of what I've been able to do has been provided through affirmative action—though I wouldn't use that term, I would use 'equal opportunity.' " Her experiences at Cal Poly–Pomona, at USC, and in Washington, D.C., reinforced the lessons that began in La Puente. "The standards for graduating from those schools didn't change, I still had to meet those standards and in some ways work harder to catch up. But through those programs I was given the kinds of support systems that other people already have, people whose parents have money, or who have had other family members go to college before them who could explain to them how it works."

On returning to Los Angeles from Washington, Solis worked for a time on the groundbreaking senate campaign of Democrat Art Torres, who would become the first Latino to enter the state senate. Torres and another Latino pathbreaker, Los Angeles County Supervisor Gloria Molina, would eventually become her political mentors. But Solis was not yet thinking of electoral politics for herself: "After leaving the Reagan administration, I wanted to get away from all that. I was very civil service–oriented at that point." Solis worked for several years as the director of California Student Opportunity and Access, a state-sponsored program designed to provide grants and assistance, like that she herself had received, to minority and low-income students who wished to enroll in college.

Solis saw her first run for elective office, in 1984—for a seat on the board of the Rio Hondo Community College—as an extension of this work, trying, in the face of decreasing state funds, to ensure educational opportunity and access for everyone. Such a small, local position hardly portended either the accomplishments or the trajectory of Solis's next decade. But in her capacity as a board member she worked very closely with the people of her community and became directly aware of their day-to-day problems and concerns—not only about education but also (at the time, perhaps, primarily) about the threat of environmental pollution and contamination from the Puente Hills landfill, which the Los Angeles County Sanitation District was then proposing to expand.

In 1992, several members of her community who were not satisfied that their current representative was voicing these concerns in Sacramento persuaded Solis to run for state assembly from the 57th district, representing Avocado Heights and Hacienda Heights, part of unincorporated Los Angeles County. "I was a little fearful about running," Solis says, adding, "not a little fearful, a lot. Where was I going to get the money, even the minimum amount I'd need to run a campaign, to make photocopies and phone calls? In politics it, unfortunately, often comes down to economics. I wasn't well known. I represented a poor community, working class, where the average family income was about $10,000 a year. People here aren't used to writing checks, to helping candidates with money."

But she was eager to continue what she was beginning to realize she'd been working toward since she had left home for Cal Poly–Pomona: trying to bring something back to the place from which she came—education, a passion for the ideal of equal opportunity, and a desire to make government more directly responsive to the needs of the people it represented. The example of one of her heroes helped show her the way. "I kept thinking about Gloria Molina and how she had been the first Latina elected to the assembly. It made me think that this could be won. It was going to take some work, but it could be done." Solis and an army of volunteers—community and labor leaders, students, and people from the neighborhoods—walked the district, knocking on doors, handing out leaflets, and putting up posters. This classic grassroots effort proved successful.

Solis had run on the issues she thought her community wanted and needed to hear more about: "When I ran for the assembly in '92 I stressed education issues. I offered myself as an example of what education could do, how it could help people make life better in our community. But mostly I ran on the environmental platform, that we not forget about preserving the quality of life of people in the district. I asked questions like, 'Why are we taking in everybody's trash? Why are we allowing the degradation of our water supply? What are we going to do about this Superfund site [the Puente Hills landfill] we've got sitting here on the other side of town?' "

Solis's education and the ground-level experience she had acquired working in state and federal agencies helped her effectively "work the system" in the state assembly. She successfully pushed legislation on health care, domestic violence, and labor issues. She guided through the passage of several key measures on the environment—among them a bill to restrict the size of the Puente Hills landfill, a victory won over the opposition of the immensely powerful county Sanitation District and 75 mayors, and bills requiring the collection of scientific data on the health impacts of waste facilities on poor and minority communities.

She had served in the assembly for two years when, in 1994, Art Torres announced that he would be vacating his state senate seat. This seat included Solis's home district. She decided to try to carry her concerns to the larger stage of the California senate—a step that would necessitate her building a broader coalition on the issues that were important to her. "The seat was not exclusively Latino, and I had to learn to work with other groups: with the larger environmental and conservation community in the state, with labor groups, with women's groups. All of these people shared my basic concerns, but sometimes with a more general focus, or coming from another angle."

Solis's coalition brought her to office in 1994. She was the first Latina senator in the history of the state; she was also, at age 37, the youngest senator in Sacramento. As a member of the senate's Natural Resources Committee, Solis began laying the groundwork for her comprehensive environmental justice legislation, Senate Bill 115. She was stunned at the level of opposition she faced. The corporate and business lobbies pulled out all the stops: "I suddenly found myself pushing against the oil, gas, and waste companies—big money, big business. The Chamber of Commerce came out against the bill. They put out a newsletter every month telling their people what bills to call up their representatives and complain about, and my bill had a red circle with a slash through it. They organized down to the local level. They went into each district and warned companies and developers about the bill. They said I was trying to come in the back door and put restrictions on their business opportunities. The bill would complicate and potentially jeopardize many of their projects." And yet Solis was able to marshal enough support in both the assembly and the senate to get the bill passed (in its original incarnation, AB 1113). This bill, however, was promptly vetoed by Governor Pete Wilson, who stated, somewhat disingenuously—Wilson's rise to power had been built upon flogging societal concerns into political movements—that he did not think the California Environmental Quality Act (an environmental law already on the books, to which SB 115 would be an emendation) should "become a vehicle for social movements."

Solis had crossed swords earlier in her career with the bullishly conservative Wilson and business interests. In 1996, she had written legislation to raise the state's minimum wage to $5.75 an hour. This bill, like SB 115, was hotly contested, was passed even against a monied and highly organized opposition, and was in the end vetoed by Governor Wilson. In what would become a hallmark of her quiet but thorough and diligent leadership style, Solis did not give up; she, along with other politicians, labor leaders, and constituents, rethought and reorganized: Solis co-chaired a statewide referendum initiative to raise the minimum wage, Proposition 110, which passed with 63 percent of the vote.

Solis similarly refused to give up on SB 115. She would endure, in the process of that fight, a hailstorm of sophisticated and not-so-sophisticated attacks on the bill and, sometimes, herself. "The opposition was very intense, very nerve-wracking. The environmental movement and communities of color were truly underdogs. The business lobby said that we were striking at the core of the state's economy, and that we were, in fact, going to endanger the economic life of our own constituents. Somebody labeled the bill 'The Inner City Job Killer.' We didn't have the public relations apparatus, the mailing programs, or the money to make phone calls or bring people to Sacramento to persuade members to go our way. There was immense pressure put on to stop us, and, quite frankly, we were getting ready to drop the bill. You just get so mad, so frustrated. A lot of people on both sides were angry. I didn't want to carry forward a bill that was watered down. But we kept on."

The environmental justice movement, to supporters like Solis, addresses fundamental questions of fairness in American society—viewing freedom from chemical waste, air pollution, and dirty water not as a question of the haves versus the have-nots in a zero-sum game, but as a right shared equally by all. Current arrangements in environmental quality-of-life issues can be construed as arrangements whereby everyone benefits from, say, garbage collection, but only some suffer the long-term problems from society's waste disposal, as they are forced to live near dumps, landfills, and incinerators: in Los Angeles County, to take one example, 90 percent of all waste-producing sites are located in minority communities.

Community leaders like Solis are arguing that the locations of these sites should not be selected through an expedient calculus based on which communities lack the resources necessary to combat them or the incomes necessary to move away. Whether or not one accepts this premise may depend on one's political inclinations, or perhaps on where one lives, but the general question raised by Solis and others remains on its face compelling: Aren't all Americans entitled to clean air and water, to an environment free of carcinogens and ambient taint? And if they aren't, how—or, more to the point, by whom—is this decided?

Solis fought for environmental justice during this period not only through SB 115 but also through several successful conservancy bills such as SB 216, which created open space and urban parks; and through specific reclamation projects like SB 244, which provided for the future utilization of mining pits in the district as open space and for commercial development. Solis counts another such bill, which formed the San Gabriel Conservancy, as her proudest single achievement. This conservancy will create parks, restore land, and buy open space along the San Gabriel River; Solis lobbied and negotiated for three years to satisfy all the towns, citizens groups, and business interests involved.

In 1998, California politics crept again to the left, and Solis found a more congenial atmosphere in the statehouse for the consideration of SB 115. Again displaying her skills as a legislator—tirelessly working the system of committee meetings, researching facts, cultivating personal relationships with senators and their aides, discovering common ground, and building bridges while keeping her end goal in mind—Solis guided the law to passage despite a fierce second round of business opposition. And this time, on October 7, 1999, Governor Gray Davis signed Senate Bill 115, Environmental Justice, into law. SB 115 requires that regulators take into account the already-present pollutants in an area before approving new building, waste-management, and other projects there. The bill, to quote from its own language, calls for "the fair treatment of people of all races, cultures, and incomes with respect to the development, adoption, implementation and enforcement of environmental laws." California Senate Bill 115 had been sponsored and shepherded by a woman of uncommon talent, compassion, and vision, and it represented the culmination of a series of courageous political moves executed with diligence and conviction.

Reflecting back on the struggle, Solis admits to some ambivalence. "To be honest, I wish the bill could have been stronger." But she does not regret the effort or the personal costs involved. "People in the business community may not appreciate what I do, in fact I'm sure they don't. But the people who elected me are tired of being affected by decisions made in other parts of the state without their understanding, and therefore without their consent. That's what they elected me for, that's what I'm bringing to the table—a request for a fair shake. Why should the people in my community be treated any differently from the people in Beverly Hills? We want to have access to opportunity, to clean air, clean water, better housing, jobs, school construction, libraries, books—we want some of the good things, basically the same things that everybody else wants. Everybody wants the same things for their children." She sees a strong future ahead for the movement she represents: "Once our communities wise up and begin to assert themselves, given opportunity and choices, they will meet the challenge. So there is hope."

New times require new leaders—leaders who can sense and articulate changing social, economic, and political landscapes, heroes willing to look beyond the concerns of the present day, and sometimes their own personal interests, to find and define the good of all. Hilda Solis, in her stand for environmental justice, proved herself one such leader. She has demonstrated what John A. Kouwenhaven describes as "a commitment to the idea that there are no fixed or determinable limits to the capacities of any individual human being and that all are entitled, by inalienable right, to equal opportunities to develop their potentialities. Democracy in this sense is an ideal, not a political system, and certainly not an actual state of affairs." But it is a possibility, something that can be suggested and worked toward. Solis's inclusive, commonsense vision of democracy—*doesn't everybody want the same things?*—reveals another way for our ever-changing society to heal racial and class injuries while also underscoring, through the opposition it faced, the still considerable barriers that exist to block such healing.

Money has come to play a fateful role in our politics, and not only in our politics but in our national life. It has become exceedingly difficult for one person, one voice, to stand up against what seem to be invincibly organized and moneyed interests in a time when hundreds of millions of dollars are routinely spent by political parties and corporate and other lobbies in election cycles (and outside of them, on issues such as health care and taxation). Hilda Solis has shown that such stands can succeed when they are principled and brought forward in a spirit of inclusiveness that encourages civic thinking and citizen participation.

In returning home to the San Gabriel Valley with the knowledge and experience she had gained from her schooling and from working in Los Angeles and Washington, D.C., Hilda Solis became a model, again heroic, of the politician as educator: moving up, securing power, helping her constituents without selling them out to money politics. It is difficult to overstate the importance of this message, that one voice can make a difference, that a true leader can illuminate the possibilities for progress and change in the United States—the message of Cesar Chavez, Dolores Huerta, Martin Luther King, Jr., and Robert Kennedy.

In the end, the questions raised by Solis's career and leadership style extend even beyond environmental issues, as crucial as such issues are to the future. Solis's law, California Senate Bill 115, born in idealism and brokered in compromise, changes the dialogue of civil rights in our society. It is a model that opens up possibilities for future discussions on what often seem to be intractable issues. Hilda Solis was able, in her modest, steady, incremental fashion, to unite disparate economic and cultural groups into coalitions that could understand one another's interests—safe neighborhoods, good schools, clean water and air—and work together. Solis has said, "All I can do is promise to be a voice." Living up to the implications of that promise—using that voice both to educate and articulate, in the America of gated neighborhoods, overflowing prisons, incredible income disparity, and racial fractiousness, and most importantly not giving up—is both courageous and heroic; and by definition, rare.

President Kennedy understood that courage is not something to be gauged in a poll or located in a focus group. No advisor can spin it. No historian can backdate it. For, in the age-old contest between popularity and principle, only those willing to lose for their convictions are deserving of posterity's approval.

Half a century ago I entered politics because of a big idea. Rejecting the Midwestern isolationism of my youth, I learned on a combat aircraft carrier in the South Pacific that leadership carries with it a price—a price measured in the twentieth century by eternal vigilance against those who would put the soul itself in bondage.

[A]midst all that is new, may I suggest that you never lose the old faith—President Kennedy's faith—in an America that is better, fairer, and more humane with each generation. For all our imperfections, we remain very much a work in progress. I hope you will reject those on both extremes who mistake the honest clash of ideas for a holy war. The bigger the issue, the greater the need for political courage.

—GERALD R. FORD, 2001

Gerald R. Ford

by Bob Woodward

VERY LATE ON Sunday morning, September 8, 1974, I awoke in a New York City hotel room to the jarring ring of the telephone.

"Did you hear?" the voice on the other end asked insistently. It was Carl Bernstein, my colleague at the *Washington Post* and my collaborator on Watergate. He sounded unusually agitated.

"About what?" I replied somewhat defensively, not wanting to appear overly uninformed.

"The son of a bitch pardoned the son of a bitch," Carl said.

And with that masterful economy of words, at once direct and characteristically irreverent, Carl seemed to have it about right as he provided my introduction to the sudden and surprising decision by then-President Ford, who had been in office only a month, to pardon his predecessor, Richard Nixon.

The decision seemed baffling, shocking. Though there had been some published speculation that Ford would pardon Nixon, conventional wisdom, which I embraced, held that Nixon was radioactive. To touch him, let alone to short-circuit the legal process, would be unthinkable. The decision about Nixon's criminal culpability was in the hands of Watergate Special Prosecutor Leon Jaworski. Eventually, more than 40 people would be indicted or go to jail, including Nixon's top White House and campaign officials.

After all, upon assuming the presidency August 9, Ford had declared a new regime and a return to openness. "My fellow Americans, our long national nightmare is over," he had said, eloquently dividing the Nixon past from the Ford future. In his first press conference as president on August 28, Ford had said he might consider a pardon for Nixon—implying strongly that any decision was down the line, after a possible indictment of Nixon, who had not been charged. "Until any legal process has been undertaken, I think it is unwise and untimely for me to make any commitment." And, he had added, "Until it gets to me, I make no commitment."

Why had he jumped in so soon, somewhat contradicting his own words? I wondered. Watergate had been more than two years of one surprise after another. Ford seemed at that moment to have joined in, even one-upping Nixon himself. I started making some phone calls, returned to Washington, and went to the *Washington Post*.

The wire reports said that Ford had attended church that Sunday morning, sitting by himself in a pew at St. John's Episcopal Church on Lafayette Square, across from the White House. He took Holy Communion. Then back at the White

House at 11:05 A.M., he went on television to announce the pardon to the country and the world.

Dealing with Nixon and his family, Ford said, "Theirs is an American tragedy in which we all have played a part. It could go on and on and on, or someone must write the end to it. I have concluded that only I can do that, and if I can I must." As president he had the power to grant a full and unconditional pardon for crimes that might have been committed. The main reason for the pardon was to put both Nixon and Watergate in the past, to put a second, more definitive end to "our long national nightmare." He had said it was over, but the continuing obsession with Watergate amounted to "bad dreams that continue to reopen a chapter that is closed." Just before reciting the official pardon proclamation, Ford read a sentence that he had added in his own hand: "I feel that Richard Nixon and his loved ones have suffered enough."

The statement was compassionate and strong, but Ford had misjudged public sentiment. The surprise element defeated any sense of sympathy for Nixon. The pardon seemed to be almost entirely on Nixon's terms. In a statement accepting the pardon, the former president had not acknowledged that he had committed crimes or even impeachable offenses.

I was deeply dismayed. The implied promise of the Ford presidency was a cleanup. The pardon seemed secret and dirty. There were obvious questions. What discussions had taken place between Ford's lawyers and Nixon's representatives? Was there a deal of some kind—a secret or implied promise by Ford or someone on his behalf that if Nixon resigned he would be pardoned? Why should Nixon, the leader of Watergate and its many poisons, be spared the consequences of his criminal actions when dozens of his aides were already in jail or heading there? Why a seeming about-face from his own press conference? Most important, what events, information, or discussions had triggered Ford's decision?

The timing—a Sunday morning surprise—made it look as if Ford were trying to sneak it through, under the radar. There had been no prepping of Congress or the public for such a monumental decision. His action set off precisely the reaction he hoped the pardon would leaven. It refocused attention on Watergate and Nixon. Jerry terHorst, Ford's press secretary and friend of 25 years, announced his resignation as a matter of conscience. In his letter of resignation, terHorst protested the pardon and said he could not understand why Nixon was "more deserving of mercy than persons of lesser station in life whose offenses had had far less effect on our national well-being."

During that first press conference of his presidency on August 28, only 9 of 28 questions were about Nixon's future. But at Ford's first press conference after the pardon, there were 22 questions overall, and 15 were either about the pardon or about an agreement on what would happen to Nixon's papers and tapes. Of the 4,000 letters received at the White House in that first week after the pardon, fewer than 700 were at all favorable. In that same span, Ford's public approval rating had plummeted from 71 percent to 49 percent.

Many in the Democratically controlled Congress were outraged. Responding to the uproar and in an attempt to quell it, Ford eventually decided to take an unusual step and testify personally about his decision before a House subcommittee.

There would be no oath and each subcommittee member would have five minutes to question the president.

On October 17, Ford appeared, reading a statement for 43 minutes. He disclosed that Nixon's chief of staff, General Alexander M. Haig, had come to his vice-presidential office on two occasions eight days before Nixon resigned. In the second key meeting, when no one else was present, Haig informed him that a smoking gun tape had been discovered that implicated Nixon directly in the illegal Watergate cover-up. Nixon had decided to resign.

Haig in effect added, *Was Ford prepared to assume the presidency within a very short time?* Ford was stunned. Haig, according to Ford's testimony, then laid out six options—half of which included a pardon for Nixon. But Ford insisted there was no pre-arrangement with Nixon or Haig. "There was no deal, period, under no circumstances," the president testified.

The newspaper accounts noted that Ford's disclosure about meeting with Haig was new, but no one made much of it. In the meeting, Haig had dropped one of the bombshells of all time—that Ford, who less than a year earlier had been a representative from Michigan, was about to become president. Why had so much time been spent in the discussion on options dealing with Nixon's future and not the momentous transition problems and issues facing Ford?

If the mood in Washington was suspicious, it also included somewhat paradoxically an exhaustion with suspicion. Republicans and Democrats were tired of scandal. House Speaker Carl Albert, the Oklahoma Democrat, had promised Jack Marsh of Ford's staff that Ford would not be hurt. The

House subcommittee conducting a pardon investigation voted a month after Ford's testimony to close its inquiry.

The Watergate scandal was a classic example of how long it takes for a more complete version of history to emerge. In the days following the break-in at the Democrats' headquarters at the Watergate office building on June 17, 1972, Nixon Press Secretary Ronald Ziegler labeled it a "third rate burglary" and ridiculed any suggestion that the Nixon reelection campaign or the White House were involved. Some 26 months later, Nixon resigned because of it. The history of the Ford pardon decision is another example of the truth slowly emerging.

During 1974, the *New York Times*, and Carl and I separately, were able to publish sketchy reports that Haig and former Nixon staffers had played a greater role in urging a pardon for Nixon than at first disclosed. For example, we learned that Leonard Garment, a Nixon White House counsel and former Nixon law partner who remained briefly on the Ford legal staff, had written a memo to Ford on August 27, 1974, saying that Nixon's health was declining and Nixon could not withstand the continuing threat of criminal prosecution, implying that Nixon might take his own life. Absent a pardon, Garment wrote, "The whole miserable tragedy will be played out to God knows what ugly and wounding conclusion."

As his presidency evolved, Ford never fully recovered from the lingering doubts about the Nixon pardon. The questions, the sheer starkness of letting the guy at the top off, cast a shadow over his administration.

And Watergate would not go away. Following the initial post-pardon convulsions in 1974, a secondary series of convulsions erupted in 1976 when Ford sought election as president in his own right. Jimmy Carter, the former Georgia governor and the Democratic nominee for president, wrapped Watergate around Ford's neck like a tire iron. By pledging never to lie, Carter reminded the nation's voters of Watergate and the pardon. He not very subtly referred to the previous four years as the "Nixon-Ford administration."

The Watergate special prosecution force was still in business. The fourth Watergate special prosecutor, Charles F. C. Ruff, launched an investigation into whether Ford had years earlier accepted improper cash payments from a small maritime union, tainting the president for three weeks before he was cleared two weeks before the November election. Carter beat Ford by two percentage points. Ford wondered, at first privately and later publicly, if the pardon of Nixon was the deciding factor.

The march for fuller disclosure about the pardon proceeded—aided principally by Ford. In 1979, Ford released his autobiography, *A Time to Heal*. The opening chapters disclose that after Haig's meeting on August 1, 1974, Ford told three of his top and most experienced aides more detail about what Haig had proposed. All three, Robert Hartmann, Jack Marsh, and Bryce Harlow, concluded that Haig had effectively offered Ford a deal. They insisted that Ford call Haig the next day and declare that nothing they had talked about the previous day should be given any consideration in whatever decision Nixon might make about resigning. It was their attempt to walk back any suggestion that a pardon would be forthcoming if Nixon resigned.

Ford describes how he wrote out a statement in longhand to read to Haig over the telephone on August 2, 1974. "We agreed that the only thing I could do would be to call Haig in the presence of witnesses . . ." Such was the level of distrust coming out of Watergate. Ford said he told Haig, "I want you to understand that I have no intention of recommending what the president should do about resigning or not resigning and that nothing we talked about yesterday afternoon should be given any consideration in whatever decision the president may wish to make." Still Ford concluded that Haig had not offered a deal. In his version, it was possible that Haig came bearing a deal, but he didn't think so—even though Ford and his aides felt it necessary for Ford to make the extraordinary telephone call to Haig.

In his 1980 book *Palace Politics*, Hartmann, who had been Ford's top aide, asked these crucial questions: Why, on the afternoon of August 1, 1974, was Haig so intent on seeing Ford alone? How many people did Haig report to after the meeting was over? Had Ford deliberately been drawn into a compromising situation?

Hartmann goes on to say that Ford had told Haig that he "needed time to think about it," after Haig mentioned the resign-pardon option. Ford had left open the possibility that he might be willing to make a deal; he hadn't slammed the door shut. Hartmann believed it was a "monstrous impropriety" for Haig even to have mentioned a pardon in Ford's presence, and he details his own efforts to show Ford how dangerous the situation was for him politically.

Hartmann wrote that he found Ford almost in a state of denial about it. The lasting implication of Hartmann's book is that Haig had certainly been sent to test Ford's reaction to the pardon suggestion, probably by none other than Nixon himself. And Ford hadn't made the whole thing any clearer by both acting indecisively and being somewhat politically naïve. Whatever happened, it was certainly improper and nobody had yet to explain it fully.

Then in 1992 I picked up a copy of Haig's full memoir, *Inner Circles*, a book full of significant disclosures that have been largely overlooked. Near the end, on pages 518–19, Haig wrote that before Ford's October 1974 testimony to the House subcommittee about the pardon, Haig received a phone call from J. Fred Buzhardt, Nixon's White House Watergate lawyer who had remained at the Ford White House during the transition.

Haig's book recounts: " 'Al,' said Buzhardt, 'I think you'd better come over to the White House. These boys have prepared sworn testimony for the president that could very well result in your indictment.' "

"Angry and bewildered," Haig's book continues, "I got into my car and drove to the White House. There I read the draft testimony, prepared for Ford by his inner circle, that suggested that I had offered Gerald Ford the presidency in return for a pardon for Nixon." Haig said it was a lie. He insisted on seeing President Ford and said if he didn't, he would call a press conference in the White House pressroom. Within minutes Haig was in the Oval Office meeting with Ford.

"What do you want?" Ford asked.

"The truth," Haig replied. "That's all."

"You'll have it, Al," Ford said.

I later learned in interviews with Haig and Ford that Ford had then handed Haig a yellow legal tablet and said, "You write that portion as you remember."

So the conclusions of Ford's top aides that a deal had been offered were initially in the famous testimony but were excised at the insistence and threats of Haig. Nixon's former White House chief of staff had called the shots on the disclosure and interpretation of the August 1, 1974, meetings with the then-vice president. That meeting was one of the critical turning points in Watergate. In a sense the presidency was in play that day as power was shifting from Nixon to Ford with Haig as the intermediary.

As Leon Jaworski said in 1981, Haig was "our 37½ president," serving between Nixon, the thirty-seventh, and Ford, the thirty-eighth.

What a story that would have been in 1974! Or 1975 or 1976. But it was 1992, and few seemed to notice or care. With these disclosures, history was being substantially rewritten, but the resulting record was still murky at best. No one had taken the public record and the documents now available in the Ford library and then interviewed the participants and re-interviewed them to sort out the contradictions and the motives, to assemble a better version of what had happened.

In 1997, nearly 23 years after the Nixon pardon, I decided to attempt that as a part of a book on the legacy of Watergate for the five presidents since Nixon—Ford through Clinton. The project eventually became my book *Shadow: Five Presidents and the Legacy of Watergate*. I hoped to replow the ground as thoroughly as possible and in a sense interrogate the full record and those involved.

I interviewed Ford's living aides and tested their memories. In several long interviews, Hartmann and Marsh (Harlow was deceased) reiterated to me their conclusions that Haig had offered a deal. During two interviews, Haig denied such a deal had been offered. But under questioning about his own memoir and that of others, he added a key piece of the puzzle. At about 1:30 A.M. on August 2, just 10 hours after his critical meeting with Ford, the vice president called him. Ford had discussed the Haig options with his wife, Betty, who said he had to disengage from any decision about a Nixon resignation. In the unusual phone call, Ford said, "Al, our discussion this afternoon, I hope you understand there was no agreement, no decision and no *deal*" (emphasis added). Haig said he went through about 30 minutes of anguish in the middle of the night, concerned that Ford thought he had offered some kind of "deal." He also explained how he then at about 2 A.M. phoned Fred Buzhardt, the Nixon lawyer who had laid out the six options, to berate him. "Goddamnit," Haig said he told Buzhardt, "what did you do to me?" Haig was disturbed that Ford thought there was some kind of "deal" or "arrangement." He felt trapped and was deeply worried.

"Why did you, if this man thinks there was some deal offered, how the hell did you give me the advice you gave?" Haig said.

"I didn't do anything to you," Haig quoted Buzhardt as saying, "Al, that's all we did was give the options."

Buzhardt was deceased. Jeff Glasser, my assistant then, and I reviewed many of the newspaper stories about Ford's presidency, read the memoirs and the other books and spent days looking at the voluminous papers and files at Ford's presidential library in Ann Arbor.

In this process, I arranged to do my first interview with Ford himself. Despite my years of covering Watergate and the

Ford presidency, I had never interviewed Ford before. His assistant suggested that we meet at 10 A.M., Monday, September 22, 1997, at the Waldorf Towers in New York City. Ford was in the city for a meeting of one of the boards on which he served.

I was a bit nervous as I went up in the elevator. Half a dozen from his Secret Service detail were turned out in the hall around his suite and I worried that Ford might be joined by a horde of secretaries, aides, and a public relations person. I feared I was about to meet with and interview a committee—the worst conditions for a talk designed to elicit new information and candor about controversial issues. Instead, he came alone into a modest parlor. He was relaxed and friendly, not in a hurry and focused, the image of Midwest simplicity and straightforwardness. It was Ford, myself, and my tape recorder.

He had just turned 84. He seemed completely confident in himself and in what he recalled. He would later tell me that he had given up drinking alcohol in 1979, a year after Betty quit. That perhaps helped him retain some of the brain cells that others lose at that age, or earlier. He was unusually attentive and sharp.

He talked comfortably in paragraphs about Nixon and Watergate. We moved to the pardon. I asked Ford whether he thought Haig had offered him a deal.

"Well, I guess I was naïve," Ford said. "I was naïve that anybody would offer a deal, because all my political life people never came to me, I'm going to give you a political donation, I expect something in return. People never came to me that way because they knew damn well I wouldn't be a part of it." It seemed to be something of a standard answer. He went on: "So when Al Haig comes with those six terms, I just didn't visualize him as one making a proposition to make a deal. It never went through my mind."

In a certain sense, what Ford was saying here squared with what the others had said of him: that the deal was offered but he would not necessarily see it. Perhaps he was too optimistic about people; he also had been informed by Haig that he was about to become president—an office he had not sought and in fact did not want. It was quite a day by any standard.

And even after his aides had him write out a statement to read to Haig in response to the purported deal offer, Ford says, "I still contended when he was there with me alone, that he wasn't doing it. I mean, that's my nature. I just never lived in that world. Nobody ever came in my office thinking they could put X dollars on the table and walk out and he has a deal." He said he trusted Haig, and that he didn't understand the potential consequences until Hartmann, Marsh, and Harlow sat him down.

And then he said that Haig had nothing to do with his final decision to grant the pardon: "There's no connection between the Haig meetings and my decision four weeks later. They were totally disconnected." This is the crux of his claim: Whatever happened in that meeting with Haig, whatever interpretations others might put on it, whatever Haig might have intended, hoped for, or imagined, it had no relationship with his eventual decision to grant the pardon. In fact, the matters and events that caused him to grant the pardon had not yet occurred. They occurred after the August 1 meeting—from roughly August 9, when Ford became president, to August 30 (two days after the press conference), when he said he decided to grant the pardon. During these three weeks he had seen the Nixon-Watergate obsession too clearly and decided he had to put an end to it. Otherwise the country could not move on. In my view this is more than a plausible claim.

Of his testimony before the House subcommittee, he said, "I never said [Haig] offered me a deal, because I didn't believe that he did."

I continued to press Ford. Did he agree when all the facts and conclusions are examined now two decades later that Haig offered a deal? "Do you agree with that now in retrospect, looking back?" I asked.

"I would agree," Ford said, "because after talking to Hartmann, Marsh, and Harlow, I wanted the record clear that I did not agree to consummate . . . So that it has to be very clear that, yes, on paper, without action it was a deal, but it never became a deal because I never accepted."

And so there it was. He had finally acknowledged, on the record, that he had been offered a deal. It was something many had suspected all along, but it had been a long, roundabout road to finally getting there.

He also acknowledged that some of his friends and advisers disagreed with his entire approach to the pardon decision, saying he should have waited until later, until after an indictment or a conviction, or even the appeals process. But he said that his decision was made after the press conference in which he felt like 90 percent of the questions were about Nixon (even though only one-third were). "So as I walked back over to the

Oval Office, I said we can't have this for the next two and a half years."

Yet as he always did, Ford took complete responsibility for the decision. "The truth is, this was a decision 99 percent on my own, which is typical of my way that I make decisions. But I make my own decisions. And sometimes I make wrong ones. And when I do I'm kind of stubborn about still believing I was right. But in this case, I have never equivocated in my own mind that I did the right thing."

He said he believed it was "very proper" to do it on a Sunday morning.

"Why pardon Nixon and not the others?" I asked. "He was the number one guy, he led the cover-up, according to the evidence."

"I wanted to get the major issue out of the White House. The others were minor players. I had to get the big problem away. Gone. The others were, as I looked at it, I didn't have my time preoccupied with them . . . It was Nixon's problems that were preoccupying my time. The only way for me to concentrate 100 percent [of the time on] 260 million people [the population of the United States] was to get the big problem away."

Then after more research, interviews and cross-referencing the accounts, I went to interview Ford again eight months later. We met on Wednesday, May 20, 1998, at 3 P.M. at his office in his home in Rancho Mirage, California, on a golf course in the midst of the desert. It was very hot but not humid, creating a slowness in the atmosphere. He offered a friendly greeting and he was alone, again unafraid of the tape recorder I stuck nearby. He was unhurried, conveying the sense that he had all afternoon. It was a somewhat large, dark office crowded with papers and memorabilia. Ford was calm, sincere, and unworried. It was in the middle of the Monica Lewinsky investigation.

"My administration had our share of problems, but I'll take ours compared to the ones that exist today," he volunteered.

He brought up his pardon decision, noting that no president had "caught as much hell as I did." His recollections were clear. I suspected he had replayed them many times in his mind and in conversation. "I was overwhelmed with the public reaction," he said. "I guess I anticipated a lot but not to the extent that happened. But at no time, despite that public outcry, did I in any way ever feel I'd made the wrong decision. It didn't faze me one bit. If anything, it made me more stubborn that I was right."

Why didn't you make sure that Nixon's statement accepting the pardon went further? Nixon's statement said, "No words can describe the depth of my regret and pain at the anguish my mistakes over Watergate had caused . . ."

"It could have been better," he responded, "but we were under a time pressure." Once he'd made the decision to grant the pardon, they had to move quickly. "The longer it took to resolve some of these things, the more likely that the issue would have come to the surface and it could have been a different ball game."

I said I agreed, it would have leaked. But presidents always operate under time pressure. Why didn't he press Nixon harder for an admission of guilt? A forthright acknowledgement by

Nixon could have ended the historical debate on that question. Why didn't Ford make more of the *Burdick v. United States* Supreme Court decision of 1915 that held that accepting a pardon is tantamount to confession of guilt?

"I still carry it around in my pocket, that statement." Ford said. He reached into his pockets. "I've got it in my wallet here because any time anybody challenges me I pull it out. I've got it here some place." He searched around in his wallet, and finally located it.

He handed me a folded, dog-eared piece of paper. It was a portion of the 1915 Burdick Supreme Court decision that he'd been carrying around for years. I began to read aloud. "Most important, the justices found that a pardon 'carries an imputation of guilt, acceptance, a confession of it.' "

Ford landed on the last phrase, and he repeated it: " 'Acceptance, a confession of it.' " See, Nixon had confessed, he said. "That was always very reassuring to me."

Ford continued to make the case that there was no deal. "Another aspect of it that people fail to realize, I was going to be president anyhow. At that point I didn't have to make a deal if I wanted to be president. The die was cast. It was inevitable that he was either going to have to resign or he was going to be impeached so there was no incentive for me to make a deal. Didn't have to."

This is the accepted wisdom today now that hundreds of hours of additional Nixon tape recordings have been released, with many providing evidence showing beyond question that Nixon was directing the Watergate cover-up. But in early August 1974, even after the smoking gun tapes were released, it was still a dicey situation. Nixon was not known to be a quitter. At that time I was among those who knew the most about Watergate, and I was not sure the die was cast by any means. In fact, Nixon's resignation was a huge surprise to me.

By the time of my interviews with Ford in 1997 and 1998, I had come almost full circle in my conclusions about the pardon. I was close to thinking that Ford had done the right thing in pardoning Nixon. After the interviews, I was completely convinced. Ford was wise to act. What at first and perhaps for many years looked like a decision to protect Nixon was instead largely designed to protect the nation. Watergate was a poison that would not go away. There was more to it than I saw at the time. Over the years the periodic release of new Nixon tapes shows new criminality and smallness.

Ford wanted to protect his presidency, a proper goal because the president is an extension of the nation. The only way out of the Watergate atmosphere was to move fast, to short-circuit the process. Preoccupation with Nixon's fate could have continued for years.

At the time, one of the chief arguments against the pardon was that in halting the judicial process Ford had stopped the flow of information about Nixon's actions. The absence of a trail would leave a void, no clear resolution, allowing Nixon to wage war with history. History would be ambiguous. But the tapes have provided more incontrovertible, conclusive proof of guilt than any possible indictment or trial of Nixon.

Significantly, it was Ford who decided that the Nixon tapes

had to be preserved. After resigning, Nixon wanted all his papers and tapes shipped to his home in California. Traditionally, a former president owned all his papers. Before issuing the pardon, Ford sought advice from a longtime friend and former Justice Department lawyer, Benton Becker, who had assisted him during his years in the House of Representatives. Becker, then only age 36, immediately saw the trap for Ford. Returning all the tapes and papers to Nixon would make Ford a co-conspirator in concealing the truth of what had gone on in the Nixon White House. Becker told Ford, "You will be writing the history of your presidency in the first week, and history is going to say Jerry Ford participated in the final act of the Watergate cover-up." Becker knew Ford was naturally a Republican team player who would want to help Nixon. But he kept pressing, and finally Ford authorized Becker to negotiate an arrangement so the government would retain the tapes. "That history must be preserved," Ford told Becker. "Do whatever you have to do, but it must be preserved. I'm not shipping that stuff out."

Becker worked out a complicated arrangement in which Nixon and the government had joint custody of the tapes for 10 years. Congress and the courts eventually saw that the tapes were preserved. A plan for gradual public release is still being carried out today.

To history, the tapes and Nixon records are more important than any possible prosecution or conviction. Ford's decision to pardon Nixon and to preserve the tapes and records for the public and for history reflect what might be called acts of instinctive courage. The last 27 years have proven their wisdom. Courage is not always wise. In this case it was.

The irony is that had Ford been more candid early on about his decision to pardon Nixon, he might have avoided the damage it did to his own reputation. And he might have been elected president in his own right in 1976. Suppose before granting the pardon, Ford had gone public and described in detail his August 1 meetings with Haig, the shocking conclusions of his top aides that a deal had been offered, and phone calls to Haig saying there was no agreement. Then Ford could have said he was going to grant a pardon anyway because the nation had to move beyond Watergate and Nixon. All hell might have broken loose. There would have been investigations and Haig might have gone ballistic. But Ford would have emerged a truth teller. That, of course, is one of the critical lessons of Watergate—early and full disclosure of even embarrassing details generates respect.

Instead, during the first three months of his presidency, the period from August 1974 to October 1974, Ford hedged, dodged, and was much less than forthcoming.

For example, on August 3, two days after the critical Haig meeting, Ford was traveling and held two press conferences, one in Hattiesburg, Mississippi, and then in New Orleans. His press secretary had mentioned that Ford had met with Haig a couple of days earlier, so reporters asked him about it. "It was not an extraordinary meeting, if that's what you want me to say," Ford said. "It was an ordinary meeting of the kind that we frequently have and has no extraordinary implications."

Not only was the meeting extraordinary, but there had never been one like it in American history. The vice president was told he was going to become president within a week. Ford should not be given a pass for telling such a whopper.

But those were extraordinary times, and it is easy to understand the pressure, stress, and confusion he must have felt. For the first time the American presidency was about to become a resignable office. It was indeed uncharted territory, and no doubt Ford was being careful in public. He could hardly declare the Nixon presidency over in Hattiesburg or New Orleans.

After his White House years, Ford really began his effort to assist history and those who would try to pry out a fuller, better version. Ford's courage has been more durable than just the actions he took in office. He has permitted and encouraged the inquiry to continue. Instead of closing the door and falling back on canned answers, he really opened up. It's unusual for anyone, especially a former president.

In 1999, my book *Shadow: Five Presidents and the Legacy of Watergate* was published. In it, I reviewed the details of the pardon decision and provided new information. I concluded that Ford had made the right decision in pardoning Nixon, adding that "a pardon was the only way of ending the public and media obsession with his predecessor's future. The problem with the pardon was in Ford's execution. To be successful, the pardon required elaborate orchestration. The public, Congress and the media needed to be prepared. Ford should have mustered all of his sense of decency to explain his actions to the public. He should have seen the danger and avoided the discussions of a pardon with Haig. He should have required Nixon to sign a statement admitting his guilt and released it with the pardon."

It was a long list of criticisms. I did not expect to hear from Ford, or if I did that it would be to disagree.

About a month after the book was released I received a one-page, handwritten letter dated July 6 from Ford. He thanked me for the autographed copy I had sent him. "I have carefully read the Ford part," he wrote, "and congratulate you on your professionalism in presenting a very controversial and complicated scenario." He said he greatly appreciated the comments I made about the pardon being the right thing. "These should be reassuring to many critics of the pardon."

Nowhere was there a complaint or disagreement about any of my unfavorable judgments. He closed, "With my admiration and gratitude, Jerry Ford." Having spent more than three decades dealing with situations and figures like these, let me just say that Ford's generous reaction is exceedingly rare, if not unique. So he isn't a son of a bitch. I was wrong.

As it may take time, even decades or more, for the hidden details of history to come out, so it may take as long or longer for the *meaning* of those details of history to be clear. If Ford mishandled some of the details and disclosures, he got the overall absolutely right—the pardon was necessary for the nation.

On May 23, 2001, Ford gave a speech as part of the Senate Leader's Lecture Series. He referred to the 1976 presidential campaign:

"Because the specter of Vietnam, on the one hand, and Watergate, on the other, loomed so large, I found myself, in effect, running two campaigns: the first to win a full term, and the second to restore the shattered confidence of the American people in their democratic institutions. I was unsuccessful, as we all know, in the first. But as I left Washington, I could take some consolation in knowing that the national mood was different from what it had been just a few years earlier."

Ford's ambition for the country was larger than his own ambition. Restored confidence was more important than his reelection. That's courage.

NOTES

MUCH OF THE work and research that supports my conclusions about Ford and the pardon was conducted between 1997–1999, for my book *Shadow: Five Presidents and the Legacy of Watergate* (1999). The first three chapters of *Shadow* are devoted exclusively to Ford's pardon of Nixon and a reexamination of the circumstances that surrounded it. I tried to interview everybody I could who had been involved, and aimed for as exhaustive an account as possible, given the passage of time. See *Shadow*, pp. 3–38.

294 *"My fellow Americans"*: Ford's inauguration speech found in Public Papers of the President, Gerald R. Ford, August 9, 1974.

294 *"Until any legal process"*: Ford quoted from "The President's News Conference of August 28, 1974," Public Papers of the President, Gerald R. Ford, 56–66.

295 *"Theirs is an American tragedy"*: Ford quoted from "Remarks on Signing a Proclamation Granting Pardon to Richard Nixon," September 8, 1974,

Public Papers of the President, Gerald R, Ford, 101–103.

295 *in his own hand:* Reading copy of Ford's statement with Ford's insertion, folder "Sept. 8, 1974, Presidential Pardon Message," Office of the Editorial Staff, Reading Copies of Presidential Speeches and Statements, 1974–1977, Box 1, Gerald R. Ford Library, 7.

296 *"more deserving of mercy":* terHorst letter quoted from Gerald R. Ford, *A Time to Heal* (1979), 175–176; Jerald F. terHorst, *Gerald Ford and the Future of the Presidency* (1974), 236–237.

297 *On October 17, Ford appeared:* See "Pardon of Richard M. Nixon, and Related Matters," Hearings before the Subcommittee on Criminal Justice of the Committee on the Judiciary, House of Representatives, October 17, 1974, 95.

298 *Nixon Press Secretary Ronald Ziegler:* Ziegler quoted from Carl Bernstein and Bob Woodward, *All the President's Men* (1974), 26.

298 *we learned that Leonard Garment:* Garment information taken from Bob Woodward and Carl Bernstein, "Ford Disputed on Events Preceding Nixon Pardon," *Washington Post*, December 18, 1975, A1; direct quotation of the memo taken from James Cannon, *Time and Chance* (1998), 370.

299–300 *In 1979, Ford released:* Description and quotations taken from Gerald R. Ford, *A Time to Heal*, 13.

300–301 *In his 1980 book:* Hartmann's questions and opinions taken from Robert T. Hartmann, *Palace Politics* (1980), 124–138.

301 *Then in 1992:* Haig quoted from Alexander Haig, *Inner Circles* (1992), 518–519.

302 *As Leon Jaworski said:* Jaworksi's statement in the January 1981 issue of *Armed Forces Journal International* quoted from *Inner Circles*, 517.

302 *I interviewed Ford's living aides:* author interviewed Alexander Haig, November 6, 1997, and February 5, 1998; Robert Hartmann, December 10, 1997, and January 7, 1998; Jack Marsh, October 23, 1997, and March 18, 1998; Phil Buchen, April 8, 1998; Benton Becker, April 22, 1998.

303 *During two interviews:* Ford-Haig-Buzhardt conversations quoted from author's interviews with Alexander Haig, November 6, 1997, and February 5, 1998.

311 *Ford sought advice:* Ford-Becker meeting quoted from author's interview with Benton Becker, April 22, 1998.

312 *"It was not an extraordinary meeting":* Ford's August 3, 1974, press conferences in Hattiesburg, Mississippi, and New Orleans, Louisiana, found in folder "Nixon Pardon Hungate Subcommittee: Background Material (2)," Phil Buchen files, Box 33, Gerald R. Ford Presidential Library.

313 *In 1999, my book* Shadow: description and quotations taken from Bob Woodward, *Shadow* (1999), 3–38.

Courage is a reflection of the heart—it is a reflection of something deep within the man or woman or even a child who must resist and must defy an authority that is morally wrong. Courage makes us march on despite fear and doubt on the road toward justice. Courage is not heroic but as necessary as birds need wings to fly. Courage is not rooted in reason but rather Courage comes from a divine purpose to make things right. . . .

When you stand up to injustice. When you refuse to let brute force crush you. When you love the man who spits on you or calls you names or puts a lighted cigarette in your hair. You come to believe that righteousness will always prevail. Just hold on.

We—and I mean countless thousands and even millions of Americans—changed old wine into new. We tore down the walls of racial division. We inspired a generation of creative nonviolent protest. And we are still building a new America—a Beloved America, a community at peace with itself. . . .

As we begin a new century, we must move our feet, our hands, our hearts, our resources to build and not to tear down, to reconcile and not to divide, to love and not to hate, to heal and not to kill. I hope and pray that we continue our daring drive to work toward the Beloved Community. It is still within our reach. Keep your eyes on the Prize.

—JOHN LEWIS, 2001

John Lewis

by Teresa Carpenter

THERE'S A PHOTOGRAPH. You've probably seen it, though you may not remember. A young black man in suit, tie, and dress shoes, his hands thrust into the pockets of his light tan raincoat. His expression is neither submissive nor hostile. Only resolute. Advancing upon him and the narrow column of civil rights marchers filed across the bridge behind him is an army of Alabama State Troopers. Moments after that photo was snapped, a billy club smashed into his skull and he slumped to the ground, unconscious.

Although film clips from Bloody Sunday—Selma, Alabama, March 7, 1965—flooded into millions of living rooms, very few Americans recognized the young man being beaten as John Lewis, one of the early Freedom Riders, an organizer of the student sit-ins at Nashville lunch counters, and leader of the Student Nonviolent Coordinating Committee. Few white Americans, in fact, would have even recognized his name. He wasn't an outstanding orator in the tradition of Martin Luther King, Jr. He wasn't as handsome as Julian Bond or as polished as Andrew Young. He didn't disturb the sleep of white people like Stokely Carmichael or H. Rap Brown. He had a slight speech impediment and never quite mastered the art of the sound bite. And yet in his quiet, stubborn way Lewis pushed, and sometimes pulled, the civil rights movement forward.

His capacity for punishment was legendary; he was arrested and jailed forty times. He was beaten repeatedly, kicked in the ribs and face so many times, he lost count of the injuries. Yet he never struck back. Not physically. His weapons of choice were fearless effrontery and a gift for what he called "creative disruption." During SNCC's turbulent passage from nonviolence to Black Power, he clung firmly to the principles of pacifism, causing him to be cast aside as an "anachronism." He rose from the ashes to high political office. In 1986 he was elected congressman from Georgia's fifth district and was returned to office seven times, eventually appointed to the post of chief deputy Democratic whip.

His extraordinary success has baffled those who first met him as a kid fresh off an Alabama dirt farm. He didn't enter the adult world with many natural advantages. The son of a sharecropper, he was shy, physically awkward, and halting of speech. He was a child who was not supposed to succeed at anything. But then, people were always underestimating John Lewis.

In his lyrical memoir, *Walking with the Wind*, Lewis recalled the world of his boyhood in Carter's Quarters as "small and safe," peopled by dozens of cousins and kindly uncles named Rabbit and Goat. Yet it was also a life of extreme poverty and rural isolation. No one in his family had more than a few years of elementary school. A black child's academic career in those days was more often than not cut short by a call to the cotton fields. Until the age of six, he never saw a white person except the mailman and a traveling salesman.

From the start, however, John Robert Lewis seemed different from his six brothers and three sisters. A strangely formal child, he insisted upon wearing a bow tie and calling his mother "Mrs. Lewis." He was also very determined. When the family visited his elderly grandmother, she would point the children to a hole about 10 feet up in a chinaberry tree where the hens nested and instruct them to check it for eggs. It was always John who shinnied up the trunk first. "It wasn't that I was bigger or faster," he would recall. "It was simply that I wanted it more."

The spring he turned five, his mother placed him in charge of the family chickens. Their helplessness aroused his pity. "I felt the need to talk to them . . . " he later wrote, "I'd speak softly, gently, as if I were hushing a crying baby, and very quickly the cackling would subside, until the shed was as silent as a sanctuary. There was something magical, almost mystical, about that moment when those dozens and dozens of chickens, all wide awake, were looking straight at me, and I was looking back at them, all of us in total, utter silence. It felt very spiritual, almost religious."

When times made it necessary to trade a hen for sugar or baking powder, John would cry and refuse to eat. His parents were not amused, nor did they approve of his strong opinions, which, as they saw it, challenged the natural order of things. There was no way, he would argue, that a person could get ahead as a tenant farmer. A man could pick a fifth of a ton of cotton and receive less than two dollars. "Even a six-year-old," he later wrote, "could tell that this sharecropper's life was nothing but a bottomless pit."

So John Lewis played hooky from the fields to attend school, a two-room shack supported mainly by fish fries and community picnics. "The thrill of learning to write was intense," he would later recall. Books he found there put him in touch with a world beyond Pike County. He devoured biographies of black Americans such as Booker T. Washington, Joe Louis, and Mary McLeod Bethune. He also discovered periodicals such as the *Baltimore Afro-American* and the *Chicago Defender*, which in 1954 were publishing articles about *Brown v. The Board of Education*. This supposedly meant he could go to school with the whites, but fourteen-year-old John Lewis noticed the decision had no effect at all upon Alabama. He still rode a bus 20 miles a day to the same segregated school. At movie theaters, he had to sit with other blacks in a balcony called "Buzzard's Row." Most humiliating to him was the discovery that he was not allowed to check books out of the public library. That was a privilege reserved for white patrons. In what he recalled as the first formal protest of his life, he walked into the Pike County Public Library and asked for a card. Turned down, he circulated a petition—signed mainly by his cousins—and mailed it to the county. He never got a reply.

In December 1955 an event took place in Montgomery that would change his life. Rosa Parks refused to give up her seat on a bus to a white passenger. The bus boycott that followed lasted for a year and fifteen-year-old John Lewis followed it with keen curiosity. Although his parents were openly disapproving of "that young preacher" who was behind it, Dr. Martin Luther King caught and held his imagination, and Lewis decided to become a minister. He applied to and was accepted by the American Baptist Theological Seminary in Nashville, and later received his bachelor's degree from Fisk University.

On the morning he left home, his mother saw him only as far as the porch. "Be particular," she said. Then she turned and went inside.

"Change," Lewis would later write, "was not something my parents were ever very comfortable with . . . Theirs was, as the Bible says, a straight and narrow way . . . What change there was [was] usually for the worse. It's not hard to understand at all the mixture of fear and concern they both felt as they watched me walk out into the world as a young man and join a movement aimed, in essence, at turning the world they knew upside down."

John Lewis, however, was not cut out to be a preacher. His speech difficulties and natural shyness didn't lend themselves to "whooping," the exuberant vocal orchestration of the best black Baptist ministers. Neither could he sing. His natural inclination, rather, lay in the direction of social action. He was so stirred by the nonviolent protests of black high school students against segregation in Little Rock, Arkansas, that he asked the president of the seminary if he could start a local chapter of the NAACP. No, he was told. The school relied upon the support of the white Southern Baptist Convention. It didn't want to be associated with troublemakers.

Lewis, however, was restless to place himself, as he later put it, "in the path of history." Early in his sophomore year, he found what he was looking for in a man named Jim Lawson. A Methodist missionary and committed pacifist, Lawson had spent time in India studying the nonviolent philosophy of Gandhi. Every Tuesday evening he held seminars in a brick chapel near the campus of Fisk University.

Nonviolence, Lawson explained to the 10 or so students who came to hear him, was not a mere tactic of combat, it was a principle that had to be internalized. Even as your enemy ground a burning cigarette into your neck, you had to love him, a feat that required an absolute "inner certainty." These were, Lewis recalled, "incredibly powerful ideas . . . We were being trained for a war unlike any this nation had seen up to that time, a nonviolent struggle that would force this country to face its conscience." Lawson was arming them with a "soul force" that would bring about what he and Dr. King called the Beloved Community.

As more students joined the original ten, "The New Gandhians" as they came to be called, were eager to put their principle to the test. Their first target: Nashville's department stores, whose lunch counters were closed to blacks. The students planned their campaign carefully. The men would wear coats and ties, the women skirts and blouses. They would be polite and orderly. They would bring books and schoolwork. But they would not be removed except by force. They would probably be arrested.

It's hardly possible now to imagine the terror that the prospect of arrest held for a black teenager in the South during the late fifties. The students planning the Nashville "sit-in" had no reason to expect kindness or respect from the authorities. Anything might happen once they were behind bars and out of public view. The fact that they were young would not protect them. Most had been in their early teens when Emmett Till was lynched. Till was a fourteen-year-old who, in the summer of 1955, made a flirtatious remark to a white woman in Money, Mississippi. He disappeared and was later found at the bottom of the Tallahatchie River, shot through the head, an eye gouged out, and the cord of a seventy-five-pound cotton gin fan wound around his neck. In setting themselves up against the white Southern establishment, the Nashville youngsters knew that they were, quite literally, placing their lives on the line.

It was one thing for a single black man or woman to disappear, but quite another for 10, or 20, or 100 to drop out of sight. Nashville, moreover, was reasonably progressive as Southern cities went, and the students were hoping that the city fathers could be shamed by the spectacle of so many youngsters, black and white, being loaded into paddy wagons.

The students, led by a Fisk University coed named Diane Nash, made a tentative test of lunch counters and were, of course, turned away. They became more assertive, parking themselves for hours at the counters of the Kress and Woolworth stores. White hecklers appeared, shouting racial insults

and pouring ketchup and mustard over the heads of the protestors. At the counter of a Woolworth's, a crowd of white
toughs hit Lewis in the ribs, knocking him down. He was arrested for "disorderly conduct."

"I could see my mother's face now," he would write. "I
could hear her voice. 'Shameful. Disgraceful.' But I felt no
shame or disgrace. I didn't feel fear either." He was, in fact,
almost giddy as he was led away to the open doors of a paddy
wagon. "The drama of good and evil [was] playing itself out
on the stage of the living breathing world."

Following the lead of Nashville's liberal daily, the *Tennes-
sean*, the national media also took notice of the Sophoclean
drama unfolding at Southern lunch counters. And over the
course of four months so much pressure was applied on Nashville that the city, by face-saving increments, finally opened its
counters to blacks. What should have been celebrated throughout the civil rights movement as a great victory, however, had
the effect of accentuating the divisions within it. The students
found themselves at odds with members of the conservative
black bourgeoisie who formed the movement during the for-
ties. No less venerable a figure than Thurgood Marshall—at
the time a lawyer for the NAACP—condemned as a dead end
the tactic of getting oneself jailed and refusing bail. Activists,
he said, should take their grievances through the courts. As
Lewis listened to Marshall speak in Nashville one spring evening in 1960, he became convinced that the "revolt" that had
started at lunch counters was as much against traditional black
leadership as it was against the white establishment. Eleven
days later in Raleigh at a conference organized by the Southern
Christian Leadership Conference, a core of young dissenters

organized the Student Nonviolent Coordinating Committee, SNCC—or simply "Snick."

John Lewis had witnessed firsthand the power of civil disobedience, and for the rest of his life would remain a believer in creative disruption. His twenty-first birthday he spent behind bars after trying to integrate a Nashville movie theatre. When in the spring of 1961 SNCC called for Freedom Riders, he was among the first to volunteer.

Late the preceding year, the U.S. Supreme Court had ruled in *Boynton v. Virginia* that a federal statute forbidding segregation on interstate trains and buses now extended to the terminals. In theory, the "whites only" signs would have to come down from restrooms and water fountains. SNCC was eager to test that new law. Lewis was the youngest of 13 original volunteers—white and black—to board a bus in Washington, D.C., for New Orleans.

In Anniston, Alabama, the bus was firebombed. The riders miraculously escaped without injury, but the organizers, principally the Congress of Racial Equality, wanted to airlift them out of Birmingham to avoid a calamity. John Lewis, Diane Nash, and a handful of others were strongly opposed. The movement, they argued, could not appear to be retreating in the face of violence. The new administration of President John F. Kennedy seemed reluctant to test the new law for fear of offending Southern Democrats. It would be necessary to make it more inconvenient for the government *not* to enforce *Boynton*, than to enforce it. Diane Nash placed a phone call to CORE's national chairman, James Farmer, announcing that she, Lewis, and several other Nashville students would be continuing the ride. And they did. All the way to Jackson, where, after entering the station, John Lewis was taken into custody for trying to use a urinal still bearing the hateful designation "whites only."

The arrests caused national outrage. Busloads of sympathizers poured into Jackson. Soon the cells of the city jail were overflowing with the new arrivals. Lewis and about two dozen of the original Riders were driven in the dead of night to Parchman Farm, Mississippi's state penitentiary with a reputation for brutality.

"We were led," Lewis recalled in his memoir, "into a cement building where deputies with cattle prods stood by while we were ordered to strip naked. For two and a half hours we stood wearing nothing, while we waited for . . . well, we didn't know *what* we were waiting for. I could see that this was an attempt to break us down, to humiliate and dehumanize us, to rob us of our identity and self-worth. I had read that such methods were used by oppressors throughout history. When we were finally led, two by two, into a shower room guarded by a sergeant with a rifle, I thought of the concentration camps in Germany. This was 1961 in America, yet here we were, treated like animals for using the wrong bathroom."

During the month that Lewis spent in Parchman, he and other inmates were blasted with streams of icy water and denied exercise. One of the female prisoners miscarried while a guard watched. On July 7, after the state of Mississippi felt it had made its point, the prisoners were released. They found themselves heroes.

John Lewis found his "measure of fame" a novel and

somewhat intoxicating experience. He had no ambitions to become a leader, he would later claim. He had, nonetheless, placed himself in "the path of history." And in June 1963, he was drafted to fill out the remaining term of SNCC's chairman, Chuck McDew. It was a role for which he was not fully prepared. Only one week after his election, he was invited to the White House.

The administration's earlier fears of offending Southern whites had been offset by the possibilities of cultivating the black vote. And so President Kennedy summoned the nation's top civil rights leaders—the so-called Big Six—mainly moderates such as Roy Wilkins of the NAACP and the SCLC's Martin Luther King. John Lewis, as the representative of SNCC, was—in theory at least—the most radical voice among them. Lewis's experience to date, however, had been on the front lines. He was unaccustomed to the trappings and exercise of power. He was frankly cowed by his first visit to the West Wing.

Of that day, he later recalled that John Kennedy seemed rushed. (He was due in Vienna to meet with Nikita Khrushchev for the first time since the Cuban Missile Crisis.) The president was blunt. He wanted the Six to call off a massive March on Washington set for August. He was worried that it would damage the prospects of his Civil Rights Bill, legislation that would ban discriminatory hiring practices, prohibit segregation in public places and guarantee equal housing.

When John Lewis carried this message back to SNCC, the rank and file were infuriated, charging that the administration was not, in fact, throwing its full weight behind the bill and now the president was trying to silence dissidents. While the

March on Washington came off on schedule, it was fraught with internal conflicts. SNCC had envisioned the day as an orchestrated series of "sit-ins" and "lie-ins" that would bring Washington to a halt. It would, however, be Martin Luther King's "I Have a Dream" speech that set the idealistic, don't-rock-the-boat tone of the day. When a draft of John Lewis's own proposed remarks circulated among march organizers, it set off alarms. As an estimated half-million demonstrators marched down Independence Avenue, Lewis huddled with a committee of fretful rewriters who methodically deleted from his text all criticisms of the president. In years to come, Lewis would downplay the havoc wrought upon his speech. SNCC, however, resented what it saw as nothing less than censorship. Lewis took heat for not being combative enough, for not "standing up" to King and the moderates.

In fact, Lewis had deeply conflicting emotions about Martin Luther King. The "young preacher" who led the Montgomery boycott was his boyhood idol. As Lewis came of age, King treated him with kindness, courtesy, and respect, offering him a seat on the board of the Southern Christian Leadership Conference, which he accepted gladly. To an extent, Lewis shared King's preference for conciliation and compromise. The tactics of moderation were, however, anathema to the rank and file of SNCC.

After the March on Washington, weeks passed, and the Civil Rights Bill idled helplessly in Congressional committees. It seemed that the crucial legislation might die for lack of attention from the White House. On November 22, 1963, when Kennedy was cut down by an assassin in Dallas, there was a fierce debate within SNCC as to whether it might not indeed, be hypocritical to make a public show of grief. Even a face-saving proposal to visit the grave of John Kennedy *and* Medgar Evers was voted down. In the weeks after the president's death, however, it became clear that civil rights had lost a great champion, and that under an administration by his successor, SNCC was on its way to becoming *non grata*. When Lyndon Johnson summoned civil rights leaders to the White House for a briefing, John Lewis was not invited.

As a matter of style, Lewis generally kept a low profile—too low to suit SNCC communications director Julian Bond, who urged the chairman to insinuate himself more aggressively into the limelight. Indeed, whenever Lewis posed for a photograph with the Big Six, he ended up on the far end, scowling and looking painfully earnest. John Lewis was simply not a creature of the media. He was a man of action. It was as a grassroots leader that he excelled.

For months before SNCC's massive voter registration project in Mississippi, Lewis traveled tirelessly to northern college campuses recruiting volunteers. He beguiled students, according to civil rights historian Taylor Branch, "as the irresistible Negro man-child, awed by everything and nothing." He could be very amusing—"a gifted mimic," according to Branch, who described in his Pulitzer Prize–winning book, *Parting the Waters*, how Lewis would entertain a circle of admirers with "imitations of Robert Kennedy's choppy, distracted discourse."

Most of the incendiary summer of 1964 Lewis spent with hundreds of volunteers going door to door, canvassing potential black voters. He was arrested in Americus, Georgia; Selma, Alabama; and Hattiesburg, Mississippi. In one particularly revealing passage of his memoir he wrote, "Some of the deepest, most delicious moments of my life were getting out of jail . . . finding my way to the nearest Freedom House, taking a good long shower, putting on a pair of jeans and a fresh shirt and going to some little . . . side-of-the-road juke joint where I'd order a hamburger or cheese sandwich and a cold soda and walk over to the jukebox and stand there with a quarter in my hand and look over every song on that box because this choice had to be *just* right . . . and then I would finally drop that quarter in and punch up Marvin Gaye or Curtis Mayfield or Aretha, and . . . I would let the music wash over me . . . I don't know if I've ever felt anything so sweet."

SNCC had its eye on the Democratic National Convention in Atlantic City where it hoped to unseat the all-white Mississippi delegation and replace it with an integrated slate of its own. For this purpose it entered into an uneasy alliance with the Liberal Wing of the Democratic Party. When, midway through the convention, that white liberal support evaporated, Lewis was personally "devastated." Bob Moses, another SNCC leader and the revered architect of the Mississippi voter project, was so disgusted he changed his name and eventually moved to Africa. Many black SNCC members called for whites to be excluded entirely from the organization. Lewis, a committed integrationist, argued against it, urging his brothers to remember how the whites had shared their prison cells and slept on the same lumpy mattresses and eaten the same meager meals at Freedom Houses throughout the South. But he found himself in the minority. What had begun as a movement of student pacifists was falling under the sway of black nationalists such as Stokely Carmichael and H. Rap Brown. Reports filtered back to Lewis that SNCC staffers were abusing their positions and misspending money. Drug use was on the rise.

"I didn't even know what marijuana smelled like," he would insist. By the seventies, he had apparently found out but was purportedly never tempted to toke. "It made me nervous," he said. "If I was around someone who lit up a joint, I'd push a towel against the bottom of the door and spray the room with Right Guard." Lewis was dismissed within his own ranks as a "square" and a "Christ-loving damned fool."

SNCC had become so alienated, so insular in its newfound militancy, that it refused to respond to a cry for help—from Selma.

Shortly after the disappearance of activists Schwerner, Chaney, and Goodman, Congress had passed the Civil Rights Act, which appeared on its face to be a document with teeth. Lyndon Johnson, had, in fact, come through on a promise made after the Kennedy assassination to place his personal prestige behind the bill. That July when the ink on the president's signature was barely dry, a group of youngsters in Selma had tried to test the new law by entering a downtown movie theater. They were arrested for trespassing. When a crowd gathered in protest, deputies repelled them with tear gas. The spurt of violence focussed national attention upon Dallas County, where almost 15,000 black voters remained unregistered. The bar in many cases was fear, in others a so-called "literacy test" that required black applicants to answer ridiculously obscure questions about the Alabama State Constitution. Illiterate whites could make their mark, no questions asked.

On the green marble steps of the courthouse, blacks walked a picket line. Teachers, undertakers, beauticians, all marched, and were, in turn, manhandled by Selma's irascible sheriff, James Clark, and his posse of white supremacists. During one nighttime march, a twenty-six-year-old army veteran, Jimmie Lee Jackson, was shot and killed trying to pull his mother to safety. The angry crowd that formed in the wake of the murder vowed to carry the casket to Montgomery and lay it on the capitol steps.

Jackson, in fact, was buried within days of his death, but the idea of a march to Montgomery took on a life of its own. Martin Luther King announced he would lead it. SNCC considered Selma its own turf and resented the fact that King and his Southern Christian Leadership Conference could sweep in trailing TV cameras and take the event over. The rank and file of SNCC refused to march, which put John Lewis in a painful position. He was their leader; but he was also a man of strong personal conviction. If he could not march representing SNCC, he finally told his followers, then he would march without them, as a private citizen.

The following Sunday morning between 400 and 600 hundred marchers gathered at Brown's Chapel to wait for their leader. But anxious hours passed and Dr. King did not appear. Lewis heard later that he had been deterred by a death threat. Andrew Young, King's chief lieutenant, later explained in his own memoir that the minister had a speaking engagement that he couldn't break. More likely, King was stalling for time, awaiting a federal court order that would have allowed the marchers to walk the 52 miles to Montgomery legally and with the nominal protection of Alabama State Police.

Word arrived that Dr. King wanted to postpone the demonstration. Lewis knew this was impossible. Hundreds of marchers were waiting for the signal to move. The people needed a leader. Without fanfare, he walked to the head of a long orderly column and took his place next to King's surrogate, Hosea Williams. Together they began a march into history.

"There was no singing or shouting," Lewis later wrote in *Walking with the Wind*, ". . . just the sound of shuffling feet. There was something holy about it." The column moved in solemn progress down Water Street, then to the river and to the foot of the Edmund Pettus Bridge. "There was a small posse of armed white men," Lewis recalled. "They had hard hats on their heads and clubs in their hands. Some of them were smirking . . . I didn't think too much of them as we walked past. I'd seen men like that so many times. . . .

"When we reached the crest of the bridge, I stopped dead still . . . There . . . stood a sea of blue-helmeted, blue-uniformed Alabama state troopers . . . dozens of battle-ready lawmen stretched from one side of U.S. Highway 80 to the other . . . Behind them were several dozen more armed men—Sheriff Clark's posse—some on horseback, all wearing khaki clothing, many carrying clubs the size of baseball bats."

John Lewis looked over the side of the bridge into the river, a drop of 100 feet. He didn't know how to swim. Then, as he recalled, "all hell broke loose . . . troopers and possemen swept forward . . . like a human wave, a blur of blue shirts and billy clubs and bullwhips." He received a sudden blow to the side of his head. "I didn't feel any pain," he recalled, "just the thud . . . and my legs giving way." He raised his arms and curled into a ball, but couldn't block the next blow to his head. He lapsed into semiconsciousness.

He heard people choking on tear gas; mothers called out for their children. Swinging clubs broke bones. The marchers fell back stumbling and coughing, with the posse on their heels. As they retreated to Brown's Chapel, men and children from the neighboring projects threw bottles and bricks at the advancing officers.

John Lewis never returned a blow. Not physically. But he fought back, this time with words delivered in strong, clear, unfaltering speech—aimed directly at the president. "I don't know how President Johnson can send troops to Vietnam," he proclaimed angrily at an ensuing rally. "I don't see how he can send troops to the Congo. I don't see how he can send troops to Africa, and he can't send troops to Selma, Alabama."

The image of John Lewis being beaten on the bridge sparked a national outrage. There were demonstrations in 80 cities. For the next week, a crowd of protestors parked themselves outside the White House chanting in support of a Voting Rights Bill. On March 15, a beleaguered Lyndon Johnson addressed Congress and the nation making what Lewis later described as, "the strongest speech any American president has ever made on the subject of civil rights." Comparing the events in Selma to the struggles for freedom at Lexington, Concord, and Appomattox, he vowed to "defeat every enemy" of equal rights.

When, one week later, Martin Luther King led a peaceful army of 3,000 out of Selma on a five-day march to Montgomery, they were escorted by 1,800 armed Alabama National Guardsmen, 2,000 U.S. Army troops, 100 FBI agents, and another 100 U.S. Marshals. A little over four months later, Lyndon Johnson signed the Voting Rights Act—legislation that eliminated literacy tests and polls taxes—into law.

John Lewis's stubborn courage had forced the hand of a president. Yet his followers remained angry that he continued to defend Martin Luther King. In May 1966 they voted him out and replaced him with Stokely Carmichael.

"I felt abandoned," he later recalled, "cast out . . . I was able to forgive this . . . [but] I will never be able to forget."

At the age of twenty-six, he was out of a job and repudiated by those he'd considered family. He had no wife, no children, no job, and, to his way of thinking, no skills. He held an "executive session" with himself. He vowed not to become bitter, and never, never to give in to despair.

For a time he lived in New York City, where he had found work reviewing grant applications for a philanthropic foundation. When a job offer from the Southern Regional Council came his way, he jumped at the opportunity to return to the South. In Atlanta, he met a young librarian named Lillian Miles. To that point, there was a part of John Lewis that had seemed to remain a child, isolated and lonely. Now, he found himself in a stable, supportive, adult relationship. "It made everything," he would later recall, "a little fuller, a little richer."

In the spring of 1968, when Robert Kennedy announced his candidacy for president, John Lewis felt stirrings of political excitement. Kennedy opposed the war in Vietnam, something that Lewis, on the strength of pacifist principle, had done for many years. (After applying for conscientious objector status, he was declared "morally unfit" for duty because of his long arrest record.) He sent a telegram to the candidate offering his support, and, a short time later, was recruited to get out the black vote. The campaign, which began so hopefully, however, was decimated by tragedy: Martin Luther King was shot in Memphis, Bobby Kennedy in Los Angeles. "So . . . that awful year ended," Lewis recalled, "with Richard Nixon about to move into the White House . . . It was a dark, dark time."

Late in 1968, John and Lillian were married, and they settled in Atlanta, then 60 percent black. No black congressman had been elected from the South since the Reconstruction era, so when in 1972 Andrew Young ran and won, Lewis and other Southern activists were elated—only to be let down when, after the election of Jimmy Carter, Young resigned his seat to become U.S. ambassador to the U.N. The Democratic Party in Atlanta cast about for a potential successor. John Lewis threw himself into the breach.

Lewis was under no illusions about his shortcomings as a media personality. "I was not charming nor charismatic," he wrote disarmingly in his autobiography. "I always preferred to walk the walk rather than talk the talk." But unlike the SNCC days when his relative inexperience and shyness held him back, he now had a potent new ally, his wife, Lillian, who knew not only knew how to write a speech but how to work a crowd.

In that special election in the spring of 1977, Lewis lost the primary to a white candidate. But he gave a rousing concession speech in which he declared, "This is only the beginning!" Nearly a decade passed before he made his second run. In the interim, he served as associate director of the federal volunteer service ACTION, then a couple of terms on the Atlanta City Council. In 1986, he made his move. This time his chief opponent in a crowded field of twelve primary candidates was former SNCC communications director and onetime friend, Julian Bond.

Bond, now a Georgia state legislator, was heavily favored. Glib and photogenic, he enjoyed the national endorsements of Mayors Tom Bradley, Ed Koch, and Marion Barry. Moreover, celebrities from Miles Davis to Hugh Hefner were falling over themselves to raise funds for him. The only civil rights leader to endorse Lewis was Ralph Abernathy. Even his former champion Coretta Scott King remained neutral.

Local Democratic kingmakers looked with disfavor upon Lewis's bid. They wanted to pick the candidate who would fill what was now informally designated as a "black" seat. Lewis objected in principle to kingmakers—black or white—and set himself up against the powers that be. That race drew national attention and became a contest between the Darling of the Radical Chic and the Frog Prince of Principle. The polls gave Lewis no real chance. But he was not daunted. "People," he later recalled, "had always underestimated me."

He rolled up his sleeves and set to work. With no money in his war chest, he was up and out on the streets every day at 5:00 A.M., leafleting, talking to voters at bus stops and grocery stores about more federal involvement in education, universal health care, plans for creating more jobs and protecting the environment. He accepted every speaking invitation that came his way, making as many as six appearances an hour. A born-again raconteur, he regaled crowds with tales about his days in the movement and his life back on the farm—leading one local black leader to quip, "Not that *chicken* story again."

To the dismay of the Bond camp, Lewis polled strongly enough to force a run-off. Then the front-runner made a blunder: He invited Lewis to debate. It was widely believed that television would show the Georgia legislator off to his best advantage. What Bond apparently failed to realize was he was dealing with a more experienced, politically sophisticated John Lewis than he'd known during their days together in SNCC. This time, Lewis was prepared. He had drilled with a speech coach. Then he drilled and role-played with an image consultant. Over the ensuing five debates, Bond's lead slipped. The contest peaked when Lewis challenged his opponent to step outside and take a drug test. Bond, who sidestepped the question, in effect declined. That 1986 election night was a cliff-hanger, until the early hours of the morning when the city's predominantly white northern precincts were counted. They went 90 percent for Lewis. He won by a margin of 4 percent.

John Lewis's special brand of courage remains immortalized in that photograph from the Edmund Pettus Bridge. The stoic resistance, devoid of malice, that monumental certainty. What the photo did not suggest, perhaps, was the maturing man; the more resilient, philosophical nature of the freshman legislator who took his seat at the Hundredth Congress. As he made his triumphal entry into Washington, he was hailed on one hand as a "national treasure" and "living saint"—a designation that always caused him to chuckle. Skeptics, on the other hand, dismissed him as a neophyte who would be out of his depth in the intrigues of Foggy Bottom. Once again, they had underestimated John Lewis.

The "moderate" liberal views that he brought to Washington were the same ideals of pacifism and integrationism he had lived out every day of his adult life. And in the House they found a natural forum. One of Congressman Lewis's first acts was to oppose the Gulf War. During the Republican Revolution of 1994, he went on the attack against a fellow Georgian—Newt Gingrich—accusing him of alleged fund-raising improprieties. The Republican majority, in turn, attacked Lewis for destroying the "comity" of the state delegation, suggesting that his outspokenness might hurt the prospects for future federal projects in his district. "I will not be silenced," Lewis shot back in an angry press release. "Anyone who knows my background . . . knows that I will not be intimidated."

He opposed the nomination of Clarence Thomas to the U.S. Supreme Court. "The fact that he is black did not matter to me," Lewis later wrote. "The fact that his politics are conservative was not the issue. But like most of the black conservatives I know, he is a direct beneficiary of the civil rights movement, and the fact that he now stood poised to deny to others the kind of opportunities he enjoyed was appalling to me."

Lewis also broke with the Congressional Black Caucus, which supported the Million Man March led by Louis Farrakhan. He objected to the Nation of Islam's doctrine of "racism, sexism and anti-Semitism." This caused a furor within the black community, causing critics to charge that Lewis wasn't "black enough" . . . he was too friendly with the white liberal establishment . . . too chummy with the president.

John Lewis was, in fact, loyal to Bill Clinton, whom he considered a friend. During the Lewinsky scandal, he argued against the release of confidential ethics reports on the president—an act that caused critics to point to his earlier efforts to get a report of an investigation on Newt Gingrich made public and charge that he was playing politics. Lewis brought his principles into alignment by conceding he should have been more forgiving of the Speaker.

But no one ever doubted John Lewis's sincerity. And those who accused him of "not standing up to the president" had apparently forgotten how he'd opposed Clinton on the North American Free Trade Agreement and welfare reform, and how he'd broken Democratic ranks in 1994 to vote against the administration's crime bill—he felt it would have expanded the use of the death penalty and he opposed killing in any form. Lewis rode out the impeachment controversy, to remain one of Congress's most revered members and the "political conscience" of his party.

Many of the leaders of the civil rights movement are gone now. Some are dead; others simply burnt out. John Lewis is still standing. Still battle-ready. As the new millennium dawned, the adversaries he found staring at him from the other end of the bridge were not troopers in riot gear but a conservative administration and a Supreme Court whose waning moral authority threatened to usher in another dark time for civil rights. But Lewis was not a man given to despair. His weapon of choice was—as ever—perseverance.

"I tell young people today," he explains, " 'you must pace

yourself for the long fight.' It's not a struggle that lasts for one day or one week or one month or one year. It is the struggle of a lifetime . . . to build a society at peace with itself. People say I'm too hopeful, too optimistic. People say 'Nothin's changed.' But I say, 'Come walk in my shoes. Come back to Selma, back to Birmingham, back to Montgomery with me.' I assure you things have changed. It's a different world."

The author drew upon *Walking with the Wind: A Memoir of the Movement* by John Lewis with Michael D'Orso; *Parting the Waters: America in the King Years 1954–63* and *Pillar of Fire: America in the King Years 1963–65* by Taylor Branch; *An Easy Burden* by Andrew Young; and *The Children* by David Halberstam. Also "Saint Lewis," by David Grann, *The New Republic*, Oct. 5, 1998; "The Last Integrationist," by Sean Wilentz, *The New Republic*, July 1, 1996; "The Lives Behind the Dream," by John Meacham, *The Washington Monthly*, May 1998; "Those Were the Days," by Garry Wills, *The New York Review of Books*, June 25, 1998; and contemporary accounts from *The Atlanta Journal-Constitution*, *The Washington Post*, *The New York Times*, *The Wall Street Journal*, *Newsday*, *Newsweek*, *Time*, *People*, *The Hill*, and *The Congressional Record*. Special thanks to the Museum of Television and Radio for making available the television documentary *Eyes on the Prize* and to Congressman Lewis for his insights and cooperation.

Terror is not a new weapon. Throughout history it has been used by those who could not prevail, either by persuasion or example. But inevitably they fail, either because men are not afraid to die for a life worth living, or because the terrorists themselves came to realize that free men cannot be frightened by threats, and that aggression would meet its own response. And it is in the light of that history that every nation today should know, be he friend or foe, that the United States has both the will and the weapons to join free men in standing up to their responsibilities.

—PRESIDENT JOHN F. KENNEDY

Address to the United Nations, September 25, 1961

PROFILE IN COURAGE AWARD 2002

by Caroline Kennedy

THE PROFILE IN Courage Award is different this year for it is impossible to think about courage now as something apart from 9/11. The heartbreaking events of that day brought to our families, to our communities, and to our nation overwhelming loss. But in those terrible moments thousands of ordinary men and women put their own lives on the line in order that others might be spared, making real the face of courage and inspiring a new generation to want to serve others. The Profile in Courage Award honors the heroes of September 11.

We also honor two men who have used the power of their offices to battle the kind of ignorance, hate, and greed that have brought the world to this precipitous juncture. One, a mayor of a small, average American town, the other a world leader. Dean Koldenhoven, the mayor of Palos Heights, Illinois, staked his political career on a fight for religious tolerance. Kofi Annan, the Secretary-General of the United Nations, has relentlessly challenged individuals and nations to take moral responsibility for creating a more equitable world.

HEROES OF SEPTEMBER 11

THE EXTRAORDINARY BRAVERY of our public servants—firefighters, police, medical teams, and our elected officials—saved thousands of lives. They ran toward danger to keep us safe, toward death to make sure we survived, and their sacrifice has ennobled us all.

These men and women put their lives on the line, as they do every day, and a new generation recognized that there are no greater heroes than those who serve others.

A note left at an improvised firehouse shrine spoke for all of us. It said, YOU RAN IN WHEN WE RAN OUT. WE ARE GRATEFUL FOREVER. It is true that a firefighter's job is to go where no one else will, to run into burning buildings while people are running out. And if you ask them, they will say that they are just doing their job. Yet on September 11, they did more than their job or any job requires. In New York City, 353 brave men died that day while doing their jobs. Until then, no fire had taken the lives of more than 12 firefighters at one time.

The firefighters of New York suffered the greatest losses. But they were not alone. The Profile in Courage Award honors the New York police, the medical rescue teams, the sanitation and cleanup workers, the police of the Port Authority and the Pentagon, and the mayor who led his city even as he told the people of New York, "The number of casualties will be more than any of us can bear."

We honor too all those civilians who demonstrated the most extraordinary bravery in New York, at the Pentagon, and in the sky. They became public servants in the very best sense of the word, saving each other, protecting the rest of us, and giving their lives for their country. As the poet wrote:

Near the snow, near the sun, in the highest fields,
See how these names are feted by the waving grass
And by the streamers of white cloud
And whispers of wind in the listening sky.
The names of those who in their life, fought for life,
Who wore at their hearts the fire's center.
Born of the sun, they travelled a short while towards the
*   sun,*
And left the vivid air signed with their honour.

They have been joined by the men and women of our Armed Forces who make courage their career, who face danger halfway around the world because they believe freedom is worth dying to defend.

The Profile in Courage Award honors all these heroes. Across this country, it is no longer possible to see a firefighter, a police officer, or a soldier the same way we did before September 11. Their courage has changed the way we think of public service. They showed us that the capacity for courage is within us all. We must not let them down. We must keep their faith.

MAYOR DEAN KOLDENHOVEN

THE PROFILE IN Courage Award also honors the former mayor of Palos Heights, Illinois. Even before September 11, Dean Koldenhoven risked his political career for the principle of religious tolerance upon which our country was founded, and for which President Kennedy battled during the 1960 campaign.

Dean Koldenhoven worked as a bricklayer most of the time that he served as a City Council Zoning Committee member and Republican precinct captain in his hometown of Palos Heights, a Chicago suburb, population 12,000. He was elected mayor in 1997, promising to bring respect to the town. Today, he speaks with pride of the new police station and millions of dollars in social service grants that he helped to attract during his time in office.

But the battle of his career began in March 2000 when he found out that the Al Salam Mosque Foundation, representing the town's 450 Muslim residents, had signed a contract to buy a building that a Christian congregation had outgrown. Shortly afterward, at a zoning committee meeting in which the Muslim group was seeking city approval for the building's continued use as a religious institution, the town came apart. Council members and residents tried to block the sale, attacking the Muslim religion and its practices. One City Council member called the Friday day of worship "like upside down," another compared the danger of postponing city action to the appeasement of Adolf Hitler. Residents suggested to their Muslim neighbors that they "go back where you came from."

Mayor Koldenhoven condemned the comments and spoke out on behalf of the mosque. "I can understand a fear of heights and a fear of flying. But when it is a fear of a person, they have to get over it," Koldenhoven said of the intolerant in his community.

But Koldenhoven did more than speak out for religious freedom. When the City Council voted to buy the church building for a recreation center, although the space had previously been rejected as too small, Koldenhoven objected. "We don't want to be known as the town that kicked the mosque out," said Koldenhoven. "People have got to look in the mirror. This is not who we want to be."

After Koldenhoven blocked the sale to the city, the City Council then voted to buy out the mosque, to pay the Islamic group to drop the whole idea. Even though the City's offer was accepted by the Islamic group (who were no longer sure that Palos Heights was the right community for their mosque), Koldenhoven vetoed the deal. He called the buyout offer "fiscally irresponsible" and an "insult to the Muslim community." In response, the Mosque Foundation sued the city and named Koldenhoven as a defendant. The following year Dean Koldenhoven came in last in a three-way race for mayor.

"The incident raised some significant issues in people's lives that they have not had to struggle with," said Rev. Peter Semeyn, the pastor of the congregation selling the church building, in August 2000. In words that seem eerily prophetic today, he continued, "Unfortunately when people think of Muslims they think of the people who bombed the World Trade Center. They don't think of the people who live across the street. The question is how do we all get along with each other?"

Dean Koldenhoven recognized that the answer lies in religious tolerance and respect for diversity. Well before September 11, he spoke out against discrimination against Muslims. He made a decision of conscience that brought on the wrath of his constituents and his colleagues, yet he never wavered in his convictions. He risked his political career to do what was right for his community, and he paid the price.

In 1960, while campaigning for President, John Kennedy said, "I believe in an America where religious intolerance will someday end—where all men and all churches are treated as equal—where every man has the same right to attend or not attend the church of his choice—and where Catholics, Protestants, and Jews, at both the lay and pastoral level, will refrain from those attitudes of disdain which have so often marred their works in the past, and promote instead the American ideal of brotherhood." Mayor Koldenhoven promoted that ideal, and our country is better off because of him.

SECRETARY-GENERAL KOFI ANNAN

JUST AS THE events of September 11 transformed America, so they transformed the world. They seared our hearts, and they confronted us with a new world order. The first Profile in Courage Award presented to an international leader recognizes the renewed importance of global understanding. As President Kennedy recognized more than 40 years ago, the fight against terrorism will call upon all citizens and states to stand up to their responsibilities. Since his election as Secretary-General in 1996, Kofi Annan has been doing just that.

In a quiet voice, with a gentle dignity, Kofi Annan has challenged nations and individuals with uncomfortable truths. Most recently, he has reminded the United States that in the struggle against terrorism, "there is simply no alternative to international cooperation. Terrorism will be defeated only if the international community summons the will to unite in a broad coalition, or it will not be defeated at all." At the same time, Annan has claimed a critical role for the United Nations, encouraging member nations to take their own steps to combat terrorism and criticizing countries that have historically supported terrorism, and has assumed a leadership role in rebuilding Afghanistan.

Kofi Annan's consistent record of speaking the truth with moral clarity has been demonstrated throughout his tenure as Secretary-General. Annan has confronted the rich and powerful nations with the cost their wealth exacts from those who live in poverty. He has called upon nations, businesses, and individuals to take greater responsibility for the crises of world poverty and AIDS. At the same time, he has challenged the countries of the developing world to assume greater responsibility for their own progress. Within the United Nations itself, Annan has tackled the entrenched bureaucracy of 54,000, provoking the opposition of longtime colleagues whose support he needs to achieve his larger goals.

In a singular act of courage, backed by years of personal commitment, Annan has claimed peace as the birthright of all individuals, and warned nations that "the sovereignty of states must no longer be used as a shield for gross violations of human rights." Now known as the "Annan Doctrine," he has put the world on notice that "a global era requires global engagement. In a growing number of challenges facing humanity, the collective interest is the national interest . . ." Annan has made it clear that our common humanity overrides "the desire of those in power to protect their position at any cost," and that the United Nations will intervene. This new moral force has emerged from the humanitarian tragedies of the 1990s when the world community did not act to stop genocide and ethnic cleansing. Annan has led by example, assuming personal responsibility for the U.N.'s inability to prevent the genocide in Rwanda and the massacres in Bosnia, yet he has not stopped there.

Kofi Annan has challenged all of us to ponder these global human tragedies, and our own part in them. "When we recall tragic events such as those of Bosnia or Rwanda and ask Why did no one intervene? the question should not be addressed only to the United Nations or even to its member states. Each of us as an individual has to take his or her share of responsibility. No one can claim ignorance of what happened. All of us should recall how we responded, and ask, What did I do? Could I have done more? Did I let my prejudice, my indifference or my fear overwhelm my reasoning? Above all, how would I react next time?"

By interweaving the lives and conscience of each individual into the fabric of our common destiny, Kofi Annan has redefined the role of the United Nations in the twenty-first century. When he accepted the Nobel Peace Prize in December 2001, Annan spoke of the chances of a baby girl born in Afghanistan that very day, "a child who would be fed, comforted and cared for by her mother, yet who would begin life centuries away from the prosperity that a small part of humanity has achieved." He went on to say that "the mission of the United Nations will be defined by a new more profound awareness of the sanctity and dignity of every human life, regardless of race or religion. . . . We must begin with that young Afghan girl, recognizing that saving one life is to save humanity itself."

As Secretary-General, Kofi Annan has provoked the powerful and the powerless. He has stood fast for the principles of human dignity and the quest for a peaceful world. A soldier without an army, he must depend on the power of moral leadership. His consistent career of conscience has made him a true Profile in Courage, not just for our time but for all time.

Primary sources: Pete Hamill in *The Daily News*, 9/17/01, 9/23/01, 11/22/01, 12/31/01; John F. Kennedy, Speech to Greater Houston Ministerial Association, 9/12/60; Martha Irvine, "Mosque Issue Forces Chicago Suburb to Examine Its Motives," Associated Press, 7/20/00; Pam Belluck, "Intolerance and an Attempt to Make Amends Unsettle Chicago Suburb Muslims," *The New York Times*, 8/10/00; Martha Irvine, "Chicago Suburb Fighting Over Plan for Muslim Mosque," Associated Press, 6/22/00; Serge Schmemann, "Nobel Peace Prize Is Awarded to Annan and U.N.," *The New York Times*, 10/13/01; Press Release, "Secretary-General Presents His Annual Report to the General Assembly," 9/20/99; Kofi Annan, 2001 Nobel Peace Prize Laureate, Nobel Lecture given in Oslo, Norway, 12/10/01; "Reflections on Intervention," Ditchley Foundation Lecture, given at Ditchley Park, England, 6/26/98.

"The Truly Great" by Stephen Spender. Reprinted with the kind permission of the Estate of Stephen Spender and Faber and Faber Ltd.

PROFILE IN COURAGE AWARD 2003

by Caroline Kennedy

———

As America battles the war against terrorism around the world, there remain issues that divide us here at home. One of those is the symbolic power of the Confederate flag. To some, it represents a link with a proud historical tradition, to others it is a symbol of racism and intolerance. Although this may seem like an argument about the past, in some Southern states it is a red-hot political issue that reaches even to the level of presidential politics. During the 2000 GOP South Carolina primary, both George W. Bush and John McCain refused to oppose the display of the Confederate flag. After he lost, Sen. McCain went back to South Carolina to apologize, declaring this was the campaign moment he most regretted. In the 2004 presidential campaign, the flag is emerging as a polarizing issue once again with Democratic candidates under pressure to declare their positions.

The Profile in Courage Award winners of 2003, former Governors Roy Barnes of Georgia and David Beasley of South Carolina, are recognized for their principled efforts to diminish the divisive symbolism of the Confederate emblem and bring unity and tolerance to their states. One is a Democrat, the other a Republican. Both men knew that taking on the flag issue would be politically disastrous. Both knew that they were risking the careers they had worked so hard to build, but they did it because they believed it was right.

Although this debate is often framed in terms of the Civil War, the Confederate battle flag began flying over Southern state capitols only during the Civil Rights era. A symbol of white resistance to integration, it was added to the Georgia flag in 1956 following the Supreme Court's decision outlawing segregation in *Brown v. Board of Education*, while South Carolina unfurled the flag in 1962 as desegregation efforts intensified across the South. As the modern South has become more diverse and prosperous, the flag has come to be perceived as a retrograde and inflammatory symbol by many.

GOVERNOR ROY BARNES

In January 2001, Georgia Governor Roy Barnes introduced a new flag. The Confederate symbol was reduced in size and incorporated into a new design featuring other emblems of the State's history, including the flag of the Confederacy and the flag of the United States. Barnes knew that a similar effort in 1993 had nearly doomed the reelection of his predecessor, Zill Miller, and had led to the defeat of two other Southern Governors in the 1990's. Barnes' internal polling also showed that the move would be disastrous. White voters from rural areas who had strongly supported Barnes were vehemently opposed to any change in the flag, as were most other white voters. Nevertheless, Barnes decided to risk his governorship on the effort. He believed it was morally right, and he feared the consequences of inaction. Barnes saw the Confederate flag as a barrier to Georgia's future prosperity, and the new flag as a symbol that Georgians were ready to unite behind a vision of tolerance and prosperity.

In his speech to the Georgia legislature introducing the flag compromise he said:

> Forty years ago, faced with court orders to integrate and with demonstrations by Georgians who wanted the University of Georgia and the state's public schools closed instead, the people who stood in our places did the right thing. . . .
>
> While the government of Arkansas used the armed forces of the state to prevent nine black students from enrolling at Little Rock's Central High School, while the Governor of Alabama stood defiantly in a schoolhouse door, Georgia quietly concentrated on growing our economy, on the goals that bring us together rather than those that can tear us apart. And, in the process, Georgia established itself as the leader of the New South. . . .
>
> Georgia moved ahead because its leaders looked ahead. Anyone who doesn't realize that's why Georgia has become the fastest growing

state east of the Rocky Mountains does not understand economic devel-opment.

I am a Southerner. . . .

I still cry when I hear "Amazing Grace."

My great-grandfather was captured at Vicksburg fighting for the Confederacy, and I still visit his grave in the foothills of Gilmer County.

I am proud of him.

But I am also proud that we have come so far that my children find it hard to believe that we ever had segregated schools or separate water fountains labeled "white" and "colored."

And I am proud that these changes came about because unity prevailed over division.

Today, that same effort and energy of unity must be exercised again.

The Confederate battle flag occupies two-thirds of our current state flag. Some argue that it is a symbol of segregation, defiance, and white supremacy. Others that it is a testament to a brave and valiant people who were willing to die to defend their homes and hearth.

I am not here to settle this argument—because no one can—but I am here because it is time to end it.

To end it before it divides us into warring camps, before it reverses four decades of economic growth and progress, before it deprives Georgia of its place of leadership—in other words before it does irreparable harm to the future we want to leave for our chil-dren. . . .

Defeating this compromise will confirm the worst that has been said about us and, in the process, dishonor a brave people.

Adopt this flag and our people will be united as one rather than divided by race and hatred.

Adopt this flag and we will honor our ancestors without giv-ing aid to those who would abuse their legacy.

Georgia has prospered because we have refused to be divided.

We have worked together, and the nation and the world have taken notice. . . .

Barnes won the vote, and the new flag was adopted. Heading into his campaign, Barnes looked difficult to beat. Virtually every political pundit and expert predicted a Barnes victory. He had improved the transportation problems and traffic congestion that plague Atlanta and pushed hard for education reform. But Barnes' opponent, State Legislator Sonny Perdue, made the flag a central issue. Confederate flag supporters began disrupting every Barnes campaign appearance, and his own internal polling showed that his popularity had not recovered. Nevertheless, he expected to win. In an upset victory on Election Day, however, Sonny Perdue became Georgia's first Republican Governor since 1871.

There is little doubt that the flag was the crucial issue in Barnes' defeat. According to the *Atlanta Journal-Constitution*, Barnes' support in Atlanta and other metropolitan areas increased or remained steady, but his support among rural white voters dropped 25 points. Even the "flaggers" weren't satisfied with Barnes' defeat, but continued to heckle him up until his last day in office, shouting epithets as he left the Governor's mansion for the drive to his new home. "There was this huge undercurrent of resentment and anger about the flag, but I think it's something we all missed because it's not something people discuss in the open," said Merle Black, a political scientist at Emory University in Atlanta.

The day after his defeat, the *Atlanta Journal-Constitution* wrote: "Barnes paid a price for changing the state flag, a brave move that will earn him an honored place in the history books, if not yet in the hearts of his fellow Georgians."

Since leaving office, Barnes has worked full-time for the Atlanta Legal Aid Society. Governor Sonny Perdue, who promised that he would put the flag issue to the voters in a statewide referendum, has postponed any referendum until 2004. In the meantime, he has asked Georgia's favorite son, former President Jimmy Carter, to help navigate the volatile racial controversy, underscoring the difficulty of this emotionally charged issue.

GOVERNOR DAVID BEASLEY

A few years earlier, and at the opposite end of the political spectrum, conservative Christian David Beasley of South Carolina had also staked his political future on the flag issue. In the 1994 campaign, Beasley promised to keep the Confederate battle flag flying above the State House dome. However, in 1996, a series of church burnings and the racially motivated shooting of three black teenagers prompted a change of heart.

Framing the issue in biblical terms, Beasley addressed South Carolina's citizens on statewide television, asking them to help pressure lawmakers to remove the Confederate flag: "I'm asking that we come together as a people, to honor and understand each other, to forge a ministry of reconciliation that extends to every citizen. . . . The Bible tells us to love our neighbors as ourselves. It is time for the races to compromise on the Confederate flag, to show Judeo-Christian love that will bring the races together."

Beasley proposed a compromise that would keep the Confederate flag on State House grounds, though not above the dome: one flag would fly next to a Confederate soldier's monument in front of the capitol, and a second Confederate flag would fly behind the State House at a monument to women of the Confederacy. The initial response from the Civil Rights community was favorable; in January 1997, 500 clergymen marched in support of the Governor's initiative.

But, the negative reaction was immediate and extreme. Beasley's proposal alienated his Republican supporters and split the state party. Prominent Republicans followed him on television and raked him over the coals. Legislators in his own party called removing the flag "cultural genocide," and compared Beasley to Neville Chamberlain. Others accused him of ignoring South Carolina's losses in the Civil War in which 65 percent of South Carolinian men were killed or wounded. Even some Democrats opposed him, feeling that the emotion unleashed by the flag issue would be destructive. School protests and lawsuits began taking place across the State. The legislature refused to deal with the controversy, rejecting Beasley's proposal, but letting alternatives languish. Beasley was forced to abandon his efforts.

By 1998, although the State's economy was booming, Beasley faced a tough reelection campaign. He had alienated his core supporters by taking on the flag issue, and after Beasley announced his opposition to video gaming and a state lottery, the huge gaming industry threw its financial support behind Democrat Jim Hodges. Although Beasley was bitterly disappointed, in an interview the day after he lost, he said: "I didn't run for election to be reelected, and I didn't want to be Governor to be popular. I wanted to be Governor to get the job done."

STATE REPRESENTATIVE DAN PONDER, JR.

The 2003 Profile in Courage Award was also awarded to former Georgia State Legislator Dan Ponder, Jr., whose passionate speech in support of hate-crime legislation galvanized the Georgia Legislature. On March 16, 2000, the Georgia House of Representatives had voted 83–82 to shelve a bill enhancing penalties for hate-based crimes when Dan Ponder, a forty-three-year-old conservative Republican businessman from rural southwestern Georgia defied expectations and rose to support the bill. Ponder, who owns a chain of fast-food franchises, had decided not to seek reelection, but had nonetheless been expected to oppose the hate-crime legislation along with most other members of his party.

Dan Ponder's courageous speech will take its place in American history as one of the great examples of the power of language to inspire action. Just as President Kennedy's Pulitzer Prize–winning book *Profiles in Courage* brought courageous historical moments to life for later generations, so will Dan Ponder's speech live on in the hearts and minds of all who read it as a testimonial to the values of freedom, tolerance, and diversity upon which our country depends.

> *I am probably the last person, the most unlikely person that you would expect to be speaking from the well about hate-crime legislation. And I am going to talk about it a little differently from a lot of the conversations that have gone on thus far. I want to talk about it a little more personally, about how I came to believe what I believe. . . .*
>
> *But I want to tell you the real reason that I am standing here today. And this is personal, and in my five years in this House I have never abused my time in the well, and I only have two days before I leave this body, so I hope that you will just listen to this part for me.*
>
> *There was one woman in my life that made a huge difference and her name was Mary Ward. She began working for my family before I was born. She was a young black woman whose own grandmother raised my mother. Mary, or May-Mar as I called her, came every morn-*

ing before I was awake to cook breakfast so it would be on the table. She cooked our lunch. She washed our clothes.

But she was much more than that. She read books to me. When I was playing Little League she would go out and catch ball with me. She was never, ever afraid to discipline me or spank me. She expected the absolute best out of me, perhaps, and I am sure, even more than she did her own children. She would even travel with my family when we would go to our house in Florida during the summer, just as her own grandmother had done.

One day, when I was about 12 or 13, I was leaving for school. As I was walking out door she turned to kiss me good-bye. And for some reason, I turned my head. She stopped me and she looked into my eyes with a look that absolutely burns in my memory right now and she said, "You didn't kiss me because I am black." At that instant, I knew that she was right.

I denied it. I made some lame excuse about it. But I was forced at that age to confront a small dark part of myself. I don't even know where it came from. This lady, who was devoting her whole life to me and my brother and sister, who loved me unconditionally, who had changed my diapers and fed me, and who was truly my second mother, that somehow she wasn't worthy of a good-bye kiss simply because of the color of her skin.

Hate is all around us. It takes shape and form in ways that are somehow so small that we don't even recognize them to begin with, until they somehow become acceptable to us. It is up to us, as parents and leaders in our communities, to take a stand and to say loudly and clearly that this is just not acceptable.

I have lived with the shame and memory of my betrayal of Mary Ward's love for me. I pledged to myself then and I re-pledged to myself the day I buried her that never, ever again would I look in the mirror and know that I had kept silent and let hate or prejudice or indifference negatively impact a person's life . . . even if I didn't know them. . . .

To those that would say that this bill is creating a special class of citizen, I would say. . . . Who would choose to be gay and risk the alienation of your own family and friends and coworkers? Who would choose to be Jewish, so that they could endure the kind of hatred over the years that led to the Holocaust and the near extinction of the Jewish people on an entire continent? Who would choose to be black simply so that their places of worship could be burned down or so that they could spend all their days at the back of the line?

We are who we are because God alone chose to make us that way. The burdens that we bear and the problems that we are trying to correct with this legislation are the result of man's inhumanity to man. That is hardly trying to create a special class of people. . . .

Hate crimes are about sending a message. The cross that was burned in a black person's yard not so many years ago was a message to black people.

The gay person that is bashed walking down the sidewalk in midtown is a message to gay people.

And the Jews that have endured thousands of years of persecution were all being sent messages over and over again.

I would say to you that now is our turn to send a message. I am not a lawyer, I don't know how difficult it would be to prosecute this or even care. I don't really care that anyone is ever prosecuted under this bill.

But I do care that we take this moment in time, in history, to say that we are going to send a message.

The pope is now sending a message of reconciliation to Jews and people throughout this world. Some of those crimes occurred 2,000 years ago.

Mary Ward sent me a message many years ago. A message of unconditional love, regardless of the color of your skin.

My wife and I have sent a message to our children that we are all God's children and that hate is unacceptable in our home.

I believe that we must send a message to people that are filled with hate in this world, that Georgia has no room for hatred within its borders. It is a message that we can send to the people of this state, but it is also a message that you have to send to yourself.

I ask you to look within yourself and do what you think is right. I ask you to vote YES on this bill and NO to hate.

When Ponder concluded his remarks, both Democrats and Republicans rose to applaud, giving him two standing ovations. The hate-crime legislation passed by a vote of 116–49.